Scotch Verdict

Scotch Verdict*

*Miss Pirie and Miss Woods
v. Dame Cumming Gordon*

LILLIAN FADERMAN

* A verdict of not proven that is
allowed by Scottish law in some cases,
or any inconclusive decision.

COLUMBIA UNIVERSITY PRESS
NEW YORK

Columbia University Press Morningside Edition
Columbia University Press
New York   Chichester, West Sussex

Morningside Edition with new preface
Copyright © 1993 Columbia University Press preface to the Morningside Edition
Copyright © 1983 Lillian Faderman

Library of Congress Cataloging-in-Publication Data

Faderman, Lillian.
    Scotch verdict : Miss Pirie and Miss Woods v. Dame Cumming Gordon
/ Lillian Faderman.
        p.   cm.
    Originally published: New York : Morrow, 1983.
    Includes index.
    ISBN 0-231-08443-9
    1. Woods, Marianne—Trials, litigation, etc.   2. Pirie, Jane—
Trials, litigation, etc.   3. Cumming Gordon, Helen, Lady, d. 1830—
Trials, litigation, etc.   4. Trials (Libel)—Scotland—Edinburgh.
5. Homoseuxality—Law and legislation—Scotland—History.
I. Title.
KDC188.W6F32   1992
345.411'0253—dc20
[344.1105253]   93-27103
                                                                      CIP

∞

Casebound editions of Columbia University Press books
are printed on permanent and durable acid-free paper.

Printed in the United States of America

c 10 9 8 7 6 5 4 3 2 1
p 10 9 8 7 6 5 4 3 2 1

ACKNOWLEDGMENTS

I wish to thank for their kind assistance the curators and librarians of the National Library of Scotland, the Central Library of Edinburgh, the Signet Library of the Parliament House of Scotland, the Scottish Record Office, the Scottish Registry Office, the Georgian House of Edinburgh, and the House of Lords Record Office.

I also wish to thank my research assistants, Kathleen Hall and Phyllis Irwin, and my friends and colleagues who read and commented on this work in its various drafts: my writers' group, directed by Jean Pickering (with special gratitude to Suzanne Kehde); Barbara Grier, Walt Stuart, Alison Scott, Lorimar Doan, Allan Skei, Barbara Bradshaw, Harriet Perl, and Savina Teuball. For their unfailing support and encouragement I am grateful to my dean, Joe Satin; my agent, Sandra Dijkstra; and my editor, Maria Guarnaschelli.

NOTA BENE

The trial transcripts and related materials in the case of *Miss Woods and Miss Pirie against Dame Helen Cumming Gordon* consist of over one thousand pages. Several of the speeches of the judges and lawyers are over one hundred pages apiece. Because so much of the material is repetitious and written in archaic language and legalese, I have edited it considerably, but always with a concern for the accuracy of the ideas expressed in the original documents.

I have made several changes as well in the *form* of the materials that I discovered in the trial transcripts. In order to preserve some of the information from the judges' speeches without reproducing those speeches at great length, I have created out of portions of them judges' "notes" on the testimony, and I have placed those notes at the intervals in which, I conjecture, they must have been written as the judges listened to the witnesses. I have also used the "notes" of Lord Robertson to speculate on the physical appearances and personalities of the witnesses. In order to spare the reader the tedium of the lengthy third-person depositions taken of the witnesses, I have created courtroom dialogues out of those depositions, in which the voices of the witnesses, the attorneys, and the judges are all heard.

I have also made several other modifications of the transcripts. For the sake of easier reading, I have omitted or modernized many archaic and/or confusing expressions, and I have substituted terms with which American readers will be more familiar; e.g., the British terms *pursuer* and *defender* have been changed to *plaintiff* and *defendant*. Because repetitious or inconsequential testimony has been omitted, for the sake of dramatic continuity I have altered the dates of some of the witnesses' appearances (usually by less than a week or two). For simplicity's sake I have omitted the roles of the agents, clerks, and other minor figures in this courtroom drama. In addition, I have embellished some of the biographical data, always with reference to the information that was available to me. In making these changes my primary concern has been to create out of unreadable documents a readable book, while preserving the intent of my subjects' statements and their attitudes.

Finally, I have tried to present a modern perspective on this early nineteenth-century material through my first-person narrative.

Contents

Foreword to the Morningside Edition

Leila J. Rupp

Ever since I began teaching a class on the history of same-sex sexuality in the Western world, I have used Lillian Faderman's *Scotch Verdict* as a kind of centerpiece, a place to slow what proves to be a dizzying whirl through the centuries, to teeter for a while on the threshhold between "romantic friendship" and the sexual revolution and to return to the conceptual debates on the nature of sexuality with which we began. When the book went out of print I started complaining to local bookstores, nudging various publishers, and devising strategies to supply my students with this essential component of the course in some legal fashion. So it is with relief as well as delight that I greet this new edition.

The story of Jane Pirie and Marianne Woods and the case they took to court against Dame Cumming Gordon is a deceptively simple and compelling one. In 1810 in Edinburgh, Scotland, the aristocratic Lady Cumming Gordon suddenly withdrew her grandaughter, the offspring of her dead son and an Indian woman, from a school run by teachers Jane Pirie and Marianne Woods. Soon all of the parents, contacted by Lady Cumming Gordon, came to fetch their daughters as well. Pirie and Woods, their school ruined because Jane Cumming accused them of engaging in sexual acts with each other, sued Lady Cumming Gordon for libel.

Lillian Faderman's strategies for presenting the case in *Scotch Verdict* preserve the historical drama while enveloping it in an ongoing dialogue between the twentieth-century narrator and Ollie, the narrator's lover, over the best interpretation of the case. As Faderman explains at the outset, she has taken some specified liberties with the court transcripts and cut them fairly drastically, but in my opinion these changes make the text more accessible without damaging it as historical document. The reader who wants to verify the text can do so by consulting the published reprint, *Miss Marianne Woods and Miss Jane Pirie Against Dame Helen Cumming Gordon.*[1]

Faderman's insertion of her narrator and Ollie into the text raises in a direct and gripping way the question of the nature of sexuality. As Faderman's narrator investigates the case and envisages herself in Jane Pirie's shoes, she and Ollie take up opposing positions on the debate that I call, in my class, "Did They or Didn't They?" Whether or not Jane Pirie and Marianne Woods had a sexual relationship—and asking the question raises another, What qualifies as "sexual"?—may be, as Arthur Schlesinger, Jr., asserted with regard to another controversial case, that of Eleanor Roosevelt and Lorena Hickok, an "issue of stunning inconsequence," but it forces us to think about sexuality historically.[2] Ollie has what has been called an essentialist perspective: she argues for the similarity of the two Scottish women's desire and behavior to that of late twentieth-century women. The narrator, on the other hand, takes a social constructionist position, emphasizing the power of Victorian ideals to shape and constrain sexual behavior and arguing against the relevance of Ollie's comparisons between early nineteenth- and late twentieth-century women. Both see clearly the existence of love, of passion. What is at stake is the extent to which the social context shaped the expression of that love and passion. This is no simple debate in the literature on sexuality, and Faderman provides a concrete case for considering the historical ramifications of an issue that can too easily be reduced to pitting biological against social origins of same-sex sexual desire. In my class we take up again the questions we ask about ancient Greek male transgenerational relationships, about sexuality among the Native American berdache, about women who passed as men and married women in early modern Europe, about sexual relations between British sailors: What, if any, limits exist to the power of social forces to shape sexuality?[3]

But *Scotch Verdict* has not only conceptual significance for a broader study of the history of same-sex sexuality. The case also makes connections to a whole range of phenomena both preceding and succeeding its particular moment in history. Despite the insistence of one of the judges, Lord Gillies, that "the crime here alleged has no existence," there is a long, if fragmentary, history of lesbian relations in Europe to which various parties in this story refer, directly or indirectly.[4]

For example, Mary Brown, the nursery maid of student and witness Janet Munro, reportedly remarked that the schoolmistresses should be burned as punishment for their crimes, thus invoking the early modern law codes that ordered death by fire as a punishment for sodomy (and perhaps also recalling the association of witchcraft and women's sexuality).[5] And when Lady Cumming Gordon's counsel noted the precautions taken in Continental convents to prevent sexual practices among the nuns, his words recalled regulations established by the councils of Paris (1212) and Rouen (1214) prohibiting nuns from sleeping together and requiring a lighted lamp in their dormitories.[6]

In addition, the testimony of Charlotte Whiffen, the schoolmistresses' maid, with regard to an occasion on which another of the servants, pregnant at the time, put on men's clothes, seems intended to raise the image of the cross-dressed woman, an important figure in the history of female same-sex sexuality. As Faderman explains, both here and in more detail in her *Surpassing the Love of Men*, the woman who dressed and worked as a man and, whether out of same-sex sexual desire or merely to protect her masquerade, married another woman represented a particularly serious threat to the gendered social order.[7] There was, of course, no question of transgressed gender boundaries here, but this odd reference in the testimony, and the remark of Mary Brown that one of the teachers must have been a man, bear witness to public knowledge, however half-conscious, of other forms of same-sex sexuality.

These are just faint traces in the text of an older tradition, but the fairly extensive discussion of the physical possibilities of two female bodies in sexual contact shows beyond a shadow of a doubt that the men involved with this cased followed the European legal tradition with regard to sodomy. By and large they associated "sex" with vaginal penetration. For a sexual relationship to have taken place between women, there had to be a penis substitute, either a "tool" or "artificial instrument," or else one (or both) of the women had to be "endowed with an extraordinary conformation," that is, an enlarged clitoris. Despite the mention of "digitation" and "Tribades," the phallocentric model of sexuality in command here overlooks any possibility of sexual pleasure between women without a penis substitute. Historically it was women who claimed the privileges of men by both passing as male and using an "instrument" to "counterfeit the office of a husband" who were most likely to be sentenced to death for their crimes.[8]

Another possibility for explaining female same-sex sexuality, based on the libertine tradition, was that women might excite each other in preparation for "admission of the male sex." Because "it is not alleged that the scenes described in this case were in any way preparatory to receiving the male sex," Lord Meadowbank did not think that they had occurred. Contrast this with the case of Benedetta Carlini, abbess of an Italian convent in the early seventeenth century, who was accused of initiating "the most immodest acts" with a sister nun. The church authorities appended to the detailed description of these acts a brief mention of handholding and kissing between Benedetta and two priests. According to Judith Brown, who discovered this case, because "church officials could not believe that a woman's sexual preferences might be directed solely at another woman, the relations between Benedetta and the priests made the other sexual charges more credible."[9] But heterosexual misdeeds never came up in the case of Jane Pirie and Marianne Woods. Even the judges who believed that the schoolmistresses had been sexual together did not seem to assume that that activity spoke to their general sexual wantonness.

So there is no question about the judges' and lawyers' understanding that women could be sexual together. Dame Cumming Gordon's counsel provided a list of references—from the Bible to the classics to earlier law codes to libertine literature—to prove the existence of "the vice in question." Yet this very proof speaks to the central paradox of female same-sex sexuality in the European tradition: the authorities knew it existed but at the same time ignored, denied, and suppressed the knowledge. As Judith Brown has put it so tellingly, they had "an almost active willingness to *dis*believe."[10]

Because women were, in early modern Europe, considered especially lustful and weak-willed, public knowledge of female sodomy might, officials feared, have disastrous results. As a result fifteenth and sixteenth-century jurists considered this a sin that "should not be named or written" and recommended against reading out a description of the crime at the time of execution.[11] It is worthy of note that the justices in this case followed the spirit of this recommendation, hearing testimony behind closed doors, limiting duplication of the transcripts, and in general trying to conceal the nature of the case. Given the transformation of Western conceptions of women's sexuality by the early nineteenth century, this fear can be seen as both backward looking and an expression of the newer reticence with regard to sexual matters.

For the older attitudes had changed in profound ways by the time Jane Pirie and Marianne Woods took Dame Cumming Gordon to court. As commercial capitalism gave way to industrial capitalism, the family gradually lost its place as the central economic unit, although it retained its sexual and reproductive functions and even increased its emotional ones. With the decline of the family economy children became less of an economic asset and required more of a financial investment, at least for the urban middle class, leading to the separation of sexuality and reproduction. As a response to the increasing separation of male and female spheres among the urban middle class and the concomitant association of middle-class women with the home and domesticity, the tenet of women's sexual difference from men served to aid middle-class men's sexual self-control within marriage and separate good women from bad. The ideology of sexual difference, in conjunction with economic and social sex-segregation, facilitated the rise of "romantic friendship."

Scotch Verdict is rife with evidence of the acceptability of romantic friendship to men and women in nineteenth-century Scottish society. No one found it unnatural that the two teachers might choose to share a bed. As Lord Gillies put it, "Are we to say that every woman who has formed an intimate friendship and has slept in the same bed with another is guilty? Where is the innocent woman in Soctland?" Dame Cumming Gordon's counsel tried to determine from the schoolgirls if they ever saw Jane Pirie and Marianne Woods "kissing, caressing, and fondling more than could have resulted from ordinary female friendship?" In other words, he tried to establish some outer limits of the expression of affection, but could not. Although Janet Munro testified that they caressed and fondled each other more than ordinary female friends, and that she also thought they went beyond the bounds of female friendship by quarrelling more strongly than appropriate, this line of questioning was really not fruitful. The irony is that the acceptability of romantic friendship rested on the notion of women's lack of sexual desire, yet passionate relationships between women did seem to raise the spectre, however strongly resisted, of normal carresses between friends crossing the line into sexual behavior.[12]

The really crucial factor for solving the dilemma of how young innocent schoolgirls could make up such a story if it had not really happened—thus forcing the men involved in the case to believe that either two respectable teachers or several girls from good families had impossibly deviant minds—is the association of sexuality with "the lower orders." Women's lack of sexual desire, in the dominant ideology of the nineteenth century Western world, separated the upper and middle classes from the working class and white Euroamerican women from women of color. So Jane Cumming, born of an Indian mother not married to her Scottish father, raised during her formative years in India, and educated previously in a school for shopkeepers' daughters, played a pivotal role. Jane Cumming either learned about sex—heterosexual or possibly even lesbian—in India, or she was corrupted by British servants or the more knowledgeable and less supervised girls at her earlier school. As Lord Meadowbank explained it, "The language of the Hindoo female domestics turns chiefly on the commerce of the sexes. . . . It is impossible to live in Indostan without learning through observation and instruction, by the age of eight or nine, something about venereal intercourse." The servants at the mistresses' school came under a great deal of suspicion as well. It was not just a question of less trustworthy individuals, from the judges' perspective, but of a thoroughgoing association between class, race, and sexuality.[13]

So the story of Jane Pirie and Marianne Woods is firmly rooted both in the past European history of female same-sex sexuality and in the nineteenth-century context of romantic friendship, and a class and race-based conception of sexuality. But Faderman also, through her commentary, points us toward the future "sexual revolution" of the early twentieth century that would ultimately make the disbelief of some of the judges so outmoded. The dialogue between the narrator and Ollie centers on the impact of changed conceptions of sexuality—women's sexuality, in particular—on the viability of comparisons between women now and women then. And Faderman refers directly to the late nineteenth-century sexologists and their discussions of sexual "inversion," suggesting that their work might have helped the judges to understand what was going on. The fact, Richard von Krafft-Ebing and Havelock Ellis might have been as confused as the judges, although for different reasons. Both sexologists distinguished "congenital inverts"—who took on the manifestations of masculinity—from women who appeared "normal" but were susceptible to the advances of inverts.[14] But who was the invert or mannish lesbian or butch in this scenario? Certainly Jane Pirie comes across as dominant, but in a "feminine" rather than "masculine" way. Despite the new "knowledge" of the late nineteenth century, which in any case reflected rather than shaped what was going on in the developing same-sex subcultures in urban areas, the riddle of Jane Pirie and Marianne Woods would have remained.[15]

What is so perfect about *Scotch Verdict* is that it recalls all of these connections for the reader familiar with the contours of the history of same-sex sexuality but stands alone as well as powerful and absorbing drama. In my class students volunteer to represent the persectives of the different characters: the defendant, the plaintiffs, the witnesses, the lawyers, the judges, and the analysts, the narrator and Ollie. Each explains what she or he thinks happened, from the perspective of a particular character, and the rest of the class asks the difficult questions. What would Jane Cumming have told her grandmother? Why did Lady Cumming Gordon believe Jane's story? What were Jane Pirie and Marianne Woods doing in bed? Did they or didn't they?

The best thing is that there are no answers, only a wonderful opportunity to ponder the intricacies of the history of same-sex sexuality and to explore one's own assumptions about the nature of sexuality.

NOTES

1. (New York: Arno Press, 1975). This is a photoprint edition of the National Library of Medicine copy, which has manuscript notes by Lord Meadowbank, one of the judges, in the margins.

2. Arthur Schlesinger, Jr., "Interesting Women" [review of Doris Faber, *The Life of Lorena Hickok: E. R.'s Friend*], *New York Times Book Review*, Feb. 17, 1980, p. 31.

3. For succinct discussions of the complex issues involved in the essentialism/social constructionism debate, see John Boswell, "Revolutions, Universals, and Sexual Categories," in Martin Bauml Duberman, Martha Vicinus, and George Chauncey, Jr., eds.,

Hidden From History: Reclaiming the Gay and Lesbian Past (New York: New American Library, 1989), pp. 17–36; Carole S. Vance, "Social Construction Theory: Problems in the History of Sexuality," in Dennis Altman et al., eds. *Homosexuality, Which Homosexuality?* (Amsterdam: Dekker/Schorer, 1989), pp. 13–34; Steven Epstein, "Gay Politics, Ethnic Identify: The Limits of Social Constructionism," *Socialist Review* (May/August 1987), 17:9–54.

4. For a discussion of conceptualizations of lesbian desire, see Martha Vicinus, " 'They Wonder to Which Sex I Belong': The Historical Roots of the Modern Lesbian Identity," *Feminist Studies* (Fall 1992), 18:467–97.

5. See Judith C. Brown, *Immodest Acts: The Life of a Lesbian Nun in Renaissance Italy* (New York: Oxford University Press, 1986); on witchcraft, see Bonnie S. Anderson and Judith P. Zinsser, *A History of Their Own,* 2 vols. (New York: Harper and Row, 1988), 1:166–173.

6. Brown, *Immodest Acts,* p. 8.

7. Lillian Faderman, *Surpassing the Love of Men: Romantic Friendship and Love Between Women from the Renaissance to the Present* (New York: William Morrow, 1981), chapter 4. See also the San Francisco Lesbian and Gay History Project, " 'She Even Chewed Tobacco': A Pictorial Narrative of Passing Women in America," in Duberman, Vicinus, Chauncey, *Hidden From History,* pp. 183–194.

8. Faderman, *Surpassing the Love of Men.*

9. Brown, *Immodest Acts,* p. 128.

10. Brown, *Immodest Acts,* p. 9.

11. Brown, *Immodest Acts,* pp. 19–20.

12. Lisa Moore emphasizes this concern with the boundaries of acceptable behavior in her consideration of the Woods-Pirie case in " 'Something More Tender Still than Friendship': Romantic Friendship in Early-Nineteenth-Century England," *Feminist Studies* (Fall 1992), 18:499–520. She concludes that romantic friendship was not as socially acceptable as we have assumed.

13. For a discussion of this development in the United States, see John D'Emilio and Estelle B. Freedman, *Intimate Matters: A History of Sexuality in America* (New York: Harper and Row, 1988).

14. See Carroll Smith-Rosenberg, "Discourses of Sexuality and Subjectivity: The New Woman, 1870–1936," in Duberman, Vicinus, Chauncey, *Hidden From History,* pp. 264–280; and Esther Newton, "The Mythic Mannish Lesbian: Radclyffe Hall and the New Woman," in Duberman, Vicinus, Chauncey, *Hidden From History,* pp. 281–293.

15. On the lack of formative influence of the sexologists, see George Chauncey, Jr., "Christian Brotherhood or Sexual Perversion? Homosexual Identities and the Construction of Sexual Boundaries in the World War I Era," in Duberman, Vicinus, Chauncey, *Hidden From History,* pp. 294–317; for a discussion of the resistance of "deviant subjects" to pathologizing discourse, see Jennifer Terry, "Theorizing Deviant Historiography," *differences* (Summer 1991), 3:55–74.

PART I

The Accusation

MARCH 18, 1982

When I was twelve years old I took acting lessons. I wanted to be an actress, preferably a child star, and when a tiny school of drama, dance, and voice with the impressive name of Theatre Arts Showcase opened in my neighborhood, I convinced my mother to pay a dollar weekly for a two-hour class session in acting. There were four other prepubescent girls, none of them as fiercely determined as I. Our teacher was a forty-year-old mustachioed man who wore a brown belted suit and worked full-time as a shoe salesman, but the Executive Director of the school, his wife, told me that he had once been in professional theater in Chicago. I was awed enough, mostly by her, the most exquisite, sophisticated blond creature I had ever seen in our dark lower-middle-class community. She was my first love.

Her husband must have been perplexed about what to do with five little girls, four of them envisioning themselves as the Lana Turner of the next decade. There were few scripts for four twelve-year-old Lana Turners and one twelve-year-old Sarah Bernhardt, but for our second session he brought us a fifteen-minute scene in which we could at least all participate, and he kept us working at that scene for the next seven or eight months, until, one by one, all the girls but me dropped out of the class. The scene was from Lillian Hellman's *The Children's Hour*. I played Mary Tilford, an adolescent bully. He told us nothing about the play, and I aspired to thoroughness in my acting, so I went to the neighborhood library where I found and read a copy of *The Children's Hour*. I was mystified, despite my own powerful crush on the Executive Director. I understood from that first reading that Mary Tilford had fabricated a tale, claiming that her two women teachers, who operated a girls' boarding school, were doing things they were not supposed to be doing, but I could not quite understand what those things were.

The play was in the adult section of the small library, and since I only had a juvenile's card I could not check it out, so I returned to reread the play three or four times over the next months. Finally I understood that the two teachers were ruined because Mary Tilford had accused them to her grandmother of being "in love with each other," and the grandmother had informed all the other parents, who promptly removed their children from the school. No one had ever told me before that the sort of thing I felt for the Executive Director could ruin someone. I was profoundly dismayed, and I continued to be dismayed (although my devotion to the Executive Director never wavered) for the next two years, until my mother and I moved to the other side of town, where I was too far away to continue my acting lessons.

Years later, as a sophomore at NYU, I happened on the play again when I was assigned to read Hellman's *The Little Foxes* for a course in American drama. By this time I had had a couple of adventures, and I had taken on a certain patina of sophistication. There was little that would have dismayed me—or rather that I would have admitted dismayed me. But the play had now some sentimental value for me. I associated it with the days of my painful naïveté and my first love. And then I came to think of it as part of a precious cache of secret knowledge, along with books such as *The Well of Loneliness* and *Regiment of Women* and *We Walk Alone*. That the characters in these works invariably ended badly did not surprise me, nor did it disturb me as much as it should have. I was only gratified that there was some mention of the unmentionable in print. I brought them up in conversations very rarely and always carefully—only when I suspected that the other person had had experiences such as mine and I was seeking to open the subject with her. They were sort of coming-out tools.

When I and my environment had changed so that I no longer had a need for such tools, I was furious with the authors for sending their female characters off to hell or suicide or insane asylums, and then I forgot them. I had not thought about *The Children's Hour* in at least ten years, until I began research for a dissertation on the popular treatment of women under the law. I found several books by a popularizer of legal history, a Scottish law historian named William Roughead, and in one of them, *Bad Companions,* which had been published in 1930, I discovered the source for *The Children's Hour.*

I was intrigued by what Hellman had changed from Roughead's thirty-page account. She set the incident in America, in her own day. It had actually taken place in Scotland, in the early nineteenth century. In her play Mary Tilford is an American girl, her grandmother's favorite. In reality she was at least half Indian, the putative illegitimate child of a very young Scotsman who went to India and died there. The Scottish woman who accepted the title of her grandmother had many legitimate, purebred grandchildren, and she merely tolerated the girl; but she believed her tale because she could believe less that a young female under her charge could invent such a story. In Hellman's play the two women sue the grandmother for libel, lose their suit—and one of them, with all the advantages of a Freudian knowledge of neurosis, admits she has long harbored repressed lesbian passions, and she shoots herself.

I was fascinated with the legal aspects of the case as Roughead presented it, but even more fascinated with the two women, Marianne Woods and Jane Pirie. In their fictional form I, as Mary Tilford, had once done them in, and later I had called on them as secret sisters. They had lived with me through my first love in childhood and through my cunning and fear in young adulthood. And now I discovered that they had once really existed. I knew that Roughead had based his accounts on trial records that were then extant. Since the case had been appealed to the House of Lords in London, I assumed all the transcripts were there. I wrote to the Secretary of the House of Lords Record Office, with whom I had had correspondence in looking for other trial records for my dissertation, and I received from him some incomplete pages of the appeal transcript. I was sure that many more pages of transcript must exist, and that they were probably housed somewhere in Scotland. I wanted to drop my dissertation and run to Scotland and find them, wherever they were moldering, probably in the law libraries of Edinburgh.

Instead, I finished my dissertation, which included a study of 156 other women as they were treated in popular accounts of the workings of the law. And I went on to one more project, which led to another, and then another. But although I have now forgotten most of the 156 cases I once studied, I remember Miss Woods and Miss Pirie. The Woods and Pirie case was one of a dozen I came across of women before the twentieth century who were accused in the courts of lesbianism, yet only theirs really touched me—partly because of my early associations with them, I suppose. But even more, I felt somehow that I knew them, and that I wanted to know them better. They were teachers, as I am; they had been well trained in constraint and propriety, as I was; and yet Jane Pirie,

despite her training and surface calm, was fierce and given to out-
bursts of violent passion, just as I am. I wanted to know whether
they were really guilty of what they had been accused, what words
were used to make such accusations in their day, how they defended themselves, how their judges responded, what happened to
women like them after such an experience in the early nineteenth
century, what might have happened to me had I, with my temperament, lived then instead of now.

I knew that whether or not men truly believed it, whether or
not their personal experiences bore it out, the spoken consensus
about the good middle-class woman of the late eighteenth and the
nineteenth centuries in Britain was that she was passionless: both
her instincts and her socialization kept her chaste until marriage,
and once married she became a sexual being only to do her duty to
her husband and to help repopulate Britain. If it was agreed that
women had no sexual drive in relation to men, then surely it was
inconceivable that they might feel sexual passion for each other.

But I wanted to know what a woman's life would be if she did
feel sexual passion for another woman. Or if someone, perhaps
someone raised on a different social level or in a different culture,
where women were thought of as sexual creatures, less madonna
and more whore—if that person *said* she did. What if a girl raised
in India, or among the lower orders, raised where flesh was barer,
where women were segregated from men and yet exposed always
to chatter about sex, or where the delicacies and stringencies of
middle- and upper-class Anglo-Christianity had no hold—what if
such a girl (for a lark, for revenge, or in truth, like the boy in "The
Emperor's New Clothes") said that she saw two respectable
women copulating together?

What if in 1810 in Scotland she said that in the middle of the
night, night after night, in the dormitory where she slept, she had
seen two school mistresses, Christian women, in bed together, not
only kissing and caressing, but going through motions that resembled sexual intercourse? Whether she told the truth or she lied,
who would believe her? And if she was believed, what would happen to the school mistresses?

The research I did for my dissertation gave me only cursory
answers. And then I forgot about my questions for years. But tonight, for some reason—perhaps because I am between projects

now, and while my body luxuriates in leisure my mind abhors it—I thought of the Scottish school mistresses and I told Ollie about them. Talking to her, I suddenly wanted very much to find out what really happened to them. I decided to go to Edinburgh this summer.

Ollie said she would like to come with me. She needs to revise her manuscript, which she has just completed in first draft, but she thinks she would be able to work in Scotland just as well as in New York.

JUNE 7, 1982

Coming from the airport last Wednesday afternoon, our taxi sped through some residential streets not far from the university. I caught a brief glimpse of a group of about ten school girls, all dressed in green monogrammed blazers, gray skirts, and green knee-high socks. I craned to see them as we passed, wanting images I could hold in my mind for the faces of Miss Munro and Miss Stirling and all the others. The taxi moved too quickly and I could not make them out individually. I was left only with the impression of round pink cheeks and smooth brown hair. Most of them were probably ten or twelve, much younger than the important girls in my drama, but about the age of Miss Hunter and the younger Miss Dunbar. Not an Indian girl among them, but I have no trouble seeing her. Her skin is quite brown. I thought at first that she might have British features superimposed on that dark skin, but I don't picture her that way now. She is very much Indian, of the large type rather than the delicate, with heavy eyelids.

I have spent all week, since Ollie and I arrived here, peering at faces. I think if I can fix pictures of all these people in my imagination I will write about them more clearly. Fashion changes, and customs change—but faces and characters must repeat themselves through the generations. I believe I have found the modern counterparts of most of the principals in the case.

For Charlotte Whiffin, the maidservant, my image is a girl I saw Friday night in a working-class disco that we happened into after an early dinner. The place was almost empty. She was on the floor, gracelessly dancing at a distance from her partner, barely lifting her feet or moving her body. They both, but she especially, looked bored—worse than bored, lifeless, without passion or hope. She is stocky, white-skinned, pimply. Several times while she danced she nervously tucked her white blouse into her blue skirt with her thumbs. I imagine her life to be almost unalloyed drudgery. She is probably a waitress. Nothing can transform her from the drudge she has become since she left childhood, not even "going out for a good time." I think she gossips viciously, losing herself in the meanest smears, which perhaps alone have the power to give her a jolt of life. What else could claim her interest?

I found two Marianne Woodses. The first was a young Marianne, about nineteen. I saw her on a bus that Ollie and I took to the National Library the day after we arrived here. She was very erect and stately for so young a girl, lovely and cold. She sat entirely still, aloof, removed. *Noli me tangere.* Who would dare to touch her? At her stop she *glided* off the bus. She was perfect in a manner that makes me unreasonably irritated.

The second Marianne Woods I found on Sunday. I wanted to go to St. Giles's because it had been the largest Presbyterian church in Edinburgh even when Jane Pirie was alive, and I think she must have come there often, at least during her childhood since it is near Lady Stairs Close, where she had lived. The associate preacher is a woman. I almost didn't notice her until Ollie said, "There is your Marianne Woods." She was right. There was Marianne Woods at about thirty-five, still erect and lovely despite a pockmarked face that relieves her from perfection. And she had been made more human by sorrow and the years. She read the closing prayer in a voice that was self-assured and intelligent. I suppose many of her parishioners are in love with her. You would still not dare to touch her, but you might hope that from her stately position she would deign to touch you.

I could find Jane Pirie nowhere, although I searched for her harder than for any of the others. Finally, this morning, I realized that whenever I looked for her, I myself appeared in my mind's eye: not my face but—what shall I call it?—my soul, my temperament, whatever I am inside.

Ollie has a cold. I feared that would happen to one of us, since it was 96 degrees Fahrenheit when we left New York and 41 when we got off the plane in Edinburgh. Where does one find chicken soup in Scotland?

JUNE 10, 1982

I actually had my hands on the complete, original trial transcripts today in the Signet Library. When the librarian first brought them out to me, I felt so awed that I was almost afraid to touch them. She must have thought I believed I was looking at the Magna Charta. Finally I went through the whole lot, very gingerly, to see what was there. There are over eight hundred pages. I intend to read through all the transcripts first to get a clearer picture of Jane Pirie and Marianne Woods and the others. Then I will go back and examine the trial itself.

Thus far I have been able to find little about the mistresses' backgrounds. Both had been governesses before they opened the girls' boarding school. How else might they have supported themselves in that day?

If her father's fortunes remained stable a girl of the middle class in early-nineteenth-century Britain could expect to drift into young ladyhood in the same idleness she had known from childhood, awaiting the suitor who would remove her from her patriarchal home into his. If her father's fortunes became uncertain, however, or if his hold on middle-class status was never more than precarious, a young lady who was still unclaimed at the age of seventeen or eighteen might have felt obliged to seek employment. But there were few kinds of jobs open to her.

In previous centuries there had been a number of trades that were considered appropriate for females of her class, but gradually those trades were taken over by men and they were now thought neither appropriate for her nor attainable. The universities were closed to her so she could not hope to train for a profession. And most professions were anyway closed to her. If she had some literary talent she might join the ranks of the popular lady novelists who were just beginning to emerge at this time. If not, her choices were few: she could be a paid companion to a wealthy woman or a teacher of some sort—giving private lessons, teaching in a school, or living with a family as a governess.

Governesses had been fixtures in upper-class households since Tudor days, but in the late eighteenth century, with a rising middle class that had pretensions to refinement, the number of governess positions grew, so that a genteel young lady who had to support herself would have had little trouble finding employment—if not in an upper-class household, then in a home not too socially disparate from the one in which she had grown up.

Such a young lady would probably have learned the rudiments of culture in her own home. Perhaps she too had had a governess who taught her reading, writing, some history and geography, some mathematics, along with sewing and embroidering. Or perhaps her mother had taught her these subjects. She may have been sent to a gentleman once a week to learn French and to a lady to learn music. Or possibly she had been at a boarding school, which was becoming a popular option for the education of middle-class girls by the end of the eighteenth century. Wherever she had got her education, it was rarely thorough, but it was considered sufficient to allow her to teach other young ladies.

However, while she might have found a governess' position without much difficulty, the literature of the period suggests that it was not very likely she would have been happy in her role. Mary Wollstonecraft complained at the end of the eighteenth century that a governess' chances of meeting with a reasonable employer were not better than one in ten, that having hired a governess the lady of the house would "continually find fault to prove she is not ignorant, and be displeased if her daughters do not improve, but angry if the proper methods are taken to make them do so." If a governess had some pride in her attainments and resented that a woman who was her intellectual inferior and barely her social superior should have power over her, her position would have been painful. Understanding this, it is not surprising to discover that by the mid-nineteenth century, according to the Victorian writer Harriet Martineau, governesses comprised the largest single group found in insane asylums. And by the time Martineau did her research, the Governesses' Benevolent Institution, which provided housing for unemployed governesses as well as counseling and old-age pensions, had been in existence for some years. In the early nineteenth century governesses had no such benevolent institutions to look after their interests and protect them from the vagaries of tyrannical employers.

There was little hope of escape for the governess, except through marriage—unless she could become her own employer. She could teach private students if she had some particular talent like dancing or drawing, but such employment was always uncertain—she might do very well one month and starve the next. If she was especially brave during that era when women rarely entered business, she could open a school. To be mistress of her own establishment must have seemed very attractive to a strong-minded governess. If she had some capital with which to set up a school, she could live where she was in charge rather than in the home of a family where she was a stranger, she could establish rules that she thought reasonable and effective for instruction and discipline, and she could enforce them as she believed best without having to be hourly accountable to the Lady of the house. The advertisements that were placed in Edinburgh newspapers during the early nineteenth century suggest that not a few Scottish governesses sought to liberate themselves from their subordinate role by opening their own boarding school for young ladies, as did Jane Pirie and Marianne Woods.

I discovered through the transcripts that Miss Woods and Miss Pirie met in 1802, in a Mr. Dallaway's art class, which they both attended with the hope of adding art to those subjects they were already qualified to teach. Jane was eighteen at the time; Marianne was nineteen. Jane had already been a governess for a year, teaching the three daughters of General Dirom, and Marianne had worked for some months as a governess and then assisted her uncle as a teacher of elocution. At a time when young ladies of their class were so often silly and helpless little misses, they must have found a good deal to admire in each other.

Jane Pirie's father was a writer of religious books. None of his works is extant. In checking the Edinburgh Postal Directory I found that he identified himself by his profession every year throughout the 1780s and 1790s; as late as 1814 he is listed as

"James Pirie, writer." Her mother was the daughter of a Presbyterian minister. They lived in Lady Stairs Close, one of the more respectable quarters of the Old Town in Edinburgh, where Richard Steele once supped and Bobbie Burns lived briefly in his more affluent days. Jane's older sister Margaret was a governess in the household of Sir Archibald Dunbar until she married in 1807. Through a series of circumstances, Margaret's job was to become fateful for her sister.

According to letters of reference that are part of the court record, Jane Pirie refused to leave Edinburgh in 1805 and 1807 although her employers asked that she move with them. It seems that she could not bear to be parted from Marianne. I think the first letter helps confirm the theory that the nineteenth century found romantic friendships between women to be perfectly normal. Jane Pirie told her employer that she could not go to Glasgow because of a close friend, and he did not seem to think it odd. The letters also show that Jane was a competent teacher, rather authoritarian, probably quite dramatic. Does an "ardent" temper mean that even before she had Mrs. Woods' antics to contend with, she flew into rages without regard to who was listening?

Letters of Reference: Miss Jane Pirie

March 6, 1805

Dear Sir or Madam,

I feel very much regret at parting with Miss Pirie, who has conducted herself very much to my satisfaction and done every duty to my little ones. At the same time, were it even in my power, I would not be so unjust as to ask her to remove with us to Glasgow when to remain in Edinburgh where she is near a dear friend is so crucial to her happiness. She informs me that she wishes to remain in Edinburgh also in order to complete herself in those branches of education she has not yet had the opportunity to do. This will certainly, in future life, be greatly to her advantage, and will make her more valuable to her employer.

Sincerely,
(Signed) *M. Dirom*

April 12, 1807

My Dear Mrs. Campbell,

Since our household must return to the country, I am happy to find that Miss Pirie has the prospect of getting into a situation in Edinburgh, where she wishes to remain, in which her abilities as a teacher will be justly appreciated. I, from my own experience, have reason to think very highly of them. Whatever she professes to teach, she teaches thoroughly. Her endeavours to facilitate the progress of her pupil are unremitting, and consequently successful; and she has ever maintained a proper authority. Miss Pirie's language and pronunciation are uncommonly good. She is a capital English scholar, has a competent knowledge of the French language, and has, in the short time she has been with us, brought on her pupil extremely well in writing, accounts, geography, music, drawing, etc. To her character and conduct I can likewise bear the most ample testimony. Nor, though her temper is ardent, did I ever find that it ever hurried her into impatience. In all that related to her pupil, I found her always willing to receive advice and to follow any plans that I suggested; and, in a word, that she conducted herself truly to my satisfaction.

(Signed) *Mrs. Hamilton*

I have found less information about Marianne Woods. She was the daughter of an English-born clerk. Although the transcripts do not indicate why she left her parents, from the time she was fifteen she lived with her uncle, William Woods, and his wife, Ann Quelch Woods. William Woods was an Edinburgh comedy actor, and he trained Marianne in elocution, rhetoric, and literature so that she might earn her own living as a teacher. When he retired from the stage in 1802 Marianne assisted him in giving private lessons. He died at the end of that year and she went off to London, to Camden House Academy, where she had a job as an assistant mistress.

Why did she stay at Camden House for only one year? Perhaps she found London too wild or too lonesome. Perhaps she returned to Edinburgh because she felt obligated to her aunt, Ann Woods, who had given Marianne a home for four years and now was alone and had no means of support. Or perhaps she returned because she missed Jane Pirie.

Apparently they had become passionate friends almost immediately in that era when romantic friendship between women was an accepted social institution. Marianne was a year older than Jane, and the transcripts allude to her having been more "polished in manners" than Jane. But she seems to have had a careful, subdued quality about her that was very different from Jane's forthright, energetic personality. Each must have admired in the other what she herself lacked, and they also shared interests and values—in literature, art, female self-sufficiency, competence. The only discordant note in their friendship at the beginning seems to have been Jane's devotion to the Church of Scotland, her spending long hours in worship on Sunday, denying herself a hot meal until the Sabbath was over. Marianne had been loosely brought up as an Episcopalian and religion meant much less to her. Perhaps she had a modifying effect on Jane's religious practices for a while.

Maybe before Marianne left for Camden House Academy they had talked about opening a school so that they might always live and work together, and Marianne went to London to see how a boarding school for young ladies was run. Or perhaps it was not until they had known one another for many years that they decided that to be their own mistresses would be a great improvement over their present lives. Or they may not have ever discussed such a move. But one day, in the spring of 1809, after Jane Pirie had been a governess with the Campbells for two years, she went with her charges to visit their friend at Drumsheugh, near the wealthy New Town section of Edinburgh.

Drumsheugh had not long before been part of the pleasure grounds of the Earl of Moray, but at the turn of the century a large portion of the property had been sold at public auction. It stood at the west end of Queen Street. Eventually the city, with its shops and markets and offices, would encroach, but now, in the spring of 1809, it was still full of blackbirds and thrushes and there was an unobstructed view across the Firth of Forth to the northwestern mountains. A few houses had lately been built there, though most of the area remained green and lush open field. Nearby, on the bank along the Water of Leith, were thick trees, and the corncrakes chirped without ceasing in the dewy grass. One could forget that the filth and noise and crowds of Edinburgh were only twenty minutes away by foot and much less by carriage.

Perhaps Jane wandered alone there on this fateful day while her charges had tea with their friend, though surely she would have been invited to join them. But at some time during this outing she came across a house that was in its final stages of construction, and the carpenter invited her in to look. Maybe she entered out of curiosity or to pass the time. It had a spacious drawing room and dining hall and several small rooms on the lower floor. The upper floor contained two very large bedrooms and two small ones. Its new wood and glass and wallpaper and brick must have been very appealing. She must have wondered how, short of marriage to a wealthy man (which was beyond her reach), she could ever become the proprietor of such a place. Maybe it was not until Jane Pirie saw the house that she thought she would like to open a school with Marianne Woods. Perhaps the sight of the house helped crystalize for her what it was she wanted to do with her life: live together with Marianne in security and stability, without the worry that an employer might move her off to Glasgow or the country. She had only recently engaged with the Campbells to serve another term, until November, but now she seemed to believe she must have that house and nothing else would do.

She had already been working for eight years and had managed to lay aside some money. True, she was only twenty-five, but she had met with nothing but success as a governess and probably could not imagine failure. Since the Edinburgh papers of the day often carried advertisements for women who were contemplating the establishment of girls' schools, why should she believe that what so many other women dared do was beyond her? Perhaps she had the same confidence in Marianne that she had in herself because she admired her so. And after all, not only had Marianne been able to support herself through her teaching, but she had also been the very responsible, sole support of her aunt.

I suspect that Jane counted her savings upon her return to the Campbells' that evening and then sent to Marianne Woods to tell her of the house. Perhaps Jane declared that if they pooled their resources they would have enough to rent it, buy furniture and school supplies, open the doors for business, and be their own mistresses forevermore. Marianne, the more cautious of the two, may have had reservations—the idea of the school might be a good one, but they would have to skimp too much now and it would be wiser to wait and save more; their finances were not equal so she did not know how she could claim full partnership and she would probably be dissatisfied with less; she had the responsibility of her aunt and did not know how Mrs. Woods would fit in to the school; Jane would not be free until next November and should not dare break a contract as it would surely damage her reputation, and Marianne feared she would be incapable of running the school by herself.

But Jane must have had answers to everything. Of course they would be full partners, regardless of how much or how little money each put in. Marianne should believe this to be fair since she would earn the right to claim full partnership by managing the school by herself from June until November, when Jane's agreement with the Campbells would be fulfilled. Mrs. Woods would live in the house, and she could even assist Marianne with the preparations and the management—with both Marianne and Mrs. Woods working in this way, surely Marianne could see that the name of Woods must in all fairness be placed right alongside that of Pirie in everything having to do with the school: Miss Pirie's and Miss Woods' School for Young Ladies. If they delayed they would lose the house, and there would never again be one like it.

Jane and Marianne signed the lease on April 1, 1809.

According to the transcripts, Marianne and her aunt moved into the house on Whitsunday, May 15, 1809. Mrs. Woods dealt with the merchants and established their presence in the community. Marianne solicited pupils. Jane, although she still lived with the Campbells, helped pay the bills of the house. Miss Hay, Miss Sandford, who was the Bishop's daughter, and Miss Clendenning, who had studied with Marianne before, signed to begin in September. At the beginning of December, a little over a month after Jane Pirie moved into the house, Lady Helen Cumming Gordon came to them upon the recommendation of Lady Dunbar, her daughter, in whose household Jane's sister, Margaret, had been a governess. Lady Cumming Gordon offered her natural granddaughter, Jane Cumming, a native of India, as a scholar. Jane Pirie and Marianne Woods asked to meet the girl. She was dark-skinned. I can only guess what went on after that interview, but I have gone through enough of the transcripts to have some notion of what their respective attitudes might have been.

"She will drive the other pupils away," Mrs. Woods must have warned. Jane Pirie agreed.

"She is related to Dame Cumming Gordon and recognized by her as her grandchild," Marianne must have said. "If she were purple, she would not drive away pupils."

"Don't make a foolish mistake," Margaret must have warned her sister. "If you accept this Indian girl your fortune is made. One word from Lady Cumming Gordon and every fine family in Scotland will be sending their daughters to you. But if you don't accept the girl because she is dark, everyone will say how despicable your behavior is, no matter what they think in their hearts. Here Dame Cumming Gordon acknowledges her, despite Her Ladyship's sorrow over her son's actions, despite the girl's color and illegitimacy, takes the child into her noble family and into her home, and here you refuse to take her into your school. Trust me. I know these ladies. There is color and then there is color. I know what a word from such a lady can do for you."

She was persuasive and she was correct. Jane Cumming became a pupil before Christmas. By the spring, largely through Lady Cumming Gordon's recommendations, the school enrolled the two Miss Dunbars, Miss Dewar, Miss Anstruther, Miss Hunter, the two Miss Edgars, Miss Cunynghame, and the two Miss Frasers. At the end of the following summer Miss Clendenning left and Miss Stirling and Miss Munro became pupils.

Five of the pupils were day students. The others slept at the house, five girls in one of the two large bedrooms and four girls in the other. Jane Pirie and Marianne Woods each slept in one of the bedrooms, in order that the young ladies might at all times be under the observation of one of their mistresses. In another small room Mrs. Woods slept. A fourth room, which might have been used as a small bedroom, was kept instead as a general dressing room for the school.

They taught everything but dancing and writing themselves. It must have been more work than either had dreamed. Jane Pirie must have been always apprehensive that they were failing or they would fail. It was not like having charge as a governess does over one or two or even three girls. They had constant responsibility for more than a dozen girls and there were no parents to settle altercations or to intimidate their children into good behavior by their presence. The mistresses had to set the tone by themselves. If they

were not stern, so many high-spirited young ladies in such close
confines would soon take advantage and make a mockery of the
whole endeavor. Punishment for the least transgression must be
swift, they probably decided. But how were they to do all this—
prepare lessons and administer them and supervise the study time
and correct the work and prepare new lessons; teach the girls
morals, religion, and good manners and exercise them and keep
peace among them and keep them healthy? If they should fail?
And how were they to find time for each other in the midst of all
this? The conception must have seemed so easy, the reality so difficult.

But the worst of it, for Jane Pirie, was Mrs. Ann Quelch
Woods.

The Woodses

Marianne must have felt that she owed a great deal to her aunt,
and she must have wanted to honor the memory of her deceased
uncle by providing for his destitute widow. They had taken
Marianne in and cared for her from the time she was fifteen, and
her uncle, William Woods, had prepared her to earn her own
bread.

William Woods, who was born in England, had been an actor
with the old Theatre Royal in Edinburgh since it was built in the
1780s, and for ten years before that a player of Iagos and Horatios
from the Haymarket in London to wherever a Shakespearean company might travel in Scotland. Although later in his life he seems
to have cultivated an image of respectability, as a young man he
had been the boon companion of Robert Fergusson, the Scottish
poet who died at the age of twenty-four, in 1774, in the bedlam attached to the Edinburgh poorhouse. Between the beginning of
1772 and the end of 1773, during the time when Fergusson wrote
most of the poems for which he is remembered, he and William
Woods were several times locked up for rowdiness by the Edin-

burgh City Guards. Some years afterward, Woods also drank with the poet Robert Burns at Dawney Douglas' bawdy tavern in the Anchor Close, a dark, narrow alley decorated with ancient mottoes: "The Lord Be My Support," "O Lord, In Thee Is All My Trust," "Be Merciful To Me." Woods' friendship with both these literary lights is recorded on his tombstone.

In his later years he appears to have been a scholar and a gentleman, which did him no good on the boards when, as an aging man, he found the roles he had popularized going to younger and inferior actors, and even less good when he tried to bargain with the enterprising and devious John Jackson, manager of the Theatre Royal. After two decades with the Theatre Royal, Woods retired in 1802 with only a little over two hundred pounds to live on. He was forced to supplement his income by giving lessons in elocution.

While all educated Scots could write the English language, many could not speak it without the heavy accent that made them unintelligible outside of north Britain. Since the Napoleonic Wars had begun in 1796, the British were not welcome on the Continent, and wealthy Scots now often went on holiday to London or watering places such as Bath, where they were made very aware of their dialect. Accepting the chauvinistic view of the south, which purported to be the true center of culture, many of them sought instruction in speaking the language as it was spoken by the better classes in London. A famous actor with a genuine English accent would have had a considerable advantage in appealing to the Scots' sense of cultural inferiority. Apparently William Woods had enough pupils so that he required Marianne to assist him in giving lessons. But he did not live long enough to amass much money from his students. He died at the end of his first year of retirement from the theater, leaving his widow, Ann Quelch Woods, with very little.

Ann Woods seems to have had the grand style of a theatrical personage, although her career as an actress was brief and not luminous. She had once been Leonora in *The Mourning Bride* and she had played a secondary role in the tragedy of *Douglas* with Mrs. Siddons in 1784. She was seen by much of Edinburgh then, since the city came to a virtual halt with the appearance of Mrs. Siddons, the most beloved British actress of her century. Everyone flocked to the theater. The General Assembly was deserted by its members, the Court was obliged to fit its important business in on alternate days, and even clergymen stood in line at the theater from the early afternoon. Perhaps Ann Woods never recovered from the dazzle of such reflected light. But that was the heyday of her career and almost the end of it. She apparently had no great talent for the stage and vanished from it after the mid-1780s. She would have had no more place in the public record were it not for her niece's devotion to her, which brought her to the Drumsheugh school and her battle with Miss Pirie.

It was on account of Marianne's attachment to Mrs. Woods that Jane Pirie was miserable. Had Mrs. Woods simply been content to be supported by her niece, there might not have been a problem. But she saw herself as the manager of the school, and the tradesmen and merchants made their bills out to her, since it was she who had opened the accounts in the beginning. One day, about six weeks after Jane Pirie joined the school, she decided they must have a more detailed terrestrial globe and she went to Princes Street that afternoon to buy one at a shop with which the school had an account. She was told by the owner that he could not give credit on her signature, and she must send her mistress in. She explained that she was the mistress of the school. He informed her that it was his understanding that Mrs. Woods was the mistress. She must have told him that it was largely with her money that the school began. "That is no business of mine," he must have said. "Mrs. Woods has told me that she is the mistress. The account is in her name, she has paid the bills, and so, as far as I know, she is the mistress."

I think that Jane Pirie must have walked out in high dudgeon, and not seeing a carriage for hire she ran almost all the mile and a half to Drumsheugh, repeating over and over the man's insufferable words and what she would tell Mrs. Woods.

She threw open the door and shouted, "Mrs. Woods, please come here immediately," though Miss Cunynghame and the elder Miss Dunbar were in the hallway. "You must go to Whyte's at once," she said to Mrs. Woods, "and tell that monstrous man to change the account into my name right away or the school will do no more business with him."

"Surely not at once," Mrs. Woods said. "It is only an hour to dinner."

"At once," Jane Pirie said.

Marianne had gone walking with the younger girls.

"I will not be ordered to do nonsense, and that so peremptorily," Mrs. Woods replied. "I will tell Mr. Whyte to change the name, of course. I only had it put in my name temporarily, for convenience, because you were away at Mrs. Campbell's. I had always intended to change it once you came. But tomorrow or the day after will be plenty of time, certainly."

"That man insulted me," Jane shouted. "I will not allow the sun to go down on his unchallenged insult. I can be vindicated only if you go to him. Please go now," she repeated.

"You're being childish," Mrs. Woods whispered, "and the young ladies are listening." She went upstairs to her room.

That was the beginning of the war, though I see that its seeds had been planted long before. Not only had Mrs. Woods assumed the management of the school from the very start, but also her conception of what the school should be was, judging from two advertisements I discovered, nothing like Jane's conception. This is the advertisement for the school, as it was written by Jane Pirie, that was to have been placed in the *Caledonian Mercury,* the *Aberdeen Journal,* the *Edinburgh Evening Courant,* the *Edinburgh Advertiser,* and the *Edinburgh Weekly Journal:*

> An establishment is now being formed by two Edinburgh Ladies, for a limited number of young ladies who are presently, or who have the parts to be, serious scholars. They will be taught arithmetic in all its branches on the newest and most approved plan, geography and the construction of maps geometrically, writing in its various forms and uses, and they will also be given instruction in the principles of literature, history, philosophy, religion, etc.
>
> The domestic arrangements are liberal, but not expensive, and are carefully adapted to form the manners of the pupils by diligent attention to their pursuits.

This is the advertisement as it was amended by Mrs. Woods, who placed it in the *Edinburgh Advertiser* for August 18, 1809, August 25, 1809, and September 12, 1809:

33

> With the recommendation and support of several fami-
> lies who regret the want of such an undertaking in Edin-
> burgh, an establishment is forming by two English Ladies
> for a limited number of young ladies of genteel connec-
> tions only, conducted on the plan of the most approved
> schools in London.
>
> The domestic arrangements are carefully adapted to
> combine the comforts of home with the forms of polished
> society. The plan is confined to those of amiable disposi-
> tion and destined for genteel life.
>
> Forty pounds per annum will include board, washing,
> and class and private instruction. Contact Mrs. Ann
> Quelch Woods, Drumsheugh.

One might have predicted a terrible battle between two who had
such disparate ideas of what a school for young ladies should be.

Then, after the Whyte's incident, Jane probably thought herself degraded. It was clear to her that she had been represented as a
mere employee in the school, even though the school would never
have existed without her idea and efforts and money. Injustice
galled her, and this was the most outrageous injustice. Regardless
of what she felt for Marianne, how could she tolerate this—being
talked back to and made to seem insignificant by this woman who
had seldom done a lick of work in her life and was now a dependent at her advanced age because of her husband's lack of prudence and foresight and her own uninventiveness?

Mrs. Woods would not go to change the name the next day or
the next. Finally, Marianne, distressed by the anger between the
two, went herself to change the name, but that would not placate
Jane.

In the beginning the three women had always supped together. Now Marianne ate with her aunt in Mrs. Woods' room and
Jane had her evening meal alone. It seems that Jane could not forget the matter of the name and the treachery it represented to her.
On Christmas Day she told Marianne she wished a certificate from
Mrs. Woods stating the truth. Mrs. Woods handed a slip of paper
to her the evening of December 26. "You see that I am willing to
do whatever is required of me," she must have said. The paper
read:

Whereas by some mistake most of the accounts of the
school of Marianne Woods and Jane Pirie are stated and
discharged in my name, I hereby declare that I paid no
part of the furnishings of this establishment; that the
same were paid equally by Miss Woods and Miss Pirie.
And I further declare that I have no title whatever to the
said furnishings.

(Signed) *Ann Quelch Woods*

Jane probably seethed, but determined to say nothing more to her.
However, when a copy of the Edinburgh Postal Directory arrived
at the beginning of the year and she saw that her establishment was
listed as "Mrs. and Miss Woods Boarding School, Drumsheugh,"
she exploded.

What was it she wanted? Marianne must have asked. She had
Mrs. Woods' apology and her own promise that the mistakes
would never again occur. What more could be done? Jane must
have resented Marianne's not knowing how to soothe her almost as
much as she resented the injustices.

"That woman must go or I must go," Jane said in March. She
had had no conversation with Mrs. Woods since that fatal day in
December. Probably there were truces—or rather there were periods when Marianne and Jane could sit together and talk of things
as they used to, and simply be, one with the other. And Jane barely
saw Mrs. Woods during the day or evening. But invariably something would happen—perhaps Mrs. Woods would order the servant to buy pork roasts when Jane had said they must have
mutton; she would cut larkspur and peonies from the terraced garden in front when Jane had said they were skimpy there and must
be left to grow, and all the cut flowers should come from the back
garden. And the war would begin again.

"Either she or I must go," Jane would tell Marianne. Then
perhaps there would be tearful scenes, even in front of the students,
with Marianne begging Jane to have pity on her. "It is not my aunt
you are hurting when you say that," she would cry. "It is I who am
tormented. If you love me as you say you do, why do you do this to
me? Where am I to send her? Where can she go? I beg you, stop
this if you love me." Then Jane would be contrite and they would

hold each other and cry and kiss, and there would be peace for a while.

Apparently, in the summer it was better. Marianne and Jane and the Indian girl (Jane's namesake, to her great consternation) went to Portobello, a seaside town a few miles from Edinburgh, for a holiday—Dame Cumming Gordon paid handsomely for the mistresses to keep her granddaughter while she herself traveled to Bath. Mrs. Woods stayed alone in Drumsheugh. Jane must have fogotten she existed.

But when they returned at the beginning of August, they found that Mrs. Woods had redecorated. A large painting of her husband in costume hung in the hallway. In the dining room, a sideboard that Jane had never before seen replaced the one she had selected and paid for on the same day they rented the house. Knickknacks and geegaws were everywhere. "This is all I have left of my married life," Mrs. Woods must have explained, "but I wished to share them with the school. I wished to give something, since I have been accused of giving nothing."

At the end of the month Jane consulted Mrs. Hamilton, who had often been in litigation when Jane taught her niece, the Earl of Lucan's daughter, and was advised to find an attorney or an objective party who would make an amicable financial settlement between herself and Marianne. Jane told Marianne she would leave as soon as this was done. They must have wept and remonstrated and shouted at each other. Some weeks later Marianne took away everything her aunt had put up over the summer. Then Mrs. Woods said that she would be the one to leave. At this, Jane told Marianne that she would be happy even to help support her aunt: they would find a place for her to live somewhere in Edinburgh or nearby Leith, and Marianne might visit her as often as she liked. They were agreed on Marianne's birthday, October 12. Then they fought again late in October because, Jane said, Marianne had not yet made a single move to relocate Mrs. Woods. On November 4, however, Mrs. Woods said she would leave of her own accord if she might have a third of the profits of the school. Jane must have thought it a bargain, though she was probably resentful too. But at the end of that week Marianne announced that her aunt was developing cataracts and would very possibly be blind before long. She could not send her alone to a flat, even with a third of the profits. And after that they had another problem.

On Saturday afternoon, November 10, 1810, Jane Cumming went to her grandmother's home at 22 Charlotte Square, where she spent the rest of the weekend. She returned to the school on Monday. On Wednesday morning her grandmother sent a servant to fetch her and her two cousins, the Miss Dunbars. Then the Edgars' servant came for the two Miss Edgars and the Frasers' servant came for the two Miss Frasers. The next day Mr. Stirling, Mrs. Munro, and Mrs. Anstruther came for their daughters, and then Lady Cunynghame came for her daughter. By Friday afternoon not a student remained in the school.

JANE CUMMING

In 1792, George Cumming, at the age of eighteen, went to India in the service of the Honourable East India Company, as had his father and uncles before him. He was the eldest son of Lieutenant Colonel Alexander Penrose Cumming of Altyre. Because of his father's friendship with Henry Dundas, President of the Board of Control for India Affairs, George was placed in an advantageous position in Patna, and his father looked forward to his glorious career. But George died before he reached his twenty-seventh birthday. He left a natural daughter, born at the end of 1795 or at the beginning of 1796 to him and a fifteen-year-old Indian girl whose father was a minor official. The child was born about the same time George's father inherited Gordonstoun and added to his family name the last name of Sir William Gordon, the relative who was gracious enough to die unmarried.

George's daughter had been given a Christian name, Jane, and at the demand of her Indian grandfather the last name of Cumming. The old gentleman could accomplish no more for his granddaughter, although George continued to see her mother, apparently promised to restore her honor in the near future, and provided money for the baby's welfare. He also hired a nurse for her so that the Indian girl would not be tied down with the child. When Jane Cumming was four, George informed his mother, Helen Cumming Gordon, of the child's existence at the same time as he informed her that he had developed a debilitating illness. She wrote that he must return home to Scotland immediately and sent him a sum of money sufficient for the child's upkeep for the next dozen years. She also wrote to a distant cousin who resided in Calcutta, a Mr. Palmer, begging him to assist George in his return and in setting up a trust for the child. George did not return home, and he refused all Mr. Palmer's offers of assistance.

Ten months later he died, but not before he communicated with Mr. Palmer, asking him to take charge of Jane's education, and enclosing the large draft that his mother had sent. Mr. Palmer immediately met with the child's mother and grandfather and arranged to have her sent to a Christian boarding school in Calcutta. When she complained of ill treatment by the other children only weeks after her arrival—she was the only child there not entirely European—he immediately found another school for her in which there were Indian children as well as European.

George's mother was prostrated by shock and grief at his death, which she blamed on his transgression. When her husband became seriously ill the following year she also blamed her son. With her husband's growing illness she must have concluded that she could help save her son's soul if she brought his natural child to Scotland and raised her. Helen Cumming Gordon must have had no difficulty convincing the girl's Indian grandfather to have the girl sent to her. The child's mother was now settled in Bombay and had just begun a courtship with an English military man.

In 1803 Jane Cumming arrived in Scotland and went to live with her natural grandparents at Gordonstoun. In 1804 Alexander Cumming Gordon appeared to have a remission from his illness. He was also made a baronet that year. Shortly afterward, Jane was sent to a boarding school at Elgin, near the Gordonstoun estate, operated by a Miss Charles, who had once been a governess in the Cumming family and was now training daughters of shopkeepers and craftsmen. Dame Cumming Gordon had decided that her natural granddaughter should be bred to a trade such as mantua-maker or milliner, so that she might make a living by her own efforts in a reputable but inferior station in life. The girl continued at the school for almost five years, spending only occasional holidays at Gordonstoun. In 1806 Sir Alexander died, and the following year Lady Cumming Gordon moved to Edinburgh so that she might be near her favorite daughter and namesake, Lady Helen Dunbar.

In the previous century the aristocracy avoided Edinburgh unless called there by court duties or other obligations. Because there were few decent residential areas outside of George Square, where several mansions stood, people of rank much preferred their country estates. They were loath even to visit Edinburgh, and for pleasure they made frequent trips to London or the Continent. The city was almost unrelievedly ugly, with its narrow lanes and dirty streets, noisy marketplaces, and crowded, multistoried houses. The wealthy who were forced to dwell in the city because of some duty generally inhabited the intermediate floors of the large tenement houses of ten or twelve stories which were built in the many wynds and closes that connected to the High Street. They occupied the same buildings as mechanics and sweeps and dancing masters and shopkeepers, the poor classes living on the lowest floors, where the stench from the street was very noticeable, or on the highest floors, which occasioned strenuous climbs up many flights of stairs. The stairs were usually filthy and dark, and they were worn and sloping with traffic. It was no easy task for fashionable ladies to crush their hoops of four or five yards in circumference up those narrow stairs. And one had to walk the streets of Edinburgh with great care in the eighteenth century, since it was customary for the tenement dwellers to pour their slops out of the windows. Sometimes, before pouring they practiced the delicacy of calling "gardyloo" (*garde à l'eau:* watch the water), and they would halt if they heard in response, "Haud yer hand." But even the wealthy who rode in sedan chairs had no guarantee against the deafness or slow reflexes of the slop-pot emptiers.

However, all that belonged to the section of the city that came to be called the Old Town. In the late eighteenth century, the architect James Craig planned a self-contained residential area of stately streets, tree-lined walks, and lovely squares in a valley overlooking the old part of the city. In 1791 Robert Adams designed the first development, to be called Charlotte Square. The house in Charlotte Square, which Lady Cumming Gordon bought for twenty-five hundred pounds in 1806, had been built five years earlier. Like all the houses in Charlotte Square, it was three stories high, made of the best hewn stone, and enclosed by an iron railing of uniform height. Lady Cumming Gordon's neighbors were, for the most part, magistrates and titled people. Her sister, who was the wife of Henry Mackenzie, the novelist, lived close by. The Drumsheugh school was a half mile away.

The New Town was indeed lovely and placid seeming. It had no more resemblance to the Old Town, as one nineteenth-century observer noted, than if each had been built by distant nations or in different quarters of the globe. But it was exposed to very violent winds, even worse than those which raged in the Old Town with incredible fury. Houses were sometimes blown down. Large trees were torn up by the roots. People were carried off their feet.

After Lady Cumming Gordon moved to Edinburgh, Jane did not see her grandmother for two years. But one night in her Charlotte Square home Lady Cumming Gordon had a dream, and the next morning she sent for her natural granddaughter. She informed the girl that she was no longer to be educated for business. She would be introduced into the world as a daughter of the family.

Lady Cumming Gordon then determined to place the girl at an Edinburgh boarding school, believing that she would have more benefit of masters, and other advantages that could not be obtained in the country. She learned from her daughter Lady Dunbar that a new school for young ladies was to be opened at Drumsheugh, which was so near Lady Cumming Gordon's home in Charlotte Square. Since one of the mistresses was the sister of Margaret Pirie, who, Lady Dunbar said, had been the most excellent governess she ever employed for her children, Lady Dunbar had reason to believe that the school would be superior. But she must have had some reservations about her mother's new enthusiasm over the Indian girl.

How difficult it must have been for Lady Cumming Gordon to have a relationship with this girl. There was so much sadness and ambivalence in it, even from its beginning: to lose an eldest son, as Lady Cumming Gordon did, in a distant, frightening country. Whose idea of shoving him into manhood was it to send the boy there at the age of eighteen? Certainly not a mother's. In those days boys as young as eleven or twelve were sent off as midshipmen in the Navy. But what mother, especially of the upper class where there would have been no relief at one less mouth to feed, could have been happy at such a separation? And what was worse, he had been sent to the other side of the world. India was the white man's burden and loot, and it was wealthy British fathers who handed it down to their sons. So he was severed from her while he was still only a child, and it was impressed upon him that in India he must prove himself a man. Didn't white men in those days often lay their first claim to manhood in the beds of dark-skinned women, those manhood bestowers who were often themselves all of fourteen or fifteen? George Cumming found one, or perhaps he found many—but one he made pregnant (or was told he made pregnant). That must have happened often enough in India, but this young man acknowledged that the child was his, and he continued his affair with its mother after it was born. Perhaps that was as much testimony to his naïveté as to his good heart.

Had George lived, certainly the child would have been nothing to Lady Cumming Gordon, because undoubtedly he would have had many more, and of the right color. But he died, as did so many young white men in that distant country which hated them and expelled them, often by disease when it could find no other way to rid itself of the dark man's burden.

I can imagine the initial response Lady Cumming Gordon must have gotten from her husband and sons and daughters when she announced that she was bringing an illegitimate half-breed into Scotland and into her home. One did not acknowledge in Britain what went on in the heart of darkness. What the British did in India belonged in India. And now Lady Cumming Gordon proposed the insanity of mixing the two.

But how long could her family have held out against her when she insisted with a frenzy, which seemed to be born as much of superstition as of her sense of dreadful loss, that she must have the only fruit of her eldest son's seed?

Was the good lady horrified from the first moment she looked at Jane Cumming? Had she thought that the girl would resemble her son, and was she angry and chagrined when she could find no resemblance? Is that why she quickly shipped her off to a school for daughters of tradesmen? Did she recognize once the girl stood before her that it would be impossible to pass this very dark skinned child off as the genuine article, either to herself or to her narrow aristocratic circle? Or had she thought that she had shouldered enough of the white woman's burden by taking the girl from her heathen country and assuming financial responsibility for her?

It was probably nerve-racking to think what to do with the girl once she arrived. When Lady Cumming Gordon decided to send her to a school where she would learn a trade, the decision was probably made with guilt and ambivalence. Then it must have been in another frenzy born of superstitious anxiety that she determined that the girl must be treated as if she had legitimate claim to the family. During all this time the family looked on, probably with a mixture of skepticism and apprehension. How could it end well? If she were trained for a trade they would have a tradeswoman among them. Would they have to invite a tradeswoman and her tradeshusband to Christmas dinner along with the Duchess of Gordon? If she were removed from the trade school and educated for society, what could become of her when she reached adulthood? What young man who respected himself would take an illegitimate girl, and of her color too? Perhaps a fortune hunter would marry her to get hold of whatever would be the manifestation of Lady Cumming Gordon's generosity; and how could they accept him into the family? Lady Cumming Gordon must have been aware herself of the terrible dilemma that her grief and superstition had occasioned. But she must have believed that there was no way out of it.

Miss Woods and Miss Pirie had, in December of 1809, only one boarder and two day pupils in the school. Lady Cumming Gordon probably saw that the mistresses were hesitant to accept her granddaughter because she was a girl of color. She was explicit in pointing out to them that the tinge was just barely perceptible. And she more than hinted that she could be very generous if she were pleased. Just before Christmas Lady Cumming Gordon left her granddaughter at the school and went to spend the holidays at Gordonstoun, but not before she recommended the school to three other families. A few months later she also persuaded Lady Dunbar to send two of her children to the school as day scholars. With the advent of so many pupils from such distinguished families, the mistresses were grateful to Lady Cumming Gordon, believing she had made their fortune.

June 12, 1982

I think Marianne Woods and Jane Pirie loved each other. In the early nineteenth century that bare fact would not have had such power to elicit shock as it did a century later. They lived at a time when Sarah Ponsonby and Eleanor Butler, the "Ladies of Llangollen," two women who eloped together and lived for fifty-three years in romantic friendship, were looked on by the arbiters of taste and morality as "fair and noble ornaments of their sex" and "sisters in love." In 1810, not long after Jane Pirie came to join Marianne Woods in the school they had established, she gave her beloved a present of the just-published poetical works of Anna Seward, with its laudatory preface by the great lion of Scotland, Sir Walter Scott. It surprised neither woman, nor any other British reader, that many of the poems were love lyrics to Honora Sneyd, who, Anna Seward said, was dearer to her than life itself.

This was the way romantic friends wrote of each other at the time:

To Honora Sneyd

An Elegy
Honora fled, I seek her favourite scene
With hasty step, as I should meet her there;
The hasty step and the disorder'd mien
Fond expectation's anxious semblance wear.

This bowery terrace, where she frequent stray'd,
And frequent cull'd for me the floral wreath,
That tower, that lake,—yon willow's ample shade,
All, all the vale her spirit seems to breathe.

I seize the loved resemblance it displays,
With mixture strange of anguish and delight;
I bend on vacancy an earnest gaze,
Where strong illusion cheats my straining sight.

But ah, it fades!—and no relief I find,
Save that which silence, memory, hope confer;
Too soon the local semblance leaves my mind,
E'en where each object seem'd so full of her.

And Memory, only Memory, can impart
The dear enduring image to my view;
Has she not drawn thee, loveliest, on my heart
In faithful tints, and permanent as true?

Transcending all associate forms disclose
Of evanescent likeness; or each grace
The breathing pencil's happiest effort throws
O'er the bright lines that imitate thy face.

As much too fix'd as theirs too fleeting found,
The pencil but one look, one gesture brings;
But varying charms, each accent's thrilling sound
From Recollection's juster portrait springs.

Be then th' embosom'd image only sought,
Since perfect only can its magic prove!
O! rise with all HONORA's sweetness fraught,
Vivid, and perfect, as her ANNA's love.

Shew me how fair she seems, when on the gale
Her waving locks, in soft luxuriance, play;
As lightly bounding down the dewy vale,
She pours her rival beauties on the day!

How fair, e'en when displeasure's darkening frown,
And scorn itself are lovely on her brow;
Like summer shades, that sweep the vale adown,
Pass o'er the flowers, and heighten all their glow;

Yet fairer, when her brightening spirit spreads,
In blest vicissitude, the cheering ray,
As Sensibility, quick veering, sheds
Its clouds and sun-shine o'er her April-day.

But fairest when her vermeil lips disclose,
In many a magic smile and melting tone,
The varied accent through the pearly rows,
That proves the mental graces all her own.

I think that Jane Pirie may have told Marianne Woods that her love for Marianne was "vivid, and perfect," and Marianne may have said the same to Jane. I think that in opening the school they had planned to be together forever, just as Mary Wollstonecraft planned to be with her beloved Fanny Blood when they opened a girls' boarding school a few decades earlier.

Probably along with their romantic friendship Jane and Marianne, like Mary Wollstonecraft, had notions about female independence and achievement. Apparently they were both somewhat "bluestocking," although they must have known that Scottish wits called bluestockings "the very *flour* of their sex." They took themselves seriously as autonomous, thinking beings. Probably they would not have been happy in a conventional nineteenth-century marriage.

They were children during the French Revolution, which fostered the beginnings of a women's movement throughout western Europe among those who believed that great changes were coming not only for the lower classes but for women also. They may have been among that small group of women who demanded for themselves, as Mary Wollstonecraft did just before them, fulfilling work together with loving companionship outside of the constraints of tradition.

They were daughters of the middle class. Had they not grown up in the midst of revolutionary fervor, they might not have been able to formulate such a vision of what they wanted their lives to be. But had they grown up 100 years later, they would have found themselves comfortable in the midst of a large feminist movement where their revolutionary avowals to find fulfilling work and loving companionship on their own terms had become as commonplace as a slogan. Had they grown up 150 years later, after Freud became a household word, they would have found there was a name not at all to their liking for their dual desires.

In 1810, before the rise of a large feminist movement and before the advent of Freud and the Freudians, almost no one bothered with such names. If a few women wished to be proprietors of girls' schools, let them. There were not enough men with the patience and adaptability required to teach the young when more and more of the rising middle class as well as the upper class were desiring that all their young be taught. These school mistresses had a role in an upwardly mobile society. Nor did they demand that all females neglect their womanly duties in such pursuits. A few mistresses hardly made a women's liberation movement.

And that such independent women might find substitutes with each other for the marriage act was unthinkable. Good women—middle-class women—were considered to be without sexual passions. Prostitutes and actresses and French queens might pollute themselves in vile, unspeakable ways, but decent women never had such urges.

JUNE 13, 1982

I have been reading some letters that passed between Marianne Woods and Jane Pirie during the last weeks of the school's existence. They refer to other letters that were consigned to the flames in anger, so I have probably seen all that survived. The earliest piece was a note that Jane Pirie wrote to accompany a present of a Bible, which she gave to Marianne Woods on her birthday, October 12, 1810:

> Accept, my beloved, of that Book, which can give consolation in every situation; and, dearest *earthly* friend, never open it, without thinking of her who would forego all friendships, but her God's, to possess yours.
>
> Ever your own,
(Signed) Jane Pirie

They had been back from their Portobello vacation for more than two months, they had fought over Mrs. Woods' redecorations in their absence, and they had made up and fought again. Now Mrs. Woods agreed to leave their establishment and to live by herself. Jane Pirie must have seen stretched before her a great peaceful vista, where she could lay down her arms and travel on, for as long as they both lived, with her dearest earthly friend, her beloved. But when a whole week passed, and then another, and no more mention was made of Mrs. Woods leaving, Jane Pirie vented her fury again. Two weeks after Marianne's birthday, her anger must have erupted. In a letter written by Marianne on October 28, 1810, she alluded to some "papers" belonging to her that Jane Pirie had burned. I think they may have been impassioned notes that Jane had once written Marianne and then stolen from her, since Marianne demanded in exchange for the burned papers that "every note and letter be returned which I unfortunately addressed to you."

If the girls had seen Jane Pirie rifling through Marianne's possessions to find those papers, what would they have made of such a scene? How might it have affected Jane Cumming in particular? Perhaps the mistresses had come to be something like parents to her during the many weeks she was alone with them at Portobello. Whether she loved them or not, they may have represented to her the only stability she had in life now, and to see them in battle with each other must have been as jarring to her as it would be to a child who saw her parents in such combat. Maybe their instability after the peaceful hiatus of the vacation so upset her that she sought a bizarre way to punish them.

Even if she and the other girls had not seen Jane Pirie rifling through Marianne's drawers or heard their squabbles, it would have been impossible for the mistresses to hide the animosity that brought forth so cold a letter as this one that Marianne wrote to Jane Pirie, who had called her "beloved" only two weeks earlier:

October 28, 1810

Madam,

I have been made deeply sensible of my error in supposing that business might be transacted between those who are termed friends in a manner different from that between declared foes. I am willing to share the blame of this oversight with you, but I shall ever deplore its consequences. It is an old saying, but its truth is more to be trusted on that account, that it is needless to look back on the past. The experience I have gained from it, however, teaches me to prepare for the future. On that subject, therefore, I wish to address you.

Marianne goes on in this letter to propose terms by which she might "retire from this uncomfortable and unadvantageous situation": they will part at the end of the spring; they will announce their intention to the parents no sooner than three months before they separate (had she extended their union so far into the future because she hoped for another reconciliation?); they will dispose of their furniture at public auction. She also warns Jane that for as long as they continue together, "I require that all the pupils should be governed by the same rules, served with the same accommodation, treated with equal attention, and in every respect taught to consider themselves as members of one family—since discord and discontent must be the result of unequal treatment." Had Jane Pirie allowed her initial repugnance to her namesake to show again? Was it Jane Cumming's discontent to which Marianne referred—and to the discord she had sown as a result? How much more she would soon sow Marianne could not have known on October 28.

The next extant letter was written the following day. Jane Pirie does not deign to open with even so cold an address as "Madam." She simply begins, "I will not answer the greater part of your epistle till I can fully adjust myself to your willingness to sacrifice me to fame, interest, etc." One accusation follows another in this letter, whose theme is Marianne's untrustworthiness: "God sees all hearts, and He knows that I was willing to sacrifice everything on earth for her who professed to be my *friend.* But I believe that you knew the line of conduct you meant to pursue in respect to Mrs. Woods and me, and you must have told her you would sacrifice me at the same time that you were declaring sincere love and friendship for your too credulous friend. I see now that your system of establishing Mrs. Woods in opposition to my interests has been uniformly pursued from the very start of our school." Jane does not acknowledge Marianne's proposal to leave, but says that she will herself give three months' notice "before I quit this abode of misery—this is all you can reasonably expect from me." She ends, "The letters I unfortunately received from you shall *never* be left tossing about for anyone's perusal as you left mine"—which was her excuse for having gone through Marianne's papers to reclaim what she sent her. They must have exchanged proclamations of devotion in those letters or Jane would not now, in her anger, have described their receipt as unfortunate. Would the girls who read those letters that were left "tossing about" have laughed at the excess of passion in what Jane Pirie wrote, or would they have found it frightening, or would they simply have accepted it as a usual manifestation of romantic friendship?

Two days later, on October 31, the first anniversary of Jane's move to the school, she received a response to this October 29 letter, but what Marianne said we will never know. "I have just received your last production," Jane immediately wrote back, "and have tossed it to the fire where it belongs." She thanks Marianne, with bitter irony, "for sending it on an evening when you knew it would be doubly pleasant." And then she continues to harp on her old theme—that Mrs. Woods and Marianne wished to steal from her her hard-earned position as a head of the school and relegate her to being a mere servant: "I shall oblige you to consider me as your *equal,* although you have worked hard to bring me from *respectability* to a situation I think *contemptible. I* could never attempt to establish myself by degrading *you* in the eyes of the world as you have done to me. Nor could I have, by any dishonourable means, tried to establish myself as head of the school and '*Lady* of this house,' etc., since I could not have conceived of such mean intentions. . . . I pray that the Almighty will enable me to be indifferent to a person who has proved herself *unworthy* of the confidence I placed in her, and that He will make your *selfish* conduct a means of showing me to trust Him alone."

There is no evidence that Marianne had such dastardly intentions toward her friend, although perhaps she should have given more scrupulous directions to her aunt: to establish the accounts in Jane's and Marianne's names only, to advertise the school as Jane wished it advertised, to list it in the postal directory as the Woods and Pirie school rather than the Woods and Woods school.

Ollie says that Jane's concerns were petty, that it should not have mattered how the school was listed as long as it was clear between Marianne and Jane that they were equal partners. She cannot understand how Jane could have loved Marianne yet still believed she would cheat her. But Ollie's father owns a chain of restaurants all over the Southwest and she went to Bennington and Yale. I tell her that she probably has little idea of what it is like to begin with no one behind you and with nothing but your ambition, to know that you must be a self-made woman if you are to be anything at all.

"I have no trouble believing that Jane loved Marianne fiercely," I say, "but she wanted *every damned crumb* she had coming to her—because no one had ever given her anything, and she was determined that no one would take away what little she had managed to wrest from the world with her hard labor."

I found one more letter concerning the two mistresses, dated November 5. It was addressed to Mrs. Hamilton, whom it seems Jane called on for advice on several occasions and used as a confidante. In this letter, Jane was somewhat relieved because the matter of Mrs. Woods had been finally settled. Following Mrs. Hamilton's earlier advice, Jane had demanded that an impartial party be called in, and Mrs. Woods agreed to accept the services of Mr. Reid, an English clergyman and acquaintance of hers, who helped them come to the agreement that Mrs. Woods would retire with a third of the profits.

Jane says in this letter that she is gratified that Mrs. Woods is finally leaving, but she does not seem able to overcome her suspicions of her beloved friend, though she loves her still:

> In the course of this business, circumstances have arisen to shake my faith in my friend's affections for *me.* I always loved *her* as my own soul; and I would willingly have laid down my existence to increase her comforts, until my confidence in her sincerity was so cruelly shaken.
>
> When I give way to doubts, I feel miserable beyond description, but circumstances are daily occurring to prove that she would sacrifice me to her aunt's comfort and pride. Dear Madam, how should I act? I can *never* conquer my affection, should she even declare herself my enemy. I have loved her for eight years with sincere and ardent affection, and I have accustomed my mind to contemplate her as the model of every virtue. And if I cannot regard her as superior to everything that is unworthy of a great and exalted mind, I feel that misery must be my portion in this life. You must aid me with your advice, as you can enter into my feelings, and perhaps you can administer an opiate that can assuage the heart-rending sorrow I frequently experience.

Pardon this incoherent production. Permit me to see you when convenient. And believe me ever grateful.

(Signed) *Jane Pirie*

"Jane Pirie was a classic injustice collector," Ollie says. "She needed to hang on to slights, even after they had been remedied. I think she was in love with her suffering."

I believe Ollie is too hard on her. "Don't you think Jane Pirie had reason to be hurt and even suspicious, since Marianne allowed her aunt to act like a proprietor when she wasn't and to rob Jane of her little taste of glory?"

"Perhaps," Ollie says. "But there is something fantastical in her reactions—her overreactions. A kind of morbidity. She was certainly a bit odd, maybe even a little crazy."

At dinner I find my plate surrounded by half a dozen hot, buttered scones, which I love.

"They're all for you, my love," Ollie says. "All I want is the pleasure of seeing you devour them, *every damned crumb.*"

But I do not have to press her very hard to eat half of them herself.

THE BREAKUP OF THE SCHOOL

By Friday afternoon, November 16, 1810, not a student remained in the school. Parents or servants had come to fetch the girls in carriages, on foot, with sedan chairs. The house in Drumsheugh must have been in chaos, and with the appearance of each tight-lipped adult and the departure of each student, the mistresses must have gotten more and more frantic. No one would tell them why the girls were being removed. The parents and servants refused to utter anything except that they had come to take away their young ladies immediately.

It did not take long for the mistresses to discern that Jane

Cumming was the source of their ruin. Did they know because they understood that she had caught them in some guilty act—or did they assume their new tragedy was traceable to her because she and her cousins were the first to be removed upon her visit home? On Wednesday morning, November 14, the mistresses had received this terse note from Lady Cumming Gordon: "Lady Cumming Gordon presents compliments to Miss Woods and Miss Pirie. She will be obliged to them to send her a statement of the Miss Dunbars' and Miss Jane Cumming's accounts. She intends to dispatch a servant immediately for her grandchildren as she does not find it convenient to allow them to return to school any more. She will likewise be obliged to Miss Woods and Miss Pirie to send Miss Jane Cumming's and the Miss Dunbars' clothes, books, music, etc."

It came without warning, but the mistresses recognized it as the death knell of their school, and the events of the next few hours proved them right. In the afternoon of that day they sent a card to Lady Cumming Gordon, to which they received no answer: "Miss Woods and Miss Pirie beg leave to address Lady Cumming Gordon. There has been some delay in the execution of her Ladyship's commands, but as soon as possible they will be attended to. The extreme anxiety of mind Miss Woods and Miss Pirie are in can alone excuse the earnest entreaty they will now make to her Ladyship that she will candidly state to them every circumstance which has occasioned her Ladyship's disapproval, and by its consequence seems to threaten their total ruin."

By then Lady Cumming Gordon had written to the parents of some students and several girls had just been removed. Two of Lady Cumming Gordon's notes to the parents are extant. The first is dated Wednesday afternoon and addressed to the wife of General Anstruther, who, upon Lady Cumming Gordon's recommendation, had placed her daughter in the school: "Lady Cumming Gordon presents best compliments to Mrs. Anstruther. She thinks it right to inform her that she has found it necessary today, for serious reasons, to take away her grandchildren from Miss Woods' and Miss Pirie's school. As Lady Cumming Gordon recommended the school for Miss Anstruther, she wishes to give her the earliest information. Lady Cumming Gordon sent for her children home without assigning any reason but a wish to have them home. She will call and give Mrs. Anstruther her reasons for what she has done tomorrow."

The second extant note is dated Thursday morning and is addressed to Lady Cunynghame, whose daughter Mary became a student at the school after Lady Cumming Gordon had praised the mistresses to Lady Cunynghame. Lady Cunynghame did not call for her daughter until Friday, and she alone spoke to the mistresses and showed them this note: "Lady Cumming Gordon presents her best compliments to Lady Cunynghame and begs to inform her Ladyship that she has, for very serious reasons, taken her grandchildren from Miss Woods' and Miss Pirie's school. As Lady Cumming Gordon was one of those who recommended the school to Lady Cunynghame, she feels it her duty to advise her very strongly to the same measure, *as soon as possible.*"

On Friday morning the mistresses went together to Lady Cumming Gordon's home in Charlotte Square, but she refused to see them. A daughter who resided with Lady Cumming Gordon, Mary Cumming, said her mother was ill and shut the door in their faces. On Friday afternoon Jane Pirie wrote to Mary Cumming. It is clear that by now Jane Pirie had absolutely no doubt that her namesake was the cause of all that had transpired in the preceding days: "If you ever expect mercy from the God of mercy, tell what your niece has said to injure two innocent persons who have laboured for nearly twelve months to improve her in every religious and moral virtue, and who are thus cruelly repaid by her. We never did anything to offend her, except perhaps to discharge our duty towards her too rigidly and to tell her of her faults too freely. You are again implored, for the sake of that God from whom you hope for mercy, to tell us of what she accuses us. The calumny has been traced to her and she appears to be the sole author of it. If ever Christian mercy or pity had place in your heart, do not delay to state *all* she says against us, as every hour's delay increases the misery she has already occasioned." But this plea too went unanswered.

Whether or not they surmised what Jane Cumming told her grandmother, whether or not they had reason to feel guilty, they must have suffered agonies. Jane Pirie must have been utterly hysterical. But if they knew what the Indian girl had said and if there was any truth in it, their next step was bold beyond belief. How did they muster such courage, such audacity?

They took themselves to the firm of John Clerk, the most successful lawyer in Edinburgh, and they told John Clerk himself that they wished to sue Lady Cumming Gordon for libel.

JOHN CLERK, COUNSEL FOR THE PLAINTIFFS

John Clerk never married. His biographer says he died surrounded only by ten cats, his companions. Yet his contemporaries all agreed he was brilliant. At one period during his career as a lawyer, Clerk had nearly half the business of the important Court of Session on his hands. He was plain, shrewd, sarcastic. His disdainful smile was famous. A younger lawyer, who often scrutinized him in court for the tricks of the trade such observation might yield, wrote that Clerk was affected with the most delightful and balmy feelings by the contemplation of any lesser legal light, some soft-headed, prosy driveller, racking his poor brain or bellowing his lungs out—all about something that he, the smiler, saw through so thoroughly, so distinctly. How chilling he must have been in a cross-examination.

He was a man's man. Only a year or two before he took on Miss Woods and Miss Pirie's case, he had been presented with a silver trophy from the British navy because, they proclaimed, his essay on naval tactics had rendered his country indebted to him: Clerk had analyzed and invented infallible countermaneuvers to the sly naval maneuvers of the French, and now the skill and courage of the British would no longer be baffled by Bony and the "mounseers" at his back. Clerk could not fight himself—he had a deformed leg and he limped—but he was wonderful at war games.

Nor did he divert himself much with women, but in his spare time he was an artist, and he was fond of drawing Bathsheba with her foot in the water. His biographer says he disliked the sex.

He was elevated to a judgeship in the Court of Session in 1823, shortly after the Woods and Pirie case was concluded. By that time, however, he was approaching senility. It was not long after his appointment that his memory failed entirely. On one occasion he heard a lengthy debate, begun one day and concluded the next. At its conclusion he announced that he did not know what the parties were talking about and requested that they begin at the beginning. Some months later he was asked by his brother judges to leave the Court, a sad end for one who had prided himself on his superior mentality.

How did the two approach such a man? What might they have said to him the first time they walked into his office? "We have been accused of . . ." What? "We want you to say in our defense . . ." Whether or not they felt guilty, how could they present their feeling for each other or their agony over their plight to a disdainful, misogynistic war tactician who painted pictures of fat, naked Bathshebas dangling toes in the water?

They told him they had no money to pay beforehand. Why would such a successful lawyer undertake to represent two virtually impoverished women? Perhaps because, as a Whig, he had no love for the aristocracy, or he believed he might earn a great deal in a suit against a woman as wealthy as Lady Cumming Gordon. Or perhaps the case appealed to a morbid if not prurient curiosity in him. He agreed to represent the mistresses and to defer charges until he won their case for them.

PART II

The
Trial

THE INITIAL HEARING

In the Scottish legal system of 1810, a libel case went first to a hearing judge, called the Lord Ordinary, who sat in the Outer House of the Court of Session. The Court of Session judges each filled the position of Lord Ordinary on a brief and rotating basis. After some weeks he who had served as Lord Ordinary would return to the Inner House of the Court of Session, and one of his brethren would become Lord Ordinary for the next weeks.

The Court of Session was the highest civil court of Scotland. The only appeal from it was to the House of Lords in England, and the expense of such an appeal was usually prohibitive. Within the Inner House of the Court of Session there were two divisions, each consisting of seven judges (called Lords of Session) who sat together to deliberate on cases that had been sent to them by the Lord Ordinary of the Outer House. If the Lord Ordinary believed that the plaintiff had no legitimate case, or that the outcome was clear-cut, he was empowered to render a decision himself and the matter might go no further. It was upon his recommendation that cases were referred to one of the divisions of the Inner House. Jury trials were not instituted in Scotland until 1814, four years after the Woods and Pirie case was brought to the Court.

John Clerk drew up the suit for Miss Woods and Miss Pirie, which was then presented before Lord Meadowbank, who was serving during the second week of December 1810 as Lord Ordinary. The mistresses complained through their attorney that their school was broken up immediately after Jane Cumming was withdrawn, the other young ladies rapidly following. They laid the blame for their ruin on Lady Cumming Gordon by offering in evidence the card she had sent to Lady Cunynghame on November 15, 1810, urging her to remove her daughter immediately. They also complained that Lady Cumming Gordon had never informed them of the reasons that she destroyed, through her actions, both their school and their reputations, and only by dark and distant hints had they gotten a vague inkling about what she accused them of, but they were entirely without knowledge of any wrongdoing.

If their claim was truthful, they must have been overwhelmed with horror when John Clerk gave them, two weeks later, a copy of the statement submitted by George Cranstoun (the second most successful lawyer in Edinburgh), who had been hired to defend Lady Cumming Gordon:

> The defendant avers and offers to prove,
>
> 1st, That her granddaughter, Miss Jane Cumming, was boarded with the plaintiffs during the summer and autumn of 1810.
>
> 2nd, That when the school assembled after the summer holidays, the ten boarders slept in two dormitories, in one of which Miss Pirie slept, in the other Miss Woods. That Miss Cumming was Miss Pirie's bedfellow, and from the 15th day of September, Miss Munro was Miss Woods' bedfellow.
>
> 3rd, That between the time when the school assembled (which was towards the end of August) and the beginning of November, Miss Woods on various nights went into the room in which Miss Pirie and Miss Cumming slept, and lay down in bed with them. During the same period, Miss Pirie occasionally went into Miss Woods' room, and lay down in bed with her and Miss Munro.
>
> The plaintiffs are required to confess or deny this article explicitly.
>
> 4th, One night during the said period, Miss Cumming was awakened by Miss Pirie speaking to Miss Woods. Miss Pirie said, "Oh, do it, darling!" Miss Woods answered, "Not tonight, it would awaken Miss Cumming," or they respectively used words to that effect. In a little Miss Woods came into bed; upon which Miss Pirie put down her hand and lifted up her shift. Miss Woods then lay above Miss Pirie, and when in that situation said, "I would like to have someone above me," or words to that effect. Miss Woods then put down her hand, and they made a noise described to the defendant as a wet kind of noise, attended with motions of the body, quick and high breathing, and a shaking of the bed.
>
> Miss Cumming being disgusted said twice, "Oh, Miss Pirie," before the latter answered. At last Miss Pirie said,

"What?" Miss Cumming said, "What shakes the bed?" Miss Pirie replied, "Nothing," or words to that purpose passed. After that Miss Pirie covered herself with the bedclothes. Then Miss Woods went out of bed. When she had reached her own door, Miss Pirie coughed so that the opening of the door might not be heard by Miss Cumming. In a little Miss Woods was heard to cough. Then Miss Pirie said, "Oh, that is Miss Woods coughing. I must go to see her, poor soul," or words to that effect. And she went accordingly.

5th, The morning after this happened, Miss Cumming mentioned it to Miss Munro, who slept with Miss Woods. Miss Munro then informed Miss Cumming that a few nights before Miss Pirie had been in Miss Woods' bed, and she observed motions and a shaking of the bed, similar to what Miss Cumming described.

6th, On a subsequent night during the foresaid period, Miss Cumming was awakened by a noise, motions, and breathing similar to those described in the fourth article. At that time Miss Woods was lying above Miss Pirie. Miss Pirie said to her, "Oh, you are hurting me!" or words to that effect.

7th, Another night during the foresaid period, Miss Woods being in Miss Pirie's bed, and lying above Miss Pirie, they raised their shifts. Miss Pirie then said, "Oh, you are in the wrong place!" Miss Woods said, "I know." Miss Pirie said, "Why do you do it then?" Miss Woods said, "For fun," or they used words to that effect.

8th, Another night during the foresaid period, Miss Woods said to Miss Pirie, when in the same situation as described in article 7, "Am I hurting you?" Miss Pirie said, "No," upon which Miss Woods continued the motions. When about to go away she said, "Goodnight, darling; goodnight. I think I have put you in a fair way to sleep." To this Miss Pirie replied, "No." Then Miss Woods again continued.

9th, On other occasions during the foresaid period, Miss Woods was in Miss Pirie's bed during the night, and they lay the one above the other, and kissed and embraced.

One night in particular when this happened, Miss Woods said to Miss Pirie, "Now darling, will you promise me one thing?" Miss Pirie answered, "I do not know. What is it?" Miss Woods said, "Now darling, will you promise me that you will not take me in your arms nor come again into my bed until the holidays?" To this Miss Pirie replied, "I know I will not be able to keep it," and she did not promise. But Miss Woods said, "I will not take you in my arms, or come to your bed, but you may kiss me, and I will kiss you," or conversation to this effect passed between them while Miss Woods was in Miss Pirie's bed.

10th, During the summer holidays, immediately preceding the period above mentioned, that is, the holidays in June and July 1810, Miss Pirie and Miss Woods slept together, and Miss Cumming slept in a bed at the foot of their bed. During that period Miss Cumming was frequently disturbed in the night by the shaking of their bed and the noise they made, which was similar to what she afterwards observed when they were in bed beside her, as mentioned above.

11th, While Miss Woods slept with Miss Munro, in the month of September or October, 1810, Miss Pirie came one night into their bed, and lay a long time above Miss Woods, and they made the bed shake.

12th, In the month of October last, after Miss Munro's family came to town, some weeks before Miss Cumming left the school, Miss Munro informed a servant or nurse in her father's house of what she had perceived to be improper in the conduct of the plaintiffs, as related above, and the said servant or nurse expressed her horror thereat.

13th, In the course of the year 1810, the plaintiffs repeatedly lay together in indecent attitudes, and were guilty of lewd and indecent behaviour towards each other. They were also in the habit of kissing and caressing each other before the young ladies in a wanton manner.

14th, One morning after Miss Munro was disturbed in the manner related above she rose earlier than usual and was the first in the school-room. A servant maid was doing up the room at the time: Miss Munro having said that she slept ill and had a dreadful night, the maid understood how she had been disturbed. The maid said laughing, "It is a pity they cannot get a man, but that they will never get," or words to that effect. Some of the elder girls coming into the room joined in the conversation, and the maidservant related some of the improprieties she had seen.

(Signed) *Geo. Cranstoun,*
Counsel for Lady Cumming Gordon, Defendant

Even Lord Meadowbank, the hearing judge, was overwhelmed. He had no wish to believe that two otherwise respectable women could behave in such a manner. It is apparent also from his notes that even if he did believe it, he would have preferred to suppress the case at once. If word of the accusation against the mistresses got out to the public, he asserted, the results would be disastrous: "Regardless of precautions, a discussion of this nature can produce a general contamination of that innocence of thought which is a distinguished feature of the manners of our country, a natural guardian of female virtue, and the best attraction of female youth." Girls must be kept innocent of the existence of such things. He would have preferred the luxury of such innocence himself, but he had to grapple with the facts of the case.

He concluded, first of all, that the defendant was culpable of some wrongdoing because her actions, which resulted in the breakup of the school, were taken solely on the basis of information provided by her granddaughter. Lady Cumming Gordon did not trouble to confirm the story with Miss Munro, the other young lady who claimed to have witnessed the indecencies. Nor did she make an attempt to have any communication with the washerwomen around the Water of Leith who, George Cranstoun now said at the hearing, knew of the infamous conduct of the mistresses and hooted at them whenever they passed by.

Then, he deemed it "strangely improbable that, supposing the plaintiffs had conceived an unnatural passion for each other, persons of their sense and accomplishment should have arranged their dormitories so, that each slept with a young lady; and that in order to indulge their passion, they should visit each other in bed, when they supposed the young ladies were asleep." The story, he decided, must have originated "from the malignity of some corrupt domestic." He would gladly have ordered Dame Cumming Gordon to admit her error and have advised her to settle out of court by paying the mistresses some reasonable sum.

But there was George Cranstoun, insisting that the defense could prove the truth of the story if Lord Meadowbank would allow him to call witnesses. The prospect must have been both horrifying and fascinating to Lord Meadowbank. He decided he would not take on himself the entire responsibility for placing these young girls, who were to be called, in so mortifying a position. On February 9, 1811, he referred the case to the Second Division of the Inner House of the Court of Session, to which he was returning from his stint as Lord Ordinary. His memorandum accompanying his referral shows that he did not believe—or did not want to believe—that lesbian sexual activity was even possible among British women:

To: The Judges of the Second Division
From: Allan Maconochie, Lord Meadowbank
Re: *Miss Woods and Miss Pirie Against Dame Helen Cumming Gordon*

Miss Jane Pirie and Miss Marianne Woods, the owners and operators of a school for girls at Drumsheugh, are suing Dame Helen Cumming Gordon for libel. They charge that by publicly accusing them of improper and criminal conduct, Dame Cumming Gordon has injured their reputations and ruined their school. Miss Woods and Miss Pirie are asking for ten thousand pounds in damages. Dame Cumming Gordon pleads in defence that she had been credibly informed and that she therefore believed that the plaintiffs had been guilty of indecent practices. (See accompanying statement for Dame Cumming Gordon.) On that account she had taken her granddaughters from the school, and she had notified only those parents to whom she had recommended the school that she was dissatisfied with the conduct of the mistresses.

In reporting the case, the Ordinary does not think it his duty to do more than acquaint your Lordships with the remarks he made at the hearing.

After acknowledging his natural tendency to doubt what is extraordinarily wicked and unnatural, and that his experiences and the philosophy he esteems strengthened this tendency, the Lord Ordinary said that he is disposed to believe that the crime in question, when imputed to women of the ordinary conformation of this country, for the purpose of gratification of the venereal appetite by means of copulation with each other, was equally imaginary with witchcraft, sorcery, or carnal copulation with the devil. Their private parts were not so formed as to penetrate each other, and without penetration the venereal orgasm could not possibly follow. The Ordinary was referred by the defendant's counsel to Latin and Greek terms denoting the crime. But those terms confirmed his opinion. They import the crime of one woman giving another the clitoris, which in this country is not larger than the nipple of the breast and is, furthermore, immersed between the labia of the pudenda. Therefore, as expressed in language of the Greeks and Romans, it is a crime which, in the general case, is impossible in this country to commit.

If the Ordinary's opinion is well-founded, then, according to the accusation, the plaintiffs must be endowed with an extraordinary conformation, for they are represented as alternately performing the function of the male in their visits. It is obvious, however, that so extraordinary a circumstance is utterly incredible. One woman of unusual formation does not exist among millions. That two women of such a structure should get together, after maintaining respectable female characters in genteel society, and then join in an undertaking where the greatest propriety is required, in order to practice reciprocally unnatural deeds, appears absurd.

Yet it must be admitted that there is a use that women of the ordinary conformation have made of one another for veneral purpose, *viz.* for excitements though not for gratification. These scandalous functions are often mentioned among the ancients. But such excitements are always described as merely calculated to excite the venereal appetite and prepare for the admission of the male sex. However, it is not alleged that the scenes described in this case were in any way preparatory to receiving the male sex. On the contrary, Miss Woods was supposed to have asked of Miss Pirie whether she fitted her to get a sound sleep, which implies that a full gratification of the venereal appetite was the understood object.

But beside the physical impossibilities, there appeared to the Ordinary very gross moral improbabilities. It is certainly strange that intelligent women, wishing to keep a disgraceful vice secret, should manage their intercourse by choosing a different bedfellow, and then visiting each other's bed when the bedfellow was supposed to be asleep, and there engaging in copulation accompanied by much noise and agitation, and carrying on audible conversations concerning what they were doing, and not only risking waking a bedfellow during their violent indulgences, but also risking waking four or five other girls, who could then witness their copulations. And all this when, without suspicion of the smallest impropriety, Miss Woods and Miss Pirie might have slept together every night, completely sheltered from all risk of imputation, by the established habits and known innocence of female intercourse.

It only occurs to add that the conduct and disposal of this strange, and not more strange than melancholy case, appears to the Ordinary to call for the utmost exertions of your Lordships' wisdom and prudence. Whatever you do, he hopes you will now take it into your own hands, being so extremely ill-suited, in every view, to proceeding before a Lord Ordinary.

Only a few months before this case had come to court, seven men were arrested at a male "bawdy house," the White Swan Public House, in Vere Street, London. They were accused of sodomy, tried, and all were found guilty. One, who claimed to be new to such debauched deeds, was sentenced only to one year in prison. The other six were sentenced to be pilloried and then imprisoned for three years. The public had no trouble believing they were guilty. According to newspaper accounts, on the day of the pillorying the streets around the Old Bailey were filled with thousands of spectators. The mob was so vast and rowdy that the shops from Ludgate Hill to the Haymarket were all shut up and the business of the Court came to a halt. Hucksters sold apples, turnips, and the remains of dogs and cats to be used as "ammunition" against the sodomites. The six of them were taken by cart from the Old Bailey yard through the streets to the pillory place. They were so pelted by offal and dung that, according to one newspaper account, the *London Evening Standard*'s, "they resembled bears dipped in a stagnant pool. It could not be discerned that they were human beings. If they had had further to go to the pillory, the cart would have been filled over their heads." They were each required to stand in the pillory, where they were further abused by the populace, for an hour, and then to travel through the furious mob on the way back to prison. They bled profusely, half-dead. "It is impossible for language to convey an adequate idea of the universal expressions of execration which accompanied these monsters on their journey," the *London Evening Standard* observed.

What would have happened if Miss Woods and Miss Pirie's suit against Lady Cumming Gordon had reversed itself upon them, just as did Oscar Wilde's suit against the Marquis of Queensberry at the end of the century? Wilde sued the Marquis, who was the father of Lord Alfred Douglas, Wilde's lover, for slander. The Marquis had called Wilde a sodomite. However, in the course of the trial against him, the Marquis was able to furnish many credible witnesses who testified that Wilde was indeed a sodomite. Not only was the Marquis exonerated, but the Crown then tried Wilde for sodomy, found him guilty, sentenced him to prison and hard labor, and, of course, ruined his illustrious career as the foremost playwright of his day.

Did Miss Woods and Miss Pirie fear that in the course of their suit Lady Cumming Gordon's statement against them might be proven true? Or were they certain that while society was willing to believe men capable of homosexuality, to have believed it of otherwise good women would have destroyed those sacred notions about female purity and passionlessness that had developed in the latter half of the preceding century and continued throughout the nineteenth century?

If they had been very well versed in legal history, they might have known of a few other cases that had come before the British courts in which women were found guilty of homosexual behavior, but, surprisingly, not even the judges or Lady Cumming Gordon's counsel knew of them. The most famous case had been tried by the English novelist Henry Fielding, who was also a judge. In 1746 he wrote about it in a six-penny pamphlet called *The Female Husband: or, the Surprising History of Mrs. Mary, Alias Mr. George Hamilton. . . .* The young woman in the case was a transvestite, brought before the Court when it was discovered that she had married three women while passing as a man. Fielding, who found her guilty, referred in his pamphlet to "something of too vile, wicked, and scandalous a nature which was discovered in her trunk," obviously a dildo. He claimed that it was specifically for possession of that instrument that she was indicted and convicted. She was then "sentenced to be publickly and severely whipt in four market towns within the country of Somerset, and to be imprisoned." Fielding described with great relish "her lovely skin scarified with rods, in such a manner that her back was almost flead."

But her case was quite different from that of the mistresses. She was a woman of the lower class—which meant to those who judged her that she was capable of behavior that would not be believed of women from more respectable classes. She was a transvestite—she did not look like a female, therefore the passionlessness associated with women did not apply to her: she might be considered as lecherous as any male. And she had been caught with the goods—a dildo: while men might not believe that women could satisfy each other sexually using only what nature bestowed, they could believe that if (as Montaigne said several centuries earlier in describing the prosecution of a transvestite lesbian in France) "she used an instrument to supplement the deficiencies of her sex," she could simulate the heterosexual act effectively enough.

Could a case like Woods and Pirie's occur today? Ollie believes it could. People are far more knowing with regard to sexual possibilities between women, she says, but that makes them less tolerant rather than more. They would be even quicker than Dame Cumming Gordon and the other parents to remove their daughters from a boarding school if they heard rumors of a lesbian relationship between the teachers.

I think in the 1930s, when Lillian Hellman brought a modified version of this story to the stage, such was probably the case. The sexologists' role in spreading knowledge of deviant sexual behavior resulted in the most spurious sort of liberalism, pseudosophistication, and misinformation. Relationships between women that were viewed in earlier centuries as ennobling romantic friendships were in the 1920s and 1930s examined for hints of taint. And such hints could create a furor. Hellman's play was so successful on Broadway in 1934 and 1935 because it was believable.

But times have changed. We have been through a sexual revolution and a feminist revolution. Even as early as 1962, the critics of the just-released film version of *The Children's Hour* suggested that the movie was a failure because people no longer behaved that way when they discovered sexual nonconformity between consenting adults. This morning I got from the University of Edinburgh library the March 15, 1962, review of the film by Bosley Crowther, which appeared in *The New York Times*. Crowther thought the film simply incredible. He said:

> The hint [of lesbianism] is intruded with such astonishment and it is made to seem such a shattering thing (even without evidence to support it) that it becomes socially absurd. It is incredible that educated people living in an urban American community today would react as violently and as cruelly to a questionable innuendo as they are made to do in this film. And that is not the only incredible thing in it. It asks us to believe that the parents of all twenty pupils in a private school for girls would

yank them out in a matter of hours on the slanderously
spread advice of the grandmother of one of the pupils
that two young teachers in the school were "unnatural."

I agree with Crowther. What could happen in early-nineteenth-
century Scotland could not happen in America today. But Ollie
thinks he and I have been misled by our respective insulated,
liberal-intellectual New York communities. Similar things are
probably happening right now in small towns all over America,
she says—just as they happened twenty years ago when Crowther
wrote and fifty years ago when Hellman wrote. She believes that
such places as Burton, New Mexico, where she was raised, will
never change, that sexual revolutions and feminism never affect
the Burton, New Mexicos, of America, and that their pusillani-
mous citizens will always persecute what is not orthodox.

But, of course, the issue in this case is not simply unorthodox
sexual preferences. The two women were accused of indulging
themselves in the beds of young girls. Surely there could be no
such parallels today because no modern woman would be naïve
enough to believe a sixteen-year-old so sexually innocent that she
would not understand the import of the activity if she happened to
wake up. It is conceivable, I suppose, that a nineteenth-century
woman might have faith in such ignorance.

Because the accusation was so horrendous, and the rumor of it
seemed to spread so quickly, I imagine the mistresses had no hope
of finding employment again until they were cleared. I do not
know if they looked for a job at this point, but I did find an advertisement that Mrs. Woods placed in the "situations wanted" section of the *Edinburgh Advertiser* for Christmas Day, 1810. She
poses as a mother, of Marianne presumably, perhaps to raise more
sympathy for the plight of a woman who has not only herself but
her daughter to support. There is no evidence that her plea was effective.

NOTICE

A Lady, who has been reduced by the death of her husband to great pecuniary distress, is very desirous of a sit-

uation in any respectable family as Companion to a Lady; and, if agreeable, would have no objection to take charge of, or assist in, the management of the domestic concerns of the family. The most ample and satisfactory testimony can be procured of her religious principles, good temper, and uniform good conduct through life; and her terms will be found moderate.

Until she is so fortunate as to meet with a situation of this description, she will be most grateful to those who will be kind enough to give her any employment in plain work, washing muslins, or any articles of millinery, or golfrying muslin ruffs, etc., as her own and her daughter's support depend almost entirely upon her industry and exertions. Any further particulars may be had by inquiring for Mrs. Ann Woods at her lodging at Mrs. Reed's, no. 17, North James's Street, 3rd door of the stair.

The Inner House

On February 16, 1811 the suit was placed on the Inner House roll of cases for the Second Division of the Court of Session. There were seven Lords of Session, red-robed and bewigged, who were to judge the case. According to the bits of information that have survived about each of them, they were almost all entirely unsuited to sit on such a case. Yet given the prejudices and customs of the era, was there a man in Britain who could have delivered impartial justice here? Nevertheless, what has come down to us through the judges' various biographers depicts them as a sad lot—pompous, prideful, dipsomaniacal, and unbright. Either nineteenth-century biographers generally chose to look with a jaundiced eye on the class who became judges, or these men were a most unfortunate representation of what such a noble body should be—or they simply behaved as people do in undemocratic and rough times.

THE LORD JUSTICE-CLERK, CHARLES HOPE. As Lord Justice-Clerk, Hope presided over the Second Division of the Court of Session. His portrait is one of three that hang in the entry hall of the Signet Library, the law library that adjoins the Parliament Building, where cases are still tried in Edinburgh. In the portrait he appears to be extraordinarily handsome, with a face that is both intelligent and commanding. His speeches that have survived do not seem to confirm that appearance, but he must have somehow attained the respect of his peers and superiors. Before coming to the Court of Session he had been President of the Criminal Court, where he was said to have surpassed any judge of his day or any day that could be remembered in his fearsomeness in pronouncing sentence. In 1811 he became President of the entire Court of Session. He left the Court of Session in 1836 to take the highest official position in Scotland, Lord Justice General. His biographer suggests that his personality was well revealed in his decision to continue as Lieutenant Colonel of the Gentlemen Regiment of Volunteers all during the years he was Lord Justice-Clerk, although many thought it unconstitutional.

ALLAN MACONOCHIE, LORD MEADOWBANK. Maconochie heard the case in the Outer House and again when it was placed on the rolls of the Second Division of the Inner House. He was an extremely conscientious man, but he seems to have been blinded both by pride and prejudice. He claimed to have a vast amount of esoteric knowledge—of literature, science, philosophy, linguistics, religion, agriculture—though his biographer says his knowledge was more varied than accurate. When he was a young man Maconochie resided for a number of years in Paris and thus, according to British views, should have been well versed in the existence of vices, but he preferred not to believe in them. He was appointed to the bench in 1796.

LORD DAVID BOYLE. Boyle alone seems to me to have grappled honestly with the facts of the case and to have consistently analyzed them with some intelligence. He heard the case now and once again when it was appealed in 1812. At that time he succeeded Charles Hope as Lord Justice-Clerk, an honor he deserved above all the others, judging from the evidence of his ability in these transcripts.

LORD WILLIAM ROBERTSON. Robertson was a Tory and owed his appointment to the Court at least partly to Tory favoritism at this time. His father had been the head of the University of Edinburgh. Since the publication of the elder Robertson's *History of Scotland* when he was a very young man, he had been considered the greatest Scottish historian of his day. His son, Lord William, also dabbled in prose but his literary talents went unrecognized. Lord William happened to be Lady Cumming Gordon's neighbor in fashionable Charlotte Square during the time of this trial. He retired from the bench because of deafness in 1826.

WILLIAM MILLER, LORD GLENLEE. Glenlee was also a Tory, and he was even closer to Lady Cumming Gordon than was Lord William Robertson: his son was married to one of Lady Cumming Gordon's daughters. Apparently such propinquity did not disqualify a judge at that time. His Toryism was so enthusiastic that he informed Francis Jeffrey, the founder of the Whiggish *Edinburgh Review,* that in consequence of Jeffrey's liberal politics, he would befriend him no more, even though the close bond between their families had spanned generations. When Jeffrey secured a Court appointment the two met frequently, though they never exchanged a word in twenty-five years. Glenlee must have appeared a frightening curmudgeon to the timid. He continued on the bench until the 1840s, when he was well into his eighties and had himself carried to Parliament Square every morning in his sedan chair.

WILLIAM BAILLIE, LORD POLKEMMET. Polkemmet was another staunch Tory. His family was reputed to have been among the wealthiest in Britain. He was described by one of his contemporaries, Lord Cockburn, as "a good man, but huge and brainless; in voice, stare, manner and intellect, not much above an idiot." How could such a man have procured a seat on the bench? Cockburn, who may have been antagonistic to him because of political differences, said that Polkemmet owed his appointment to Lord Braxfield, who felt indebted to his friend because he had once given Polkemmet some bad advice that caused him to lose considerable property. When another judge objected to Polkemmet's appointment to the bench on the ground that he had no rhetorical ability, Braxfield is said to have replied, "Nonsense, man. I've bargained that he's never to speak." Considering Polkemmet's performance in this case, Braxfield appears to have been serious. Polkemmet was never present during the testimony. He based his vote on the transcripts and gave no speeches whatsoever. He might have avoided embarrassing exposure this way throughout much of his career. The law required the presence of only a simple majority of the judges on a case, and it was not necessary that a judge be present during the testimony in order to participate in a vote, or that he state the reasons for his decision.

CHARLES HAY, LORD NEWTON. Newton was seventy-one in 1811. He died soon after rendering his decision in favor of the defendant. His deportment during his tenure would probably call for impeachment today, although it obviously did not in his time: those who served with him claimed he never heard a case without first imbibing six pints of claret, as had been usual among judges (who even drank on the bench) when he first came to the Court in the preceding century. Lord Cockburn, who became a judge in the Court of Session in 1834, made this observation of Newton and his contemporaries in a memoir of the late-eighteenth- and early-nineteenth-century Court, when Cockburn was a very young lawyer:

> Black bottles of strong port were set down beside the judges on the Bench, with glasses, caraffes of water, tumblers, and biscuits; and this without the slightest attempt at concealment. The refreshment was generally allowed to stand untouched for a short time, as if despised, during which their Lordships seemed intent only on their notes. But in a little, some water was poured into the tumbler, and sipped quietly, as if merely to sustain nature. Then a few drops of wine were ventured upon, but only with the water. But at last patience could not endure longer, and a full bumper of the pure black element was tossed over; after which the thing went on regularly, and there was a comfortable munching and quaffing to the great envy of the parched throats in the gallery. The strong-headed stood it tolerably well, but it told, plainly enough, upon the feeble. Not that the ermine was absolutely intoxicated, but it was certainly sometimes affected. This however was so ordinary with these sages, that it really made

little apparent change upon them. It was not very perceptible at a distance; and they all acquired the habit of sitting and looking judicial enough, even when their bottles had reached the lowest ebb.

Many of them may have been dipsomaniacs, but as long as they could appear to handle strong drink, it was not held against them. Of Newton it was remarked that when he was a young man he often drank until seven in the morning, slept a couple of hours, and then appeared in court, where his behavior was impeccable. Even in his old age his defenders were quick to point out that whatever he drank, he kept as clear a head as one who never touched a drop, and that he might often seem asleep during court proceedings, but his questions and comments indicated that he missed absolutely nothing. Lord Newton was understood not to have relished female society. He never married.

The Court of Session was conducted in what had been the Scottish Parliament House before the Union of Scotland and England in 1707. In 1810 or 1811, to get to the rooms where the cases are heard, you would pass first through two dark and dungeonlike antechambers. Then you enter by a low door into a huge hall of antique grandeur, with a multi-arched, black oak ceiling. The hall is completely filled. Advocates, the first class of legal men, who are privileged to plead orally before the Court, and solicitors, Men of Business as they are called, without the right to plead in open court, move in two different streams along the respective places that custom has allotted them on the floor.

The advocates' side of the house is by the wall. The elder and more frequently employed advocates occupy the benches that extend along the walls. Most of them wear powdered wigs. Often they are pouring over briefs or notes for speeches they will soon make, or they are complaining to each other about some decision. The younger ones, some in wigs and some without, collect in small groups near one of the two large iron stoves, often around an acknowledged wit who is holding forth.

The crowd nearest the door is made up of the solicitors. They are usually mature figures, meditating pale-faced counselors, and most of them are dressed in somber colors. Their dandyish clerks, in contrast to them, are often in the snow-white breeches that were in fashion all that winter and spring, and in smart green riding jackets, glossy velvet collars, waistcoats in a diversified dazzle of stripes and spots. They walk with a military swagger.

This is a gentlemen's club. Scottish historians say that throughout the eighteenth century the national system of education was such that even a poor man's son (although obviously not his daughter—or even a rich man's daughter, since women were excluded from university education) could go on to one of the universities as well prepared as his wealthy classmates. That was the conception—but I suspect that, as in twentieth-century America and elsewhere, the actuality was seldom as ideal as the conception. In any case, the lawyers were a closed corporation of noblemen and gentlemen, with high entrance fees and exclusive regulations. During the period 1752 to 1811, 88 percent of them came from landed families, and very few of the rest were born to tradesmen or craftsmen or tenant farmers. The Lords of Session almost always had wealth and title behind them. They were often at this time the most conservative Tories. To be examined, defended, judged by such lofty superiors in those pre-jury days must have been awesome to the average Scotsman who found himself in an early-nineteenth-century law court.

Here and there, in the great hall of the Parliament House, is a client, often dressed in black broadcloth. Some of them are farmers who have traveled far to be litigious. Many of them are squabbling Edinburgh businessmen. There is seldom a woman in sight.

Outside, however, is a statue of a woman—Justice—holding in her hand not the usual scale, but something that resembles a steel yardstick. The statue is precariously perched on an inverted pyramid. So perilous is its balance that had the artist not been a Scotsman, it might have been suspected that he intended to insinuate that the goddess had no safe footing in this court.

But no doubt all the judges in this case wished to judge wisely, and they must have believed themselves capable of transcending whatever differences of class and gender they might encounter in those who came before them. Yet, I wonder: even if they had all seven been the wisest, soberest, most objective men in Britain; even if they had been able to listen and analyze divested of all predilections; even if they had been more than human—human only in that they looked like men—would they have been able to uncover the truth then? Not only did they have their own class prejudices to contend with in this case: their difficulties were compounded by the fact that all of the principals and all of the witnesses were female. The business of the Court, in all its aspects, was entirely masculine. How overwhelmed the few females who entered this Parliament House must have been, whether they came as plaintiff, defendant, or mere witness. Even supposing the women's best intentions to tell the truth, could it have been gotten out whole in this all-masculine preserve?

Females of their day learned as a matter of course never to tell the truth to males. Miss Young said in her famous *Letters of Advice to Ladies* that a woman "must listen patiently to all a man says even though it be dull and tedious, and never must she contradict him, however mistaken he may be, for that is something a man never forgives." Most women must have had little practice in proclaiming a truth whole and for an extended period of time in the presence of men. They were trained to hold back, if not to lie.

It must have been intimidating enough to be a woman examined and cross-examined by a room full of men—but to be examined and cross-examined on the subject of sex, and moreover a variety of sex that was not supposed to have existed, must have been terrifying. If there were women who were not terrified, did they feel a cool disdain for the infernal ignorance of the male?

Females occupied one sphere and males another. But to obtain redress or to prove her innocence, a female had to plead in the males' court. She had a double burden: she had to try to reconstruct truth (or lies), and she had to do it before strangers of a different sphere. In her nervousness or her fury, what she said must often have come out skewed. Although I found only one admission that a witness could neither think clearly nor speak effectively in such imposing company, I believe that this somewhat hysterical response of Mrs. Campbell (Jane Pirie's last employer before she opened the school) was typical of what most females must have felt in this Court:

March 31, 1811

To the Honourable Lord Justice-Clerk Hope:
Sir,

At the time I was called on to give evidence regarding Miss Pirie's character I was in very great distress because a young person who had lived with me from infancy was at the height of a dangerous fever. That circumstance alone would at any time unfit me for anything. But when you also take into consideration that though I am now an old woman I never before appeared in court, that I am deaf, and that throughout my life I have always had a degree of timidity that I could not shake off, you will understand any embarrassment or stupidity that may have appeared when I was taken before your (to me) formidable Court. I believe I did not do Miss Pirie the justice she deserves. I shall now state to you, Sir, my candid opinion of her, which I am willing to swear to again, if you consider it necessary, but beg you will not take me before such a number of people again. I also beg leave to add that I have had the charge of young people for twenty years, and during that time I have had several governesses in my family. I never had anyone that I would prefer to Miss Pirie. I hope, Sir, you will forgive my giving you this trouble, but in a very short time I shall leave town, and I feel very anxious before I go home to be of all the use I can to Miss Pirie.

> I am, Sir, respectfully yours,
> (Signed) *Mrs. Helen Campbell*
> Widow of General Campbell of Strachur

THE TESTIMONY

According to early nineteenth-century court procedure, neither the plaintiffs nor the defendant were permitted to take the stand on their own behalf. Their counsel submitted a list of witnesses to be called. The Court declared that testimony was to begin with witnesses for the defendant on March 15, 1811. Lord Meadowbank urged his brethren to find means to conceal the nature of this case, for the public good, and all concurred. It was decided that evidence would be heard behind shut doors: no one not directly involved in the proceedings would be allowed in the courtroom.

Elaborate plans were made for maintaining secrecy. The Clerk of the Court was directed to keep the record of the case under sealed cover, and was not to exhibit it to any persons except counsel for the parties. When counsel needed it, the Court ordered, "it shall be lent only to the attorneys in person, and not to their clerks, and shall be put again under sealed cover when returned." What terrible debaucheries they must have feared would follow if it became common knowledge that women might be sexually intimate with one another.

MARCH 15, 1811, 10:00 A.M.

Miss Janet Munro is the first witness called by the defendant. Present are Lord Justice-Clerk Hope, Lords Meadowbank, Glenlee, Robertson, and Boyle, counsel for both parties, Marianne Woods, Jane Pirie, and Lady Cumming Gordon. George Cranstoun, the advocate for Lady Cumming Gordon, informs the Lords that Miss Munro is sixteen years of age, born of the most respectable parents, motherless from the age of nine, educated in the bosom of her family until the month of September preceding the unhappy event, intimate only with persons of the first character in Edinburgh, and esteemed and beloved by all her acquaintances. She became Miss Woods' bedfellow when she entered the Drumsheugh school, in September 1810. She is a little deaf. Solemnly sworn and purged of malice and partial counsel, she is questioned by Cranstoun:

"You were a boarder at the school of the plaintiffs since September last?" he asks.

"Yes, sir."

"And you slept with Miss Woods?"

"Yes, sir, from the beginning until I came away."

"During the time you slept with Miss Woods, did Miss Pirie ever come into your bed?"

"Oftener than once."

"And when she came into your bed, was she fully dressed?"

"No, sir, I believe her clothes were off, and one lay above the other. Miss Pirie was uppermost."

"Was there a candle in the room, Miss Munro?" Lord Meadowbank wishes to know.

"No, sir, no candle. But the first time she came into the bed there was shaking of the bed, and the bed clothes tossed about, and they seemed to be breathing high. I felt their bodies moving."

"And did you speak to them?" Cranstoun continues.

"Oh, yes. I said, 'Miss Pirie, I wish you would go away for I can't get sleep.' Then Miss Woods said to Miss Pirie, 'You had better go away, Jane, for I'm afraid you'll catch cold standing there.' But I knew she wasn't standing. She was in bed. Even though Miss Pirie said, 'I am not in the bed, I am only standing beside it.' But when she said that she was not beside it. Then she got up and went away."

"Did you tell anyone what you had observed?"

"Yes, sir. Miss Cumming."

"And did you not tell someone else?"

"Oh, yes, sir. Mary Brown, the nursery maid at home."

"How long have you known Mary Brown?"

"She has been in our family as long as I know."

"Miss Munro, tell the court what Mary Brown said to your story."

"She said, 'If it is true, it is dreadful.' And then she told me that if it happened again I must speak out and let it be known. And I must tell her too. And she said they should be burnt."

"Did it happen again?"

"Yes, sir. Some days after this. But I don't exactly recollect how long."

"Tell the court what happened, please, Miss Munro."

"Miss Pirie came again to our bed, and she lay in the same way, Miss Pirie above Miss Woods, and there was the same shaking of the bed and motions and breathing as before."

"Was there a candle in the room this time, Miss Munro?" Lord Meadowbank wishes to know.

"No, sir. But some daylight came in. The first time there was no daylight."

"Have you any idea what time it might have been?" Cranstoun asks her.

"I'm not sure, but from the light I think it was five in the morning because I could see any person in the room."

"Did you make them aware you observed them?" Cranstoun continues.

"Yes, sir. I coughed and turned myself. And then Miss Woods turned to Miss Pirie and whispered, 'I suspect she is awake.' Then Miss Woods began coughing herself and said she heard me coughing and asked if I had been long awake. When I said I had, she said, 'I'm afraid you've got a cold. If you'll get up and go to such a drawer in the room, you'll get some barley sugar.' But I told her I didn't want any. So then she asked me to get up and go to the dressing room and get her some water."

"And did you?"

"Yes, sir. But before I did I could see Miss Pirie in bed. Then when I came back with the water, Miss Pirie was gone."

"Did you discuss this incident with anyone?"

"Well, the next morning I told the maid Charlotte that I was very tired and I'd been disturbed and gotten very little sleep. I didn't have to say any more because Charlotte seemed to understand me. She said, 'It's a pity they could not get a man.' And she said that one day she had to get something that was in the drawing room, but when she tried to get it she found both the doors bolted. So, she looked through the keyhole and she found them the same way on the sofa."

"Miss Munro," Cranstoun asks, "Did Charlotte describe anything more of what she saw through the keyhole?"

"No, sir. She said she called through the door that she wanted something, and they answered that she must wait a while as they were busy."

"Did you tell Charlotte what you had witnessed the second time?"

"I don't remember, but a day or so later, before breakfast, Charlotte came down to the schoolroom and told me and Miss Cumming and Miss Stirling that she had caught them again in the dressing room on one of the beds. She said that when she went into the room Miss Pirie leapt out of bed and her face was very red, and Miss Woods hid under the bed-clothes."

"Did anyone else hear Charlotte's story?"

"Well, there were others in the room at the time, but I don't think they heard it."

"Miss Munro," Lord Boyle asks, "was the door to the dressing room not bolted as the drawing room door had been?"

"Charlotte did not say, sir. She only said she got into the dressing room."

"Did Charlotte say anything else?" Cranstoun asks.

"I don't think so, sir."

"Nothing else, Miss Munro?" Cranstoun asks again.

"Oh, yes, she said that we should notice their faces and see what they looked like when she came in with the kettle at breakfast."

"And did you?"

"Yes, sir."

"Did Miss Woods and Miss Pirie look odd?"

"I thought they seemed to avoid looking at Charlotte, and they even looked away from her. Then Charlotte looked at them and made faces at them. And when they left she said, 'Who would serve such mistresses?' "

"Were there other occasions when you saw Miss Woods and Miss Pirie behave indecently?"

"I think those were the only times."

"Have you never seen them kissing, caressing, and fondling more than could have resulted from ordinary female friendship?"

"Oh, yes, sir. I have."

"Was this before or after the first time?"

"Both, sir."

"So their behaviour struck you as extraordinary even before you saw them in bed together?"

"Yes, sir."

"Miss Munro," Lord Meadowbank asks, "had you discussed that with Miss Cumming?"

"Yes, sir."

"What had you discussed?"

"Well, we had conversations about what had happened, and in particular I mentioned how I was disturbed in bed, and Miss Cumming said she was used to being disturbed like that."

"Did the two of you decide to take any action, Miss Munro?"

"Well, we agreed that Miss Cumming should tell her grandmother. But I think we decided that first we would give them a hint that we knew what was going on."

"And did you?" Lord Meadowbank asks.

"Yes. One day we were out walking, and Miss Cumming told me that she was so tired with being disturbed in the night that she was hardly able to go on with her lessons. So she decided that when we returned from the walk she would complain. Then when we returned Miss Cumming said to Miss Pirie that she was terribly tired with being disturbed in the night time. So then Miss Pirie's face grew very red, and she turned her back and she soon afterwards went out of the room."

"Did you discuss Miss Pirie's response with Miss Cumming?" Lord Meadowbank asks.

"Well, Miss Cumming said to me, 'Do you see how guilt is on her face?' "

"Miss Munro," Lord Justice-Clerk Hope asks, "since it was agreed that Miss Cumming should tell her grandmother what had happened, why didn't you tell your own father?"

She pauses. "I didn't like to do it," she says at last.

"Miss Munro," the advocate now continues, "do you go to church regularly?"

"Yes. Miss Stevenson took me to receive the sacrament not long ago."

"Who is Miss Stevenson, Miss Munro?"

"She's the daughter of Dr. Stevenson of Glasgow, who died last year. She's had particular charge of me since I was nine. She was my governess and now she is my little sister's governess."

"Miss Munro, were you happy at the school?"

"Yes, sir. Except for being disturbed at night."

"Instruction good? Good treatment?"

"Oh, yes, sir. I had no other complaints."

"And one final question, Miss Munro. Have you discussed your testimony with Miss Cumming?"

"No, sir."

"When did you last see her?"

"Not since the school broke up, sir."

Mr. Cranstoun declares that he has finished questioning the witness.

The Lord Justice-Clerk indicates that John Clerk, advocate for the plaintiffs, may proceed.

"Miss Munro," Clerk asks, "can you tell the court exactly when you observed Miss Woods and Miss Pirie in bed together."

"I think about three weeks after I first came to the school."

"Can you set an exact date?"

"No, sir. About the end of September. So I think the second time would be early in October."

"So you never observed them in bed together upon any other occasion?"

She pauses. "Well, I don't know. Once before the end of September, I waked in a fright and I thought there was somebody in bed with Miss Woods, but I couldn't be sure of it or who it was."

"Did you ask Miss Woods what it might have been?"

"No, but I think I mentioned it to Miss Cumming. I think that was when she said that Miss Woods often visited Miss Pirie in bed, so it must have been Miss Pirie visiting Miss Woods."

"Nothing more?"

"She may have said at that time that Charlotte told her they behaved indecently—but I'm not sure it was that time."

"Miss Munro," Clerk says, "please describe for the court your morning schedule."

"You mean what we did at the school every morning—from when we got up?"

"Yes."

"Well, we—the scholars, that is—we usually rose between six and seven, and Miss Woods and Miss Pirie rose when we got downstairs."

"And what was the first thing that happened when they came downstairs?"

"After they came down there was prayers, and then we had to repeat our lessons to them, and then we had breakfast."

"Did you spend much time over breakfast?"

"No, sir. Less than half an hour I think."

"And then after breakfast you were taught your lessons. And several times a week the mistresses took you all for a walk for an hour or so, then you all ate together, then they sat with you while you worked, and they sat with you when you had tea at five, and then they gave you your lessons for the next day, and they sat with you while you prepared. Is that correct?"

"Yes, sir, I think it is."

"And what after that?" Clerk asks.

"We had prayer session."

"Please describe that, Miss Munro."

"Miss Woods and Miss Pirie took turns reading prayers, and before prayers one of us—one of the scholars—read a chapter from Miss Trimmer's *History of the Bible.*"

"And then?"

"We went upstairs."

"Did Miss Woods and Miss Pirie go with you?"

"Yes, sir. To help us undress."

"And then?"

"They didn't undress themselves."

"Weren't there prayers again, Miss Munro?"

"Oh, yes—Miss Woods heard three of the younger girls say their prayers aloud in our room, and I believe Miss Pirie did the same in the other room."

"And then it was about nine o'clock, and they corrected your written work, and prepared the lessons for the next day, and supped?"

"I don't know when they did that."

"Miss Munro, what time did Miss Woods usually come to bed?"

"About eleven I think, but I can't be sure because I was usually sleeping."

"Then on the first occasion, when you saw them in bed together, you waited up for Miss Woods?"

"No, sir. I had fallen asleep before Miss Woods came to bed, and I didn't know when she came, nor when Miss Pirie came into the bed."

"How long had you been awake before you spoke to them?"

"About half an hour I think."

"And that was when you told Miss Pirie to go away? You said nothing more?"

"No, sir. But before that I heard a great deal of conversation going on in whispers, but I couldn't make any kind of sense of what they said, though perhaps I might pick up a word here and there. I don't now remember."

"And what about the second occasion, Miss Munro, what did you say?"

"Then I also heard conversation going on between them in whispers but I couldn't understand it, unless it was, as I said before, when Miss Woods said to Miss Pirie that she thought I was awake. I coughed several times so they would know I was awake, but I didn't say anything."

"Miss Munro, have you at any other time heard Miss Woods and Miss Pirie talking in your bed?"

"Once I think I heard them conversing something about Miss Stirling, but at that time Miss Pirie wasn't in bed. I think she was standing by the bedside, and she was talking of her brother-in-law also as well as of Miss Stirling."

"Was this before or after the two occasions?"

"I don't recollect, sir. But I know I was awakened by Miss Pirie speaking. I remember that I told her a day or two after that I had heard her speaking about her brother-in-law and about some colliers and dogs, and that her brother-in-law had nearly been killed at that time."

"Miss Munro, weren't there actually many occasions when Miss Pirie came to talk to Miss Woods in the night?"

"Oh, yes. I remember one other time when Miss Pirie came to Miss Woods and sat down upon the bedside, just after Miss Woods had gone to bed. I think Miss Woods was ill then. Miss Pirie rubbed her back for a little, and they didn't have much conversation. Those are the only times I remember."

"Miss Munro, upon the first occasion, when you say you believe Miss Pirie's clothes were off, what led you to that belief?"

"Because it was the dead of night, sir."

"You had no other reason for believing that?"

"Well I'm sure they were, sir."

"How do you know?"

"It was the dead of night."

"And are you positive that Miss Pirie's legs were in bed on the first occasion?"

"Not quite positive, but I think so. I felt the legs of one of them."

"On the second occasion, are you positive Miss Pirie's legs were in the bed?"

"Yes, sir. At least she was lying in such a manner as to make me think they were, since she was below the bed-clothes. And on the first time also I think her body was below the bed-clothes."

"One last question before we adjourn," Lord Justice-Clerk Hope tells the advocate.

"We will continue along another line of questioning on the morrow, your Lordship," Clerk says.

The court adjourns until tomorrow at ten o'clock in the morning.

LORD GLENLEE'S NOTES ON THE TESTIMONY OF MISS JANET MUNRO, MARCH 15, 1811

If Miss Munro's evidence is true, it is enough to exonerate Lady Cumming Gordon. The Lord Ordinary has said that what she describes is physically impossible, that women cannot so give each other the venereal orgasm. But whatever the gratification obtained, whether it was complete gratification, a partial gratification, or no gratification at all, is irrelevant. I have no doubt that there is great enjoyment even in the gratification afforded by the imagination, in postures and other circumstances calculated to excite the passions. The women may be seeking something that is unattainable to them, but even in this there is enjoyment. It is feasting the imagination. And I have very little doubt that in all ages and countries, women have enjoyed this mode of seeking pleasure ... a very improper and irregular sensual gratification, to be sure; but it may perhaps even bring on the venereal orgasm.

Lord Meadowbank's Notes on the Testimony of Miss Janet Munro, March 15, 1811

The first hint Miss Munro seems to have had of anything improper in the mistresses' conduct was derived from Miss Cumming. After relating her opinions respecting the two meetings of the mistresses, Miss Munro admits on cross-examination that at an earlier time she awoke with a fright and thought there might be someone in bed, but could not be sure of it. Having mentioned this to Miss Cumming, she was furnished with an hypothesis to account for whatever she might afterwards observe. Thus, whatever she saw acquired in her eyes an extraordinary character, and she was blind to simple explanations that might account for events. For example, the mistresses may simply have been talking in bed, since their workday appears to have been so crowded as not to allow them any other time to talk together. Miss Pirie might conceivably have gotten under the covers to keep warm.

I am particularly struck by Miss Munro's assertion that she frequently observed the mistresses kissing, caressing, and fondling each other more than could have resulted from ordinary female friendship, and that their behaviour seemed to her extraordinary even before she saw them in bed together. I think this statement demonstrates perfectly what the defendant's counsel pleaded at the hearing of the case and what I feared would occur in the calling of witnesses: that the young ladies needed an opportunity to exonerate themselves by "proving" the truth of their imputations. Miss Munro is a prejudiced witness. She is prejudiced not only by an hypothesis that she rashly adopted, but also by her interest in maintaining her accusations against the mistresses. Why else would she prefer to ascribe their public caresses to the unknown cause of an unnatural venereal appetite, rather than to the simple, true, and natural one of warm feelings that are common among those of great sensibility?

Lord Robertson's Notes on the Testimony of Miss Janet Munro, March 15, 1811

A prissy little bit of feline flesh. Very proper seeming. Quite heartless, I would guess. I do not imagine she is too clever. Her close-set eyes, which detract from her rather commonplace prettiness, do not suggest great intelligence, nor great imagination, for that matter. And lacking these she could not have concocted such a tale. She will grow into a fat, bland matron in no more than fifteen years. Now one wants to pinch her from behind or shake her ferociously or nip her on the cheek—if only to raise a response. What might the silly little puss say? I detest such vapidity. "Naked because it was the middle of the night" indeed.

June 15, 1982

Ollie has been wandering around the used-book stores of Edinburgh while I have been at work at the Signet Library. She says she is gathering momentum to return to the revision of her own manuscript, "British Jurisprudence as a Shaper of Western Thought," but thus far she has not even unpacked it. I am not to worry about it, she says.

Today she brought home a mid-nineteenth-century reprint of Mary Wollstonecraft's *Thoughts on the Education of Daughters,* which was written in 1787. I would guess that Jane Pirie and Marianne Woods were familiar with Wollstonecraft's more famous feminist book, *A Vindication of the Rights of Woman,* and they may have known this book too. Possibly they were influenced by it.

I suspect Mary Wollstonecraft was very much like Jane Pirie. Perhaps I say that because I see myself so much in both of them. In the mid-1770s, the decade before Jane Pirie was born, Mary Wollstonecraft, then a girl of sixteen, met Fanny Blood, "the friend whom I love better than all the world beside," as Mary called her.

They became and remained romantic friends until Fanny's death, about ten years later. Soon after their meeting, Mary was writing to a correspondent, "The prospect of living with my Fanny gladdens my heart:—You know not how I love her," and reiterating that since she was averse to matrimonial ties on many accounts, it was her intention never to marry, but to stay with Fanny forever. In Mary Wollstonecraft's autobiographical novel, *Mary: A Fiction,* which was written soon after Fanny's death, the narrator observes of the title character, who becomes involved with a man after "Ann" (Fanny) dies, "Had Ann lived, it is probable [Mary] would never have loved [the man]."

Mary Wollstonecraft, coming from a class of genteel poverty probably like Jane Pirie and Marianne Woods, was a governess for a while. Then, together with Fanny, she opened a school for young ladies in 1783, in Islington, and when it failed, tried again with another school in Newington Green, which was somewhat more successful. The conception, the plans, the preparations were all Mary's. She had to convince Fanny, who was reluctant and fearful of failure, to join her in this venture, much as I suspect Jane had to convince Marianne. The Newington Green school was short-lived, despite its initial success, because Mary finally recognized in her friend a "morbid softness of temper," together with a worsening tubercular condition. Mary realized now that Fanny was unsuited for the fray of such a strenuous life. She advised her to accept the proposal of Hugh Skeys, an old suitor who was living in Portugal where, Mary hoped, Fanny's physical condition might be improved. Yet when Fanny became pregnant, about a year after the marriage, Mary went to Lisbon to be with her. Fanny died in Mary's arms on November 29, 1785, after bearing a child who also died. But the relationship was not over in Mary's mind. More than ten years later she recollected, in *Letters From Norway,* "looks I have felt in every nerve, which I shall never more meet. The grave has closed over a dear friend, the friend of my youth; still she is present with me, and I hear her soft voice warbling as I stray over the heath." Theirs was one of the saddest stories of romantic friendship. The Woods and Pirie story is another.

But Mary Wollstonecraft's *Thoughts on the Education of Daughters* must have been a staple for serious-minded early-nineteenth-century governesses and proprietors of schools for young ladies. I believe, because of her own thoroughness and commitment to learning, that Jane Pirie was as outraged as her predecessor about the trifling sorts of educations given to young ladies. Wollstonecraft observed indignantly: "Girls learn something of music, drawing, and geography; but they do not know enough to engage their attention and render it an employment of the mind. If they can play over a few tunes to their acquaintances, and have a drawing or two (half done by the master) to hang up in their rooms, they imagine themselves artists for the rest of their lives. It is not being able to execute a trifling landscape, or anything of the kind, that is of consequence—these are at best but trifles, and the foolish, indiscriminate praises which are bestowed on them only produce vanity."

Perhaps Jane Pirie raised such great resentment in Janet Munro and Jane Cumming at least partly because her system of education was so stringent, and she demanded that the young ladies—who would have been quite content with learning to play a few tunes and executing a drawing or two that they might display at home—really study history and mathematics and moral philosophy. Possibly Jane Pirie also learned from Wollstonecraft's humorless book that girls must be discouraged from vanity and an immoderate fondness for display in dress. Wollstonecraft complained about any such ornamentation, "I hate to see the frame of a picture so glaring as to catch the eye and divide the attention." That philosophy too must have been repellent to these purse-proud young ladies. What was the good of being wellborn and wealthy if you could not show it off? I would imagine that there was a good deal of tension over such issues in a school like Jane Pirie's.

MARCH 16, 1811, 10:00 A.M.

Present are Janet Munro, the Lord Justice-Clerk, Lord Meadowbank, Lord Robertson, Lord Newton, Lord Boyle, and Lord Glenlee, the counsel for both parties, and Marianne Woods and Jane Pirie.

"Miss Munro," John Clerk begins, "when did you first mention to Miss Cumming what you had observed?"

"I think it was the next morning, after the first time when Miss Pirie came into our bed. Miss Cumming and I were dressing together in the dressing room."

"Was it then that Miss Cumming told you she had observed the same kind of incident?"

"I don't remember if it was then or some other time, but she did tell me so."

"And did you tell anyone else what you told Miss Cumming?"

"At the school?"

"Yes."

"No. Miss Stirling was there when I told Miss Cumming. But I didn't tell Miss Stirling particularly by herself at any time."

"When did you tell Mary Brown?"

"When she came to town, about the beginning of October. I've already been asked about all of this, sir." She is close to tears.

"I'm sorry, Miss Munro. I'll try not to repeat questions except for clarification. Was Mary Brown alone when she came to town?"

"No, she came with my older sister. But I didn't mention anything to her."

"Did you mention anything about it to your sister at any time?"

"No, sir."

"Did you see your sister much in October?"

"I saw her a few times, sir."

"Why did you not tell her what had happened in your bed?"

"I did not like to do so."

"Did you tell Miss Stevenson?"

"I told Mary Brown to tell her."

"Why?"

"Because she was my particular friend and I had no other person to tell it to. Oh—no, I'm sorry. I recollect now. Miss Stevenson wasn't in town at the time. I told Mary to tell my aunt, Miss Isabella Murdock."

"Miss Munro, did your behaviour towards Miss Pirie or Miss Woods alter in any degree after these occasions you described?"

"No."

"When did you first suspect that they were engaged in improper conduct with each other, Miss Munro?"

"I think it was when Charlotte the maid mentioned that she had seen them through the keyhole, when she described the way they were lying, so that made me consider it improper conduct."

"What particulars did she give you?"

"I don't remember. None."

"Was Miss Stirling present when Charlotte told you of the incident?"

"Yes, sir."

"Did Miss Stirling say anything to acknowledge that she understood?"

"No, sir. But one day when we were out walking, Miss Cumming, Miss Stirling, and I were together, and Miss Cumming began to talk on the subject. Then Miss Stirling joined in, but I don't remember what she said."

"Had she ever expressed shock at what Charlotte had said?"

"Yes, she seemed to be shocked at what Charlotte told us, and she seemed to think it very wicked."

"When did she say this?"

"I can't remember now, but I'm sure she said it."

"Miss Munro, what other young ladies were in the room when Miss Pirie came to Miss Woods?"

"All who slept there. Miss Cunynghame, Miss Hunter, and the two Miss Edgars."

"Did they see what you have described?"

"I don't know whether they were awake or not."

"Miss Munro," Lord Boyle asks, "do you mean to say that with all the noise and movement in the room none of the other four girls saw or heard aught?"

"I don't know, sir. Perhaps they did. The second time it happened, when Miss Woods told me to go to the dressing room for water, I went out by the foot of the bed to get my wrapper. And then when I saw Miss Pirie in the bed, I purposely gave her a knock with my elbow when I stooped down to put my slippers on, so that Miss Pirie would know that I knew. I don't know if Miss Edgar—the elder Miss Edgar—saw, but when I returned with the water she laughed."

"And did you say anything to her?" Lord Boyle asks.

"Yes, in the morning, after Miss Woods was gone."

"What did you say?" he asks.

"I only asked if she'd seen Miss Pirie go out of the room."

"You said nothing more to her, nor told her what you had observed?"

"No, sir."

"Did she tell you what she had laughed at?"

"No, sir."

"Didn't the other pupils think anything odd was going on?" Lord Boyle asks.

"Yes, a lot of people thought they caressed and fondled each other more than you would in ordinary female friendship," Miss Munro says.

"Thank you, Mr. Clerk," Lord Boyle says. John Clerk continues, "Miss Munro, who specifically said that your teachers' behaviour was beyond ordinary female friendship?"

"Miss Cumming and Miss Stirling, and I rather think the Miss Dunbars, but I'm not quite sure."

"Anyone else?" John Clerk asks.

"I don't now recollect any others that did so."

"Miss Munro, did anything else happen to make you think that theirs was a relationship beyond ordinary friendship?"

"They quarrelled."

"You mean you thought they behaved indecently in bed together because they quarrelled?"

"No. But it was stronger than the way ordinary female friends might quarrel. Once when they quarrelled in the dressing room it was so loud that all the scholars in our room woke up. And then the next morning Charlotte the maid told me—and I think everyone heard it—that she had heard them quarrelling also, so she went up to see what was the matter, and she found Miss Woods crying and Miss Pirie standing beside her, bidding her not to cry."

"Did they quarrel often in front of the students?"

"Yes, sir. Maybe they wished to conceal those quarrels from us, but they took no pains to do so. And after a quarrel began they never left the room."

"Miss Munro, did you ever witness a reconciliation between them?"

"Yes, sir. Sometimes a quarrel would last for a week or ten days, and then they would have a reconciliation."

"How did they become reconciled?"

"Well, it was then that they particularly caressed each other."

"Now, Miss Munro, on any of the occasions when Miss Pirie came to Miss Woods' bed, did you not observe that it was for the purpose of reconciliation?"

"I don't remember. I don't think there was any coolness between them before either of the times that Miss Pirie came."

Lord Justice-Clerk Hope wishes to know if there might have been any private quarrel between them without her knowing it.

"Perhaps there might," she answers, "but I don't think that there was."

"You do not think that there was," John Clerk says, "but you do not know, do you?"

"No," she responds.

"Miss Munro," John Clerk continues, "when did you last receive the sacrament?"

"Last November."

"According to the forms of the Church of Scotland?"

"Yes, sir."

"And when had you last received it before that?"

"November 1808."

"Did you speak with any clergyman before taking the sacrament the last time?"

"No, sir."

"Did Miss Pirie advise you to have such a conversation in order to prepare yourself for receiving the sacrament? And did she not blame you for not having done so?"

"I don't recollect."

"Did you not have several conversations with Miss Pirie respecting religion?"

"Yes, I think so."

"And did Miss Pirie not give you several instructions with regard to reading the Bible, and offer to go over with you what you read and explain it to you?"

"Yes."

"Did you complain to Miss Pirie that your time was so taken up with the lessons you had to learn that you did not have time to read the Bible?"

She says nothing.

"Did you, Miss Munro?"

"I'm not sure I said that."

"Did Miss Pirie not complain to you that she thought you had made little proficiency in religious knowledge?"

"No, she did not."

"Before you took the sacrament, did Miss Pirie not tell you that Mr. Dickson, the minister, would converse with you?"

"Yes, but Miss Stevenson said she thought it unnecessary, so I didn't talk with him."

John Clerk goes to his table and brings two books to the witness. "Do you know these books?" he asks. One is Miss Pirie's Bible; the other is a book on the sacrament, *A Short and Plain Instruction for the Better Understanding of the Lord's Supper for the Benefit of Young Communicants.*

"Yes," Miss Munro answers.

"Did Miss Pirie recommend to you serious perusal of several passages in the Bible, which she marked for you?"

"Yes."

"And in the sacrament book? Kindly read this marked passage," he says and places the book in front of her.

" 'We are by nature sinners,' " she reads aloud, " 'and as such God cannot take pleasure in us. And if we die before we are restored to His favour, we shall be separated from Him and miserable forever.' "

He takes the book back and turns to another page. "Now read this marked passage," he commands.

" 'How a Christian ought to prepare himself for the Sacrament: They must examine themselves thus, Whether they repent them truly of their former sins? Whether they steadfastly propose to lead a new life? Whether they have a lively faith in God's mercy through Christ? Whether they have a thankful remembrance of His death? and whether they be in charity with all men?' "

"And here is another," he says, turning the pages as she holds the book in her hand.

" 'If, therefore, you stand in any fear of the judgment of God, set yourself seriously to consider your past life: see whether you have not lived, or do not now live, in any known sin or evil habit . . .' "

"I believe that is sufficient, Miss Munro," Lord Robertson says. "I would imagine we are all here familiar with the book."

"Were these not the pages marked by Miss Pirie in order that you might pay particular attention to the passages therein?" John Clerk reiterates.

"Yes," she answers.

"And, Miss Munro, was it not recently, before you took the sacrament, that Miss Pirie put this book into your hands? Were you not then on the same good terms of friendship with her as you had been from the beginning?"

She says nothing.

"Do you remember that after taking the sacrament you came round to the table to Miss Pirie and shook hands with her and asked her how she did?"

"No."

"You do not remember that?"

"I don't think so."

"Miss Munro, on the day when you finally left the school, do you remember coming into the small room next to the school room where Miss Pirie was sitting with the dance mistress?"

"Yes, I went into that room to ask Miss Pirie to excuse Miss Edgar some lines she was to recite."

"Did you not say to her that your papa had come for you and you wondered what he wanted?"

"I don't remember saying that. I think I supposed she knew my father had come for me."

"Did you tell Miss Pirie you were going away never to return?"

"No, I didn't know that myself at the time."

Lord Justice-Clerk Hope interrupts. It is 11:30 A.M. and the Court is scheduled to meet with the lawyers on *Crow against Mathieson* before the morning is over. They will resume listening to the testimony of Janet Munro at 2:00 P.M. on this day.

The religious differences between Jane Pirie and Marianne Woods may have caused considerable difficulties once they lived together and tried to "raise children," just as it might in a marriage if one partner or the other was fanatically religious. While Marianne seems to have modified Jane's views when the relationship was new, perhaps by 1810, at a time when a wave of Evangelicalism was pouring over Scotland, bringing a revival of religious sternness, Marianne's modifications had worn off.

It appears that the women agreed that those girls whose families belonged to the Church of England would be supervised in their religious training by Marianne, and Jane would look after those of the Church of Scotland. The plan was sensible, but its execution may not have been without conflict. From the time of the Presbyterian insurrection in 1688 to the mid-eighteenth century, Episcopalians had been severely persecuted in Scotland. In the streets of Edinburgh, Episcopalian clergymen were taunted by the school boys with rhymes such as:

> Pisky, Pisky, Amen,
> Down on your knees and up again.

At the end of the eighteenth century, Scottish Episcopalians enjoyed a relatively untroubled period, but the revivalism of the first decade of the nineteenth century appears to have stimulated some hostilities again.

Even if there was no outright hostility between Marianne Woods and Jane Pirie concerning Evangelicalism or Episcopalian persecution, Marianne would have found it hard to understand Jane's extreme upset over Janet Munro's taking the sacrament without preparation. According to Jane Pirie's early religious training, to receive communion when one was unfit to take part in the "sealing ordinance"—having broken the Sabbath or sworn profanely or put on gaudy attire or spoken lies or evil of others—was to eat and drink damnation to oneself. She must have remembered how the ministers of her childhood admonished their congregations in this regard: "Will ye seal damnation to yourselves and, as it were, make it sure ye shall be damned, and so drive the last nail in your damnation? Rather put a knife to your throat than approach. What! Will ye be guilty of His body and blood? The worst morsel that ever ye tasted is to eat and drink eternal vengeance."

Janet Munro, who appears to have been a spoiled young lady with very little religious training at home, was probably horrified by Jane Pirie's passion over what Janet was used to treating lightly. Now she was told she was not fit to take the sacrament. She would have been resentful at this stringency of the school together with all its other stringencies. If she saw what she claimed she did, the mistresses' hypocrisy must have overwhelmed her. But if the sex scenes were nothing more than her fabrication, it must have been a jolly good joke to say that those pious-acting women were more abandoned than common whores. She may not have been in a position to realize that Jane Pirie's religious fervor was not shared by Marianne Woods, and that Marianne was probably wary of the disruption and bitterness Jane Pirie's unyielding attitudes might cause the school. Marianne too must have had some contentions with Jane over her enthusiasm.

MARCH 16, 1811, 2:00 P.M.

The same parties are present as were at the session of the morning. John Clerk resumes the questioning of Miss Munro.

"Miss Munro, did you not, both before and after the time Miss Pirie came to your bed, always, whenever you happened to be near her, put your arm round her waist as expressive of kindness and affection for her?"

"No, I never did. At least I don't remember doing that."

"Were you not always anxious to sit next to Miss Pirie during the working hours?"

"Sometimes I sat next to her, but not generally."

"Were you not always anxious to take her arm while you were all out walking?"

"Sometimes I used to take her arm, and so did several of the other girls. But that was because we learned our geography with Miss Pirie, and we often used to get part of our lesson while walking with her in that way."

"However, Miss Munro, is it not true that when you found that Miss Pirie had given her arms to other young ladies for the walk of that day, you said—you often said—'Well, remember I bespeak an arm for tomorrow'?"

"Perhaps I did. I have no recollection of it."

"Miss Munro, did you not complain often of the difficulty of getting double tasks imposed by way of punishment?"

"Not more than the other scholars."

"Do you remember that Miss Pirie talked to you several times about the need of sending you to what was called 'the disgrace table,' and you responded that you dared say it was all for your own good and you would bless the day you came to Drumsheugh?"

"I think I may have said that once, but I don't remember when. And I don't remember Miss Pirie talking to me about why I had to sit there. I would just be sent there if I didn't do a lesson or something."

"During the last three weeks you were at the school, had you not been at the disgrace table more frequently than before? Several times in those weeks?"

"I don't think so. I can't recollect."

"Do you know this book?" he asks, placing before her *A New History of England* by the Reverend Mr. Cooper. "Is this not your discipline book?"

"It was the book from which we studied history."

"But when you misbehaved you were given extra work from this book."

"Yes. I had to memorize extra passages."

He turns the pages, holding the book up for the judges to see. "Here it says, 'October 11, 50 lines on Richard I for being forgetful,' and here is '50 lines on Henry III for noise on October 20,' and here is '100 lines for neglect of practising for the writing master, Mr. Mather, November 1st.' Were these your disciplines?"

"Yes, and I had to do more work than that also."

"And you resented all the work you had to do?"

"No, sir. I don't think I did. It was more than I was used to, but I don't think I resented it."

"So you liked the school and your mistresses?"

"Until I found out what they were doing."

"Did you not often confide in Miss Woods and Miss Pirie?"

"I'm not sure what you mean. I told them things you would tell a mistress."

"Didn't Miss Cumming propose that you and she become bedfellows, and didn't you tell Miss Pirie that you did not know what to say to Miss Cumming, but you did not want to sleep with her?"

She says nothing.

"When Miss Pirie told you that it was anyway out of the question to change rooms at that time, did you not tell her you were happy she prevented it?"

"I don't remember saying I was happy she prevented it. I think I remember telling her that Miss Cumming proposed we be bedfellows."

"Miss Munro, do you remember on one occasion when out on your walk that you and Miss Cumming got some apples between you, and each of you brought one to Miss Woods?"

"Yes, she was walking with us."

"And you said you picked one on purpose for Miss Woods?"

"I don't remember that."

"How long was that before you left the school?"

"I'm not sure."

"Mr. Clerk, I'm sorry to interrupt, but I must ask a question regarding some former testimony," Lord Boyle says. "Miss Munro, you said you told Charlotte the maid after the second occasion that you were very tired because you were disturbed and got little sleep in the night. Is that correct?"

"Yes, sir."

"But since day was breaking in the morning before you were disturbed, you must have had at least seven or eight hours' sleep. You could not have been very tired for want of sleep, unless I suppose you had been restless before. Why did you say that to the maid?"

"Well, I think it was because Miss Cumming told me before

that the maid knew how they behaved, so I said that to start the conversation."

"May I ask something else please," Lord Boyle says. "Miss Munro, as it was quite dark the first time Miss Pirie came into Miss Woods' bed, how did you know that Miss Pirie lay above Miss Woods, rather than Miss Woods above Miss Pirie?"

"I don't think I knew which one of them was uppermost the first time, sir."

"Well, then," he asks, "how in the dark did you know that one of them was lying above the other rather than by the side of the other?"

"My reason was that I couldn't get the bed-clothes kept on me."

"Then do you wish it understood," Lord Boyle asks, "that you had not formed your opinion of one being above the other from having felt them in that situation?"

"Oh, no sir, on the contrary. I partly formed my opinion from having felt them, since they were lying so close to me. And I thought at that time, and still think, that I felt both their bodies at the same time."

"Do any other of your Lordships wish to ask further questions?" John Clerk inquires. None do. "One further question from me, Miss Munro," he says. "On the first occasion, when you think you felt the mistresses' bodies one above the other, what were they wearing?"

"I think they had on nothing but their shifts."

"Their shifts?"

"I think so."

"Was it their naked bodies or their shifts that touched you?"

"I think both."

"Miss Munro, I understand that you are hard of hearing. How is it that you heard so much of their conversation?"

"There was much that I couldn't hear, sir. But I'm only sometimes a little deaf in one ear. But that's why I had to turn to hear what they were saying. I had been lying with my back to them, with my best ear on the pillow."

John Clerk indicates he has no further questions. They are adjourned until Tuesday next at ten o'clock forenoon.

Lord Boyle's Notes on the Testimony of Miss Janet Munro, March 16, 1811

There are contradictions and inconsistencies in the witness' testimony. First she says she believes Miss Pirie's clothes were off. When asked why, the only reason she gives is that it was the dead of night. Later she says that when she felt the mistresses' bodies one above the other they had on their shifts. When asked if it was their naked bodies or only their shifts that touched her, she says both. She contradicts herself also with regard to how and when her suspicions were first aroused, but it is in any case clear that Miss Cumming had a hand in arousing them. At a time when Miss Munro had seen nothing whatever of impropriety in the conduct of the mistresses, Miss Cumming had communicated to her that she and Charlotte had seen them behave in a way that was indecent. It is easy to conceive that Miss Munro's imagination became greatly alive to the extraordinary details which Miss Cumming must have related to her in their conversations. Miss Munro said at one point that she became sensible of the mistresses' wickedness only after Mary Brown, the nursery maid, informed her that their behaviour was indecent, but it appears to me from her testimony, contradictory as it is, that she had previously received a full communication from Miss Cumming and perhaps from Charlotte Whiffin. Her report to Brown must have been extremely strong, otherwise Brown could never have arrived so soon at her conclusion that the offenders merited burning.

It is impossible to listen to Miss Munro without observing that she has some strong grudges against the mistresses, although she seemed to have admired them as well. I would venture to guess that the harsh discipline at the school prompted her ambivalence and led directly to her finding grave fault with the two ladies.

Lord Glenlee's Notes on the Testimony of Miss Janet Munro, March 16, 1811

I think it is perfectly clear that nothing could have made Miss Munro believe that one of those women was lying above the other unless it had been the fact. Counsel for the plaintiffs is apparently attempting to point out that she was influenced in her conclusion by others—Miss Cumming, Mary Brown, Charlotte Whiffin. But will any degree of influence account for such a complete fabrication as this? I must either conclude just as Miss Munro did about the mistresses' behaviour, or I must believe that there was downright perjury, and I have seen no reason why she should so perjure herself. On the contrary, she seems to have had an amicable relationship with the mistresses and to have liked the school apart from her shocking discovery.

June 20, 1982

Who was Janet Munro? Dame Cumming Gordon's attorney tried to present her as a carefully brought-up child. But would an innocent conceive of such indirection as to knock Jane Pirie with her elbow "accidentally" to let her know she saw her, or to open so deliberately a discussion with the maid about the mistresses' indiscretions by saying she could not sleep because she was bothered in her bed? She was subtle in a way that the naïve are not. What did such subtlety signify? It might have been a sign of a malicious temperament rather than any sort of sophistication.

It is not difficult to see what would have made her malicious. There was, to begin with, a good deal of sadness in her life. Her mother died when she was nine. Her father seems to have been distant, though maybe not unusually so for a nineteenth-century patriarch. She had neither the independence granted to the oldest daughter nor the attention given to the youngest children. There was no one in her immediate family with whom she believed herself to be on intimate terms. She could speak more freely to the nursery maid, who had never even been her own nurse, than she could to her sister. Was it because she knew the nurse would be more gullible than her sister, who would perhaps have accused her of inventing such a story? The nurse's response must have been what Janet wanted, whether the tale was true or not: she expressed horror at the mistresses, she sympathized with Janet, and she passed the information on. Maybe Janet believed that filtered through the nurse, an adult, it would be treated with more credulity than it would have been coming directly from a sixteen-year-old.

She resented the discipline of the school: the work seemed to her excessive and she had never learned how to get by with going through the motions that would satisfy a teacher. Nor had she ever before been punished with the severity that was common at the school. Such punishment must have been a shock. It would have been enough to make her malicious toward the mistresses.

And how unpleasant the mistresses' piety must have been to her. They made their students pray four times a day. Both Miss Pirie and Miss Woods must have seemed to her zealous in their religious instruction. Is it possible that they only wanted to impress upon the parents that theirs was a moral establishment? They could have thought that piety was a good blind if they wished to carry on outrageously. Or might they have been genuinely orthodox in all other areas, Miss Pirie in particular, and still carried on outrageously? Maybe their wild sexual activity, if it really happened, occupied only one small dark corner of their minds. Maybe they saw it as having nothing to do with their daytime piety. Maybe they believed that Christ would forgive them their weakness, and they would try to control themselves soon. Or maybe they could find nothing sacrilegious in their physical exchanges; but if they saw them as perfectly pious expressions of their love, would they not have tried to secure the privacy that such serious acts need?

Suppose that Janet fabricated the whole thing—or helped Jane Cumming fabricate it. She would not have needed a motive so melodramatic as fearing blackmail because Jane knew she had stolen a bracelet, which is what Hellman attributes to her counterpart in *The Children's Hour*. She had never been away from home. It must have been terrifying for a young girl to find herself suddenly among total strangers. She would have wanted to ingratiate herself, especially among her peers. The oldest girls would have been the most powerful, the most important to please. Jane Cumming was one of the oldest—and then there was her connection with Dame Cumming Gordon. Janet's family was wealthy but not titled. In that class-obsessed society what influence a girl like Jane Cumming would have had among the others, despite her "tinge of colour." If she was manipulative, and perhaps hardened by frequent punishments as well as the facts of her life, what might she not have done with a pawn like Janet Munro?

The women's attorney wanted to show that Janet was enamored of them, but perhaps her seeming affection was nothing more than civility or the sentimental conventions that were considered appropriate for a school girl toward her mistresses. It is clear, anyway, that there was some duplicity on her part, although that is probably not unusual for a sixteen-year-old who must find a way to survive in an alien place. Or did she develop a love-hate toward one or maybe both of the mistresses? She would want to see them suffer because they did not treat her with enough gentleness or the attention she would have liked to have had. I wonder if it is possible to become so strongly ambivalent in the space of a few weeks.

She chose the maid Charlotte Whiffin as a confidante at the school, but would she have confided in a maid she had known for so brief a time if she really wished to unburden a heavy heart? The studied casualness with which Janet opened the conversation—admittedly to get Charlotte to talk on the subject—suggests to me that she was not in great anguish when she related her shocking discoveries. Perhaps she thought the maid as easily scandalized as she guessed the nurse at home would be; and as the only accessible adult in the house she might help Janet take action—or she might provide good entertainment. I wonder if Janet was not looking for such titillation as the judges, and most of nineteenth-century Britain, believed that sixteen-year-old virgins never sought. Jane Cumming seems to have told her that Charlotte would respond with stories of her own, so she already knew what she might expect.

But what is to be made of Janet's report of what Charlotte said? It reads like a description in a pornographic novel: two women lewd in dressing rooms and drawing rooms and broom closets. What, if anything, did Charlotte actually see to make her say, "They're at it again"? It is conceivable that she was referring to their arguments and their reconciliations, while Janet chose to interpret such remarks to mean something else. Or maybe Charlotte saw the mistresses embracing passionately, as Eleanor Butler and Sarah Ponsonby, Mary Wollstonecraft and Fanny Blood, Mme. Récamier and Mme. de Staël must have embraced in their day—but coming from a less sentimental class and (at nineteen) having had little exposure to such ladies, Charlotte might have viewed their embrace as it would never have occurred to them to view it. But who can be sure of what Charlotte really said to Janet: did she describe the women "lying" together, as Janet reports; or did she not give *any* "particulars," as Janet says at another point?

I can't imagine what the mistresses might have done out of bed that would have aroused genuine suspicion in their day. Novels and poems and diaries and letters show that romantic friends hung on each other and kissed and caressed. So how might Woods and Pirie's public kisses and embraces have been different from those of other romantic friends? Perhaps once knowing of the mistresses' bed behavior, once understanding that there are no limits to erotic possibilities between women, Janet saw in a new light what would usually have been considered normal in their daytime caresses. Not having been privy to such night scenes, most people would never have put that construction on the mistresses' embraces.

I'm fascinated by Janet's assertion that she suspected the mistresses were sexually intimate because they quarreled. Lovers quarrel in her universe. Had she observed a good deal of quarreling between her mother and father, as a young child? Where else would she have learned to connect intimacy with turbulent anger? I think I can count on the fingers of one hand the number of times Ollie and I have seriously quarreled in eleven years. I doubt that Eleanor and Sarah quarreled much.

I think Janet may have reported what she saw truly, but with skewed vision, distorted by the promptings of Jane Cumming.

Maybe she saw the mistresses together in bed all right, but they were—in combat? Shaking each other, out of fury? Maybe Miss Woods had just told Miss Pirie that she couldn't send her aunt to a flat after all because of the cataracts, and maybe Miss Pirie grabbed her and cried, "Marianne, after your promises? I believed you. Have you no regard for me? Do I mean nothing to you?" And maybe Miss Woods cried back, "Get hold of yourself, Jane. You'll wake everyone. Please, please stop. You'll ruin us." Then Miss Pirie might have controlled herself, and they might have held each other for some tearful moments. If Janet had said something to them just then, they would have been startled, and then ashamed of themselves. They would have tried to disguise their actions. Miss Pirie might have explained that she was only standing there, that they were doing nothing untoward. If they were embarrassed by their violent quarrels, that would explain why the maid had seen them red-faced. Or maybe not. Maybe the women were insane enough, distracted enough, desperate enough, actually to have sex in a bed that their sixteen-year-old student shared, or where they might be observed by anyone. Is that consistent with anything that is known of them? I think I would have been a Jane Pirie had I lived 170 years ago. I cannot believe she was less prudent than I am.

I am like Lord Meadowbank. My tendency is to doubt what is extraordinarily wicked and unnatural. Their alleged sexual play would have been neither one (not in Lord Meadowbank's world, but from my modern perspective), except that it was supposed to have been carried on in the presence of children. Either they were monsters, as Dame Cumming Gordon believed, or they were innocent.

Ollie has decided she needs some distance from her own manuscript, and she wants to let it alone for a month or so, perhaps for as long as we stay in Edinburgh. It sits on top of the little refrigerator in our flat, all six hundred pages, menacing her. I wish I could do more than give her my sympathy over it, but I can see that at this stage she needs to work it out for herself. She says she wants to "get involved" with my project for a while. I'm truly grateful. I feel overwhelmed by the mass of material I must wade through in the next two months.

March 20, 1811, 10:00 a.m.

Mary Brown, thirty, servant in the family of George Munro, Esquire, for seven years, is called as a witness. Present are the Right Honourable Lord Justice-Clerk Hope, Lords Meadowbank, Roberstson, and Newton, counsel for the defendant and the plaintiffs, Marianne Woods, and Jane Pirie. Mary Brown is sworn in. Mr. Cranstoun examines her for the defence.

"When were you first made aware of Miss Munro's complaint regarding her mistresses?" he asks.

"Well, your honour," she says, "the family of Mr. Munro came to town on the 1st of October last, and then I came on the Wednesday with the children."

"And that is when Miss Munro told you of what she had witnessed at the school?"

"No, your honor. When I came Miss Janet Munro was herself at the school. She came to visit her father at the lodgings in Edinburgh on the Saturday next, and she stayed all night."

"And it was at that time that Miss Munro confided to you what she had observed?"

"Yes, your honour. It was while I was attending the children. Miss Janet called me two times into her room and seemed anxious that she should get me alone."

"Did she get you alone?"

"Not the first time, but the second time I had just finished putting the children to bed."

"And what happened?"

"I believe that I asked her how she liked her new school. And she told me she liked it very well but there was one thing very disagreeable to her."

"Did she tell you what that was?" Cranstoun asks.

"Not right away. But I told Miss Janet she must tell me. Then she said nothing, and after a minute, being like to cry, she said that one mistress came to the bed that Miss Janet shared with the other one. She came in the middle of the night."

"Did Miss Janet tell you anything further?"

"She said she was awakened with a noise and disturbed with the bed shaking, and she could not get the bed-clothes kept on. She said she spoke to the mistress—not the one she slept with but the other . . ."

"Miss Pirie?"

"I think that was it. And she desired this Miss Pirie to go away as she could not get sleep, but Miss Pirie said that she was standing by the bedside. Then the one Miss Janet slept with . . ."

"Miss Woods?"

"I think that was her name, your honour. This Miss Woods told her friend she had better go away."

"Are those the very words Miss Janet used when she told you this during the first week in October?"

"Yes, your honour."

"Did she tell you anything else?"

"Oh, yes. She said that the one who came to visit was lying above the other."

"Did she say they were kissing one another?"

"No."

"Mary," Lord Justice-Clerk Hope asks, "did Miss Janet tell you that the mistresses lay still, or that there was any motion between them?"

"I can't remember that, your honours," she says, "but she said the bed shook."

"Was that the end of your conversation with Miss Janet that evening?" Cranstoun asks.

"No, your honour. She asked me what I thought it was, and I said that it was a wicked thing and that they were worse than beasts and deserved to be burned if it was true. And then Miss Janet answered, 'Oh, yes, Mary. It is perfectly true.' So I told her that if she ever saw the same thing again to let me know."

"And did she ever mention it again?"

"Yes, your honour. I saw her on the next Saturday when she came home and stayed all night."

"What conversation did you have with her on that occasion?"

"Well, when she came into the nursery that afternoon to inquire after the children, I then asked her if anything bad was still going on at the school and she answered, yes, it was as bad as ever, and that the mistresses had again carried on in the same manner as before."

"Can you tell the court exactly what Miss Janet said, Mary?"

"Miss Janet said that she had lain long awake and coughed and turned herself to make them understand she was awake, and that she saw the mistress who didn't belong there in bed with herself and the other lady. Then the one Miss Janet slept with desired her to get up and get a glass of water and she did so, but when she came back with it the other one had slipt out of the room."

"Did Miss Janet tell you what conversation passed then between her and her bedfellow?"

"I don't remember. I think Miss Janet fell asleep."

"After Miss Janet told you this, what did you say?"

"Why, I said it was a very dreadful thing, and one of them is certainly a man."

"Did you ask Miss Janet if anyone else had seen the same things?"

"Yes, your honour. Miss Cumming, the granddaughter of Lady Gordon, told her the same thing had happened to her, because she shared a bed with the other teacher—and the one who slept with Miss Janet often came to visit them in the middle of the night. So then I said to Miss Janet that she must not sleep with the teacher. She must get another bed for herself."

"Mary, how long have you been in Mr. Munro's family?"

"Seven years, your honour."

"Mary, what sort of a girl do you consider Miss Janet as to veracity?"

"Your honour?"

"I mean as to telling truth or lies?"

John Clerk objects to the question. His objection is sustained by the judges. "Then I have no other questions," Cranstoun says.

John Clerk rises to interrogate the servant, Mary Brown, for the plaintiffs.

"Miss Brown," he asks, "did any more conversation take place between you and Miss Munro that second Saturday?"

"I don't think so, your honour," she says.

"You may call me 'sir' or 'Mr. Clerk' " he says. "Now, Miss Brown, please take time to recollect. Something may come to you."

She pauses a minute. "No, sir. I don't remember any other conversation except that I said to Miss Janet that she ought to let it all be known to the other young ladies at the school, so that it might be found out and stopped."

"What did Miss Munro say to that?"

"I don't remember exactly what she said, but it was something about the other young ladies being all little."

"Mary," Lord Boyle asks, "did Miss Munro desire you to tell her father or elder sister?"

"No, sir."

"Did she desire you to tell anyone?"

"On the first Saturday she said that I might tell Miss Isabella Murdoch, her aunt who stayed with us, I think I asked her if I might, and first she said no, then she said yes. So that same night, when Miss Murdoch came to the nursery to see the children, I began to tell her, but she would not listen to it and went out of the nursery. I remember I was just beginning to tell her about it and she said something—I can't remember what—but she didn't seem to be listening to me. Then she left the room. And a day or two after she went to Glasgow, and she still remains there, so I never told her anything more of it."

"Did you tell any other person?" Lord Boyle asks.

"No, sir."

John Clerk resumes. "What was your reason for concealing it?" he asks.

"Because it was so strange and dreadful a story, and the other servants were all new, and I had no one to tell it to."

"What was your reason for concealing it from Mr. Munro?"

"I did not like to tell it to him, and I had no other female in the house to tell it to."

"What was your reason for concealing it from Miss Stevenson and the elder Miss Munro?"

"I could tell it to none of them. It was such a horrible thing that I could not speak of it."

"What did you think would become of Miss Janet Munro from such horrible proceedings in the meantime, and before they were discovered?"

"Why, I always hoped Miss Janet would make it public among the other young ladies, and that it would be discovered by some other way. I could tell it to nobody."

"Miss Brown, was it your real opinion that one of the mistresses was a man?"

"I don't recall whether it was. But I was very angry about it, and I thought it so peculiar, so I just said surely one of them must be a man."

"But if you did not really believe that one of the mistresses was a man, what sort of wickedness did you suppose had taken place?"

"Why, I can give no account of it, sir. I think I read something about it in the Bible—but I don't remember what it is."

"Is it in the Old Testament or the New Testament?" John Clerk asks.

"I'm not sure, but certainly I think it's in the New Testament."

"Did you ever hear of such wickedness being actually practised, or how it was practised?"

"I never did by any other women. I never heard anything about how it was done."

"Did you tell Miss Munro it was a wickedness mentioned in the Bible?"

"No."

"Now, Mary," the Lord Justice-Clerk says, "you have said the mistresses were not kissing one another. And you have said that Miss Munro did not tell you any other circumstance from which you inferred that they were lewd or indecent or criminal, except that Miss Pirie was lying above Miss Woods and that the bed was shaking. Without any explanation of those circumstances, how came you to think and say to Miss Munro that their conduct was so dreadful that they should be burned?"

"Sir, I can't say. But it is God's truth that I did think that and that I still think it was very bad indeed."

John Clerk resumes. "Miss Brown, how far had you proceeded in your story to Miss Murdoch?"

"I think I had told her there was something very wicked at the school, and that one mistress came to the other's bed. But she interrupted me, saying something like, 'Oh, Mary, is that true?' And then she left the room right away and I never had a chance to tell her the rest."

"Did you tell Miss Munro that Miss Murdoch would not listen to you?"

"I had no chance that first Saturday, but I did the next one. And by that time Miss Murdoch was already gone to Glasgow, sir."

He has no further questions.

Cranstoun is asked if he has further questions of the witness. He does not.

MARCH 20, 1811, 1:00 P.M.

Charlotte Whiffin is called as a witness for the defendant and is sworn in. She is nineteen, from the county of Kent, unmarried, former servant at the plaintiffs' school. Five judges are present, Hope, Meadowbank, Robertson, Boyle, and Newton, as well as George Cranstoun and his junior advocate, John Erskine, for the defendant and John Clerk for the plaintiffs. Marianne Woods, Jane Pirie, and Lady Cumming Gordon are also present.

In response to Erskine's questions, Charlotte Whiffin tells the Court that she has been in the service of the mistresses since the 16th of May last, and that she knows Miss Munro and Miss Cumming who were boarders at the Drumsheugh school.

"Charlotte," Erskine asks, "did you ever hear those young ladies say anything about the conduct of the mistresses in the beds they shared with Miss Cumming and Miss Munro, and did you take part in the conversation, or did you relate anything to the young ladies which you had seen or known?"

John Clerk rises to his feet and objects. The Lord Justice-Clerk sustains his objection and instructs Erskine first to examine the witness as to what she saw and not what she said.

"Charlotte," Erskine begins again, "did you at any time observe anything in the conduct of the mistresses towards each other that appeared to be extraordinary or indecent, or that led you to be surprised at what you saw?"

"No, sir," she answers.

He stares at her and then looks at Cranstoun, who also stares at the girl. "Perhaps she did not understand the question, your Lordships," Cranstoun rises to say. "May counsel for the defence repeat it?" Hope nods yes.

"I understand the question," Charlotte says tonelessly. "I

never saw them doing anything they should not be doing."

"Now, Charlotte," Erskine asks, "did you not see Miss Woods and Miss Pirie kiss each other, or show any uncommon marks of affection for each other?"

"I never saw any such thing," she states.

"Charlotte, did you ever see the mistresses lying together in the drawing room or the dressing room?"

"I never did."

"Charlotte, I want you to think more carefully," Erskine admonishes her. "Did you ever . . ."

John Clerk objects to the manner in which the question is stated. He is sustained.

"Charlotte," Erskine says, "did you not on any occasion go into the drawing room in order to speak to Miss Pirie and Miss Woods, and find the drawing room door locked or bolted when the mistresses were in there together?"

"I never went to the room and found the doors bolted."

"Charlotte," Erskine asks, "did you never observe any dispute or high words between the mistresses?"

"No."

"Oh, come now, Charlotte," he says, "you never heard them quarrelling?"

"Well—maybe I heard them quarrelling sometimes, between themselves."

Erskine turns to the judges, exasperated. "Your Lordships, since the witness denies having seen the plaintiffs together, may I now ask the questions with which I began?" He is given permission.

"Did you at any time hear the young ladies discuss the conduct of the mistresses in their beds, and how they were disturbed by that conduct? Did you not take part in the conversation?" Erskine asks the maid.

"No." She is exasperated too.

"No, what?" Erskine asks.

"Well, I had seen these young ladies together, and talking together, but I don't know what it was about, and I never told them that I had seen anything wrong in what my mistresses did."

"Charlotte," he asks calmly, "do you remember Miss Woods' birthday in October last?"

"Yes," she says tentatively.

"Do you remember anything in the way of festivities, disguising or masquerading in the house?"

"Nothing very big. The other servant put on some clothes, and she and I went upstairs together to amuse the young ladies, but we did not stay long."

"Was there a girl serving in the house by the name of Nancy?"

"Yes, that was the one I just mentioned."

Erskine stares at her. "What was Nancy wearing that night?" he asks.

"She had men's clothes on over her own clothes."

"Was there anything particular in Nancy's situation at that time?" he asks.

"She was with child, but it could not be noticed."

"Do you mean that it could not be noticed when she had on men's clothes, or it could not be noticed when she was in her ordinary dress?"

"Well, some people might and some people might not notice it in her ordinary dress. It was harder to notice when she had on men's clothes."

Erskine has no further questions. John Clerk is permitted to question the witness.

"When you entered the service of Miss Woods and Miss Pirie, did you not engage for six months?"

"Yes," she says. "And about a week before the first six months was up I engaged to serve them another six months."

"Do you know a girl called Bell Campbell?" Clerk asks.

"Yes, she come in the place of Nancy, Martinmas last."

"Did she ask you at the time she was hired if it was a good place or not?"

"Yes."

"And what was your response?" Clerk asks.

"I said it was a very good place and I had been very comfortable ever since I was in it."

"What were your duties in your job, Miss Whiffin?"

"Now they are changed," she answers, "but when the school was still going I was to wake the young ladies in the morning, and then do up the school room. Then to help with the serving of the breakfast. Then to make the beds, and then to do washing or other cleaning."

"Miss Whiffin, after the scholars assembled in the school room, what did they do?"

"Prayers was the first thing."

"Did you attend?"

"Either I or Nancy or Bell would attend, excepting on washing days."

"Would you say that your mistresses were very attentive to the behaviour and conduct of those under their charge?"

Erskine objects. The Lord Justice-Clerk overrules.

"They were very careful," Charlotte affirms. "They were always with the young ladies and they had prayers four times a day."

"Miss Whiffin, when Miss Cumming left the school for good, did you know why she was leaving?"

"Oh, no. I thought she had been coming back the same as usual. At least she said nothing different."

"When were the other scholars taken away?" Clerk asks.

"Right after Miss Cumming."

"Did you know what the cause was?"

"No, and I heard no surmise of it. I thought on the Wednesday night when they were taken away so many of them together that they were going to some ball or entertainment."

"Did you at that time hear it speculated that the school had gone bankrupt?"

"That was the first reason I heard for the young ladies being taken away."

"Miss Whiffin," John Clerk asks, "do you recollect, shortly after this, meeting Miss Cumming in Charlotte Square?"

"Yes. I saw her as I was accidentally passing through Charlotte Square on that Friday. And Miss Margaret Dunbar, her cousin, who had also been a scholar, was with her."

"Can you say what occurred on that occasion, please?"

"They came up to me and asked me if all the scholars had left the school, and I said all but two, and they seemed very glad of it. Miss Cumming turned to Miss Dunbar and clapped her hands and said, 'Do you hear, Margaret, they are almost all gone.' Then I asked Miss Cumming if she knew what was the reason, and she said she did not."

"Miss Whiffin, did you know that Miss Pirie often had back pains?"

"Yes, I know she does because I was sometimes asked to rub her back."

"Did Miss Pirie sleep with her bed gown and petticoat?"

"I know she sleeps with a bed gown. I don't know about a petticoat."

"Miss Whiffin, who made the beds in the morning?"

"I did, with Nancy and then with Bell."

"Was there anything particular in the bed in which Miss Pirie and Miss Cumming slept?"

"I don't remember anything particular, only that we used to make it last."

"Why?" Clerk asks.

"We used to throw the bed clothes open and let it get air, because we thought that bed had a smell. Also, I remember that it was a feather bed, and we always saw a big swell in the middle of it."

"What does that mean?" Clerk asks.

"Why, that the two persons who had slept in it slept at a big distance from each other."

"Miss Whiffin, did you ever hear Nancy talk of having looked through the keyholes of any of the drawing room doors, or did you ever try to look through them yourself?"

"Never. Neither one."

"Do the doors have keyholes?"

"I don't remember. I think they do."

"Did you ever hear Miss Munro accuse the mistresses of improper conduct?"

"Not any such thing."

"Did you ever hear Miss Cumming accuse them of improper conduct?"

"Not to me."

"In your hearing?"

"No."

"Do you remember what was called the disgrace table, Miss Whiffin?"

"Yes."

"Were any of the scholars sent often to the disgrace table?"

"Miss Munro was often at it just before she left the school."

"Miss Whiffin, did the mistresses know of Nancy disguising herself as a man on Miss Woods' birthnight?"

"They found out about it only when they came upstairs."

"Did you ever express to any of the young ladies any dissatisfaction with your mistresses, or use any expressions such as that you were a better lady than them?"

"Oh, not at all."

"One final question, Miss Whiffin. You said earlier that the young ladies never complained to you about being disturbed in the night, and the counsel for the defence appeared to be rather surprised at your statement. Now that you have had time to collect yourself, and you seem to be a bit more calm, will you think on the question again. Did you ever hear such a complaint from the young ladies?"

"Well, I do remember one morning Miss Munro complaining to me that she had been disturbed by Miss Woods making her get out of bed to bring some water."

"And what did you say to Miss Munro?"

"Nothing except that I wondered that Miss Woods had not rung the bell."

"And that is absolutely all you know of complaints about night time disturbances?"

"Yes."

Mr. Clerk has no further questions, nor does counsel for the defendant wish to cross-examine. The Court is adjourned until March 21, 1811, at 10 A.M.

Lord Meadowbank's Notes on the Testimonies of Mary Brown and Charlotte Whiffin, March 20, 1811

Miss Munro received instruction as to the horrid nature of the vice imputed to the mistresses from the nurse maid, Mary Brown. It is apparent that by her questions she encouraged Miss Munro to talk. Perhaps the questions helped to fabricate the answers. I have ever in my own family abstained from such examination of children, as I am confident from my long observation that it affords the strongest temptation to invention and falsehood. It appears to me that Mary Brown's testimony serves only to verify the suspicion that Miss Munro's perception was distorted by those with whom she spoke.

On the other hand, Charlotte Whiffin's denial of all knowledge that the mistresses were suspected of improper conduct by the scholars, and her further denial that she herself shared those suspicions, is unfavourable to the plaintiffs. Must she not have been coerced by the mistresses into falsehood? And what else but their conscious guilt could have prompted such a measure?

Or might it be that the maid is lying because she is trying to conceal having spoken in disrespectful and contemptuous language of her mistresses?

Yet there is another possibility to account for her denials. Maybe she is simply a domestic of little conscience. Falsehood is the ordinary vice of persons in her line of life. She may have invented tales in order to flatter any fancy that she saw was a favourite with the older scholars—tales which she knew were lies and could not stand an investigation under oath. She would be ashamed to admit that she had lied. She would wish to escape that shame, as well as the risk of detection if she attempted to insist her tales were true. She would thus conclude that it was safest and easiest to deny everything about the matter. I believe it is significant that, according to Miss Munro, Charlotte never said anything to her about the indecent behavior of Woods and Pirie until Miss Munro told Charlotte she had been disturbed. It is probable that

Charlotte, once having heard such a remark, chose to encourage it further by detailing and exaggerating circumstances which may have been quite innocent.

However, the true history of Charlotte Whiffin's conduct seems to me of little importance. The defendant may think otherwise, but she herself is to blame that it cannot now be dived into. Instead of swallowing at once a story so extraordinary and improbable in all its circumstances, she should have proceeded with due caution and made immediate inquiry of the maid and everyone else referred to in the story. Had she done that she would have been able to fasten down the truth so that it could not be controverted or disguised, as it may now be by Charlotte Whiffin or any other person.

Lord Robertson's Notes on the Testimonies of Mary Brown and Charlotte Whiffin, March 20, 1811

Whiffin is lying and very frightened, this great slatternly gawk of a girl. But what a position in which to find herself: what can she know of courts and testimony and the workings of justice and the squabbles of her betters? She wishes only to get back to her penny ghost tales and mops and dusters. Yet I do believe she told the girls that her mistresses behaved indecently. Miss Munro's account of Whiffin's stories is too clear to be manufactured. She told the tale all right. Of course, one cannot assume that what she told the young ladies was truth.

Now Brown is as like Whiffin as fin is like firmament. She is a starched, proper little person, plain looking but not unpleasantly so. I would venture to guess that her scrupulousness of appearance bespeaks a scrupulousness of behaviour: I doubt that there is a particle of prevarication in her entire being. But what has she sworn to, after all? That Janet Munro told her a particular story and that she responded to the story in a particular way. Her testimony neither proves nor disproves the veracity of the story. What does prove its veracity is its very outrageousness. Fiction lags after truth.

Lord Newton's Notes on the Testimonies of Mary Brown and Charlotte Whiffin, March 20, 1811

Brown: Miss Munro communicated to her the circumstances as they happened, *de recenti,* with a reluctance that might be expected in a matter of so much delicacy. Brown has confirmed all Miss Munro swears, to the letter.

Whiffin: Whiffin continued in the employ of Miss Pirie for a month after the school was broken up and, it is my understanding, still does occasional work for her. Counsel for the defense ought to have realized that she would be a useless witness. What can they have been thinking? The girl has clearly perjured herself in denying everything. Ought she not be sentenced to jail for perjury? Discuss in Hope's chambers next P.M. if time permits!

June 25, 1982

Most young servants of the early nineteenth century must have led lives of unimaginable tedium. It was usual for a girl to go into service at the age of twelve or thirteen and, as often as not, to be forced to make her bed on the stone flags under the kitchen table or in another spot that was equally well designed to mortify flesh and bone. Servant girls were often lured from the country to the big city by the stories of other girls who returned from London or Edinburgh or Glasgow to visit an ailing mother or to attend the funeral of some close relative. They might be dressed in their mistresses' cast-off silks and satins and laces and have tales to tell of the splendor of the Lord Mayor's show and the castle guards and all the fair and incredible creatures they saw daily. But the lot of the servant girl was often harsh. In a large household, a maid of all work, as Charlotte was, would have had to rise at 5 A.M., and lift and carry and stoop and scrub, and be at the beck and call of master and mistress and their many sons and daughters until 11 P.M. or later, all for the princely sum of five or six pounds per annum with board and a place to lay her head.

Charlotte, who was nineteen at the time of the trial, may well have had a few years of such a regimen before she came to work at the school. She would have known a good place—one where the mistresses were not on her all day, since they had work of their own to do, and where there was no master and sons and daughters to obey—and she would have been determined to keep such a job. She would not have been happy with Janet Munro and Jane Cumming for ruining this comparative sinecure for her, and of course she would have lied in court had she thought her lies could help restore the old order.

But I would guess that she was ambivalent: she really may have told the tales that Janet attributed to her; she may have said of her mistresses, "It's a pity they could not get a man," and "Who would serve such mistresses?" Having no status of their own, servants often claimed a share of their employer's status, so that the servant of a Duchess was worth more, both in her own eyes and in those of other menials, than the servant of a Baroness. The servant of two middle-class women who had no prestige above being proprietors of a girls' school must have felt tiny in this scale of things. Charlotte's hostility toward her mistresses—which was probably common enough between maid and mistress in the nineteenth century—was compounded because, as Charlotte saw them, they were barely above her in the pecking order: they too were at the mercy of wealthier employers who could tell them what to do and fire them if they did not do it. And if they dared to give themselves airs (as I suspect Mrs. Woods and Jane Pirie must have done from time to time), she would have disdained them.

There was generally a rigid hierarchy among servants, even in one household. The closer to the persons of the master and his family were the duties performed, the higher the prestige of the servant. In a large house, the higher servants dined in the servants' hall. In small households, the entire staff dined together, but the servants who held the highest posts occupied seats at the head of the table, and the others sat according to rank in descending order. In a mansion such as Janet Munro's family owned outside of Edinburgh, the nurse was usually quartered on the floor near her charges, while the common servants slept in the attic story or, if there was no room there, in nooks and crannies or in the kitchen.

Mary Brown's position would have been quite different from Charlotte's since, as a nurse hired to care for the children of a wealthy gentleman, she would have been fairly high in the servant social order; she would have sat near the head of the servants' table and had a bedroom near her charges, in a comfortable part of the house; and she would likely have been awed by those whose status raised hers and who were at the same time so far above her. She might have really believed that Janet never lied because gentlemen's daughters had no need to lie. Yet, Miss Murdoch, the aunt, thought that Janet lied, or she would not have said to the story, "Oh, Mary, is that true?"

Why did Mary persist in her total credulity after Miss Murdoch's response? Or was she so credulous? Perhaps she testified that Janet Munro never lied because, like Charlotte, she knew a good position and wished to keep it. She appeared to be quite without craft, but given class relations at that time, surely all servants needed to learn some cunning if they were to survive.

Charlotte was crafty—rather, she would have liked to be crafty, but she was often merely transparent. Or did she deny everything not out of what she thought was cunning design but out of terror? If she says, "No," "I don't know," "I never did," then she cuts the interrogation short: much, much easier to perjure herself than to have to explain what she meant by saying she was a better lady than her mistresses, or why she thought the drawing room doors were bolted. Even if Charlotte saw what Janet Munro said she claimed to have seen, would Charlotte have admitted it? Having made such an admission, she would have been forced to describe in graphic detail, in a courtroom full of men, two women flailing together. Janet Munro described it, but she had no choice. I think Charlotte must have figured she would brazen it out with denials. She put a bold face on it—she stared Erskine down and would not bend to his bullying. I am sure she was quaking within all the while.

What puzzle me completely, however, are Erskine's motives when he so persistently drew out of Charlotte the story about Nancy. He seems to have wanted to show that the mistresses were immoral enough to keep a pregnant woman in their hire (she must have been unmarried), but why did he want to establish that Nancy had dressed as a man one night? Was he trying to associate in the judges' minds cross-dressing and lesbianism? In the eighteenth century there were cases that came before the British courts of women who dressed as men and made love to other women, such as that of Mary Hamilton, on which Henry Fielding deliberated in 1746. In 1777 there was another such case in London: a female adventurer who disguised herself in male attire and, in the course of her career, married three women. She was sentenced to be exposed in the pillory (so that other women might recognize her in the future) and then imprisoned. But if Erskine had been familiar with those cases he surely would have mentioned them.

However, even though he did not know of those specific incidents, he seems to have been hinting that because the mistresses permitted Nancy to dress as a man they were tolerant of transvestism, which suggested they themselves were not above it, which proved they were indeed lesbians. But Nancy got herself pregnant heterosexually. Immorality must have been immorality to Erskine: if you permitted one kind to go on under your nose, you were yourself capable of any variety of sin. Nancy's brief transvestism must only have tickled his imagination further.

But apparently most people thought it inconceivable that two mere women could make love together: Mary said, when she first heard the tale, that one of the mistresses was surely a man. Later she claimed to know that according to the New Testament, two women could commit sexual sins together, although she had never heard of its being practiced and had no idea how it was done.

Ollie asks, "What else could she have said? Like Charlotte,

she knew that if she admitted to knowledge, she would have had to explain—in a roomful of men."

I suppose Ollie is right. Such a starched personage as Mary Brown would have been even more reluctant than Charlotte to discuss sex, especially unorthodox sex, in front of so imposing a masculine congregation. But I can believe that her innocence was genuine, that she knew nothing about what women could do together.

Ollie thinks that women always knew, about all of it, no matter what their societies tried to teach them: when they were alone with themselves or each other, their bodies taught them. I think they certainly knew about masturbation. According to the eighteenth-century Swiss doctor Samuel Tissot, women spent a great deal of time indulging themselves. But masturbation is different from sex with another person, male or female. An act done alone, without witnesses, can be denied even to yourself. If another person shares in the act, you have her consciousness to contend with as well as your own. And if you have been convinced that no one else indulges in such corruption and you should not want to, could you bear both your knowing and her knowing?

Ollie thinks I am as naïve as nineteenth-century men when I confuse what "ought" to have been with what was. But I think that for many women, what *ought* to be, in fact *was*. I have no trouble believing John Fowles' picture of Ernestina in *The French Lieutenant's Woman,* the pure Victorian girl who, whenever thoughts of coupling invaded her mind, would quickly blast them out by chanting, "I must not." Ollie says that is only what nineteenth-century men would have liked to think, and that it is as possible to blast such thoughts out of your mind as it is not to think of tigers if someone says, "Don't think of tigers."

But I do not think I am so unusual. I can stop myself from thinking of tigers.

"You are indeed unusual," Ollie says. "Most people can't."

Perhaps they can't, but they can stop themselves from acting on their thoughts—and they generally have: in the 1950s only 20 percent of the unmarried female population in America had had intercourse by the age of nineteen. In 1970 about 50 percent had. Just a couple of decades earlier, 30 percent fewer acted on their thoughts because society said they weren't supposed to. If that is true of heterosexual behavior, it must have been at least as true of lesbian behavior.

But then, there have always been that 20 percent, or 10 or 5, who did what they weren't supposed to be doing. The question is, did Marianne Woods and Jane Pirie think of tigers? And did they ride them?

Ollie says she will go with me to the Scottish Record Office tomorrow. I want to find out if Marianne Woods or Jane Pirie ever married. I cannot imagine Jane Pirie as the wife of some Scottish patriarch with a brood of half a dozen. But Marianne Woods might have sought what would have appeared to be a safe harbor after the grueling punishment of the trial. I think she was less driving, less ambitious than her friend. I think she admired Jane Pirie at the start because Jane possessed those fierce qualities that Marianne herself lacked, though living with so foreign a temperament from day to day made her miserable. After the unhappiness of their brief union, she might have considered that marriage was not so inimical to her.

THE CALLING OF OTHER WITNESSES

After Charlotte Whiffin's surprising testimony, George Cranstoun informed his client, Lady Cumming Gordon, that they must have more witnesses who would corroborate the story before they brought Jane Cumming to the stand. The maid's testimony, so fresh in the judges' minds, would counter whatever Jane might say at this point.

I would imagine that Lady Cumming Gordon was extremely annoyed with Cranstoun for having permitted the junior attorney to examine the maid. Cranstoun must have explained that Mr. Erskine was one of the most brilliant young lawyers in Edinburgh, and they had anyway been positive that Charlotte would simply corroborate all that Lady Cumming Gordon's granddaughter had said. But who might they call now to corroborate Jane Cumming's story?

Lady Cumming Gordon offered another granddaughter, Margaret Dunbar, to whom Jane Cumming said she had related the events as they occurred. Cranstoun guessed that the plaintiffs would successfully challenge the calling of Miss Dunbar because of her propinquity to the defendant—although Jane Cumming's calling could not be challenged because she was an eyewitness and not a relative under the law of the country.

Perhaps Cranstoun suggested to Lady Cumming Gordon that they might locate the washerwomen at the Water of Leith who were supposed to have hooted at the mistresses because of their infamy; however Lady Cumming Gordon would not stoop to trafficking with such creatures.

Cranstoun then requested that he be permitted to contact Mrs. Edgar, the mother of the student who was said by Janet Munro to have laughed when she witnessed the mistresses' indiscretions. But Mrs. Edgar would not see the attorney and informed him by letter that her daughter knew nothing of the situation and had nothing to say in court.

Cranstoun had gotten a delay of testimony for only a few days, and he needed to find additional witnesses immediately. He pleaded with Lady Cumming Gordon to take an active part in helping him. If they did not succeed in producing additional witnesses, he said, he felt sure the case would be lost. I can imagine that Lady Cumming Gordon announced to her family that she would fire Cranstoun and find a more competent attorney, but her son-in-law, John Forbes, who was a Lord of Session of the First Division, would have advised her that it would be very unwise to change counsel right in the midst of the trial.

Lady Cumming Gordon agreed then to appeal to Mrs. Stirling, the mother of Eliza Stirling, who, according to Jane Cumming, had often spoken with her and Janet Munro about the mistresses' conduct. Lady Cumming Gordon wrote to Mrs. Stirling:

My Dear Madam,

Seeing that the request I am about to make to you is necessary, I am inclined to make it a personal one since I think that will be less disagreeable to you than any communication from my counsel. You cannot be ignorant of the very wretched affair in which I am now involved because I acted as I feel any Christian mother would have acted in the same situation. If your daughter had told you what my poor girl told me, you probably would have been called upon to act the part that I did; you would have been the one to inform the mothers of the other children to remove their girls from a situation which would have been their ruin had they remained. Since that job fell to me, I hope you will feel now that we have a common cause. These women are suing me for damages with a view to clear their characters and to enable them to set up school again. They have many friends and the story is so horrible that although my granddaughter and Miss Munro are perfectly clear, and there are many other proofs, yet my counsel thinks it necessary to ask your daughter to say what she knows either from her own observation or from what she heard the maid say. I trust that no overscrupulous delicacy will prevent you from doing what I hope you will feel to be justice to me. It is already known that Miss Stirling has corroborated the other girls' testimony, and if we fail to establish a complete proof all who are concerned will be held responsible for inventing this horrible story. As I said before, I hope you will look on this business as a common cause in which, God knows, I have had the worst share. Let me beg your forgiveness for the trouble I have given, and I remain,

> Dear Madam, with esteem,
> your obedient humble servant
> (Signed) *Helen Cumming Gordon*

No doubt Mrs. Stirling would have preferred to be as protective of her child as was Mrs. Edgar, and a plea from George Cranstoun she might well have ignored, but not a personal plea from Lady Cumming Gordon of Altyre and Gordonstoun. However, she was anxious that her daughter not be called as a witness and probably hoped that her insistence on the girl's innocence of the matter would discourage Lady Cumming Gordon from pursuing that line any further:

> Dear Madam,
>
> I received your letter of the 22nd this morning, which distresses me extremely since I hoped all your anxiety about Misses Woods and Pirie was at an end. I know the part you have taken in this disagreeable business proceeded from the very best motive, and I am sure you will not lose your reward, however it may terminate. I would give you every support in my power most willingly, but I am quite at a loss how to make out any clear statement from my daughter. When she came home I asked her never to mention the subject and to discharge it from her mind. She never witnessed anything improper in the behaviour of Misses W. and P. Therefore anything she could say would be of no more avail than hearsay evidence. That being the case I cannot suppose anyone so cruel as to call upon her when she can be of no use. With deep regret, I have now given her your letter. She proposed answering it in a letter to Miss Cumming, which is enclosed. I have left it open for your inspection. Please return it if useless or when this unfortunate affair is settled.
>
> I enter deeply into your feelings and remain, Dear Madam, with good wishes, your obedient humble servant.
>
> (Signed) *Mary Stirling*

The enclosed letter from Eliza Stirling suggests both that she would have liked to have been invited to Gordonstoun, or at least to 22 Charlotte Square, and that she knew nothing of any significance concerning the mistresses' indiscretions:

> My Dear Miss Cumming,
>
> My mother received Lady Cumming's letter this morning. I do not think that my testimony can be of the least consequence since I myself never witnessed anything improper in the behaviour of Misses Woods and

Pirie. All that I know of the affair you, Miss Munro, and Charlotte the maid told me. I said that I could not understand what it was that they did, nor do I at this moment; and you said that you could not tell me, but that when your grandmother came home you would tell her. The maid, you may recollect, told us that she had caught them one morning in bed together in the dressing-room, and that Miss Pirie jumped out of bed with her face as red as scarlet. She also said that they might as well take a man at once. I was one night awakened by a violent knocking. I afterwards asked Miss Woods what it was. She said that she had locked the door and that Miss Pirie wanted to get into the room. You know what Miss Munro said, since you were present at the time, and I daresay that you will remember that she told us that she was disturbed in the night, and that both Miss Woods and Miss Pirie were in bed with her. As for what I said to Miss Macdowell, my cousin, I merely told her that what I had been told of the mistresses' behaviour was extremely indecent.

I am very sorry our correspondence should have begun on this disagreeable subject, which I regret we ever heard of, and I truly hope it can continue on a happier note. I remain yours sincerely,

(Signed) *Eliza Christian Stirling*

As unpromising a witness as Eliza Stirling appeared to be, she was now the only other witness who might be produced at such short notice before the calling of Jane Cumming. She was summoned to take the stand on March 26, 1811.

MARCH 26, 1811, 10:00 A.M.

Miss Eliza Christian Stirling, seventeen years old, is called as a witness for the defendant. She is accompanied into the room by her father, John Stirling, Esquire, of Kippenross. Present are Lord Justice-Clerk Hope, Lords Meadowbank, Robertson, and Newton, counsel for both parties, and Jane Pirie. Cranstoun says Miss Stirling was a boarder at the plaintiffs' school from August till November last. She is solemnly sworn and purged of malice and partial counsel.

"Miss Stirling," Cranstoun asks, "while a boarder at the school of Miss Woods and Miss Pirie, did you know a servant called Charlotte Whiffin?"

"Yes," she whispers.

"Do you remember being with Miss Cumming and Miss Munro, or either of them, at any time when a conversation about the conduct of the plaintiffs took place, and was the maid Charlotte in the room?"

"Yes," she whispers.

"Miss Stirling, you will have to speak up so that a deaf old man can hear you," Lord Newton requests.

"Yes," she says.

"I'm sorry, Miss Stirling. 'Yes' to what?" Cranstoun asks.

"Yes, Charlotte the maid talked about them often, but I can't remember who was present."

"That's better, Miss Stirling," Cranstoun assures her. "Now, do you remember anything Charlotte the maid said about them?"

"Once she said to herself, 'They might as well take a man at once.' I think I was in the room alone with Charlotte when she said it."

"Do you remember at any time hearing Charlotte say anything about what she had observed on a particular occasion in the dressing room?"

"I remember hearing something about the dressing room, but I can't remember whether it was Charlotte or Miss Cumming who told me it. Also, I think I remember that Charlotte said she saw Miss Woods and Miss Pirie through the keyhole of the drawing room door—but I'm not certain whether it was Charlotte or Miss Cumming who told me that either. I think it was Charlotte."

"Miss Stirling," Lord Meadowbank asks, "do you remember anything else that definitely came to you directly from Charlotte regarding your mistresses' improper behaviour?"

"Well—I'm not positive. I remember that when the kettle was brought in at breakfast one morning, someone said to look at our mistresses' faces. I think it was said by Charlotte, but I can't say for sure."

"Miss Stirling," Cranstoun continues, "in your letters home to your mother, did you not complain often of the conduct of the mistresses and express great dissatisfaction with the school?"

"I only remember writing two letters to my mamma. I think I did complain that one of the mistresses was not very good tempered."

"When you saw your mother in Edinburgh, Miss Stirling, did you not complain of their behaviour?"

"Yes."

"What did you complain of?"

"I complained that they were extremely nasty. I think I told my mamma that if she knew how they behaved I would never have been sent there."

"To what part of their behaviour did you allude?"

"To their improper behaviour."

"How did you explain to Mrs. Stirling of what their improper behaviour consisted?"

"I could not explain it. My mamma asked me if there was a man, and I said no. And then my mamma said she couldn't understand it either. And she said I was to stay at the school until summer since we had paid for the year."

"Miss Stirling," Lord Justice-Clerk Hope interrupts, "did you make your complaint from anything that you had yourself observed in the conduct of the mistresses, or only from the information of others?"

"Only the information of others."

Cranstoun thanks her.

"Have you no further questions, Mr. Cranstoun?" the Lord Justice-Clerk asks.

"Not at this time, your Lordship," Cranstoun answers.

133

"Very well, then. Does the counsel for the plaintiffs have any questions of this witness?"

John Clerk approaches the witness, who is trembling visibly. "Your Lordship," he tells Hope, "perhaps the witness and her father would like to stroll about for a few minutes."

"Most certainly," Hope says. They adjourn for fifteen minutes.

"Miss Stirling," Clerk begins. "When and by whom were you first informed of the mistresses' improper conduct?"

"I think by Miss Cumming, one morning in our bedroom. But I'm not certain about the time."

"Did Miss Cumming often talk to you on that subject?"

"Yes."

"Did Miss Munro also talk to you on that subject often?"

"Not as much as Miss Cumming."

"Was Miss Cumming generally present when Miss Munro talked to you on the subject?"

"I think so, but I'm not sure."

"Miss Stirling," Lord Justice-Clerk Hope says, "earlier you stated that what you communicated to your mother was solely from the information of others. Whom do you mean by the word 'others'?"

"Miss Cumming, Miss Munro, and Charlotte the maid."

"All right," he continues. "Now you also told us earlier that Charlotte said to you, 'They might as well take a man at once.' Can you remember what had previously passed between Charlotte and you that led her to make that observation?"

"I think it was the morning that I had heard, either from Charlotte or Miss Cumming, that Charlotte had seen the mistresses in the dressing room. I think that was when Charlotte said it."

John Clerk continues. "Miss Stirling, you also said before that Charlotte used to speak often about your mistresses. What did she say about them? Was it about their improper and indecent behavior with each other?"

She appears to be thinking.

"Miss Stirling?"

"The scholars were forbidden to speak to Charlotte, except on necessary occasions. So I did not speak to her often."

Lord Meadowbank wishes to know if she was aware that the

plaintiffs had frequent quarrels. She was. "Were you ever present at any reconciliation after a quarrel?" he asks.

"Yes. I think I was."

"Can you describe what you witnessed?"

She sighs. "I once went into the small parlour on the first floor, just at a time they seemed to be making up after one of their quarrels. I didn't hear what they said. But they seemed to feel warmly towards each other."

"Now, Miss Stirling," Lord Meadowbank says, "please think. At that time or since, upon reflection, after all you have heard, does it strike you that there was anything more warm or improper in their manner than became any other two friends under such circumstances?"

"No."

"Miss Stirling," John Clerk now asks, "you slept in the same room with Miss Cumming and Miss Pirie. Did you never observe anything improper take place in the bed of Miss Cumming and Miss Pirie?"

"No."

"Were you ever awakened in the middle of the night?"

"Yes, I think I was. Once by someone knocking and once by someone praying."

"In the middle of the night?"

"Yes. The person who was praying spoke very loud and was crying at the same time. I know from her voice it was Miss Pirie. And then about the knocking—I asked Miss Woods what it was, and she said that she had locked her door, and that Miss Pirie wanted to get into the room."

"Miss Woods told you this?" Mr. Clerk asks.

"Yes."

"Are you certain of that, Miss Stirling?"

"Yes. I remember because she hesitated a little before she said it. I remember that I asked her the next day. It must have been about three o'clock."

"What was the person who prayed saying, Miss Stirling?" Lord Robertson asks.

"She said, 'Oh Lord Jesus Christ,' over and over. And when I asked her if anything was wrong, she stopped. And then she started again. She was crying at the same time."

"One more question, please, Miss Stirling," Lord Meadowbank says. "When Miss Cumming first told you about observing unusual behaviour between your mistresses, did she tell you that she understood that it meant something in particular?"

"Well, first she asked me if I'd been awakened—and then she told me some things. I said I didn't understand, but she seemed to understand what the mistresses had been doing. Then I think she told me some of the conversations between Miss Woods and Miss Pirie that she overheard, but I can't remember them exactly. And about others she said she would not tell me. I think she said they always began with Miss Woods asking Miss Pirie, 'Have you on your stockings?' I don't remember anything else exactly, so I would not like to say."

"Did any other young lady at the school beside Miss Cumming and Miss Munro ever tell you that they had observed anything indecent in the conduct of your mistresses to each other? Or did any of the others appear to understand that anything improper was practised between your mistresses?"

"The Miss Dunbars were the only other ladies I talked to about it. But I think the elder Miss Edgar had some suspicion."

"Why do you say that?"

"I'm not sure. I believe Miss Munro or Miss Cumming said she knew about it."

"I have no more questions," John Clerk tells the Lords.

Mr. Cranstoun is asked if he wishes to examine the witness further.

"Yes. I have one more question. Miss Stirling, is it not true that on the Wednesday when Miss Cumming was taken away from school she told you that her grandmother would write to your mother about taking you away, and you begged her to tell her grandmother right away? You said you were very anxious about it, and you urged her to it repeatedly?"

"Yes," Miss Stirling says.

"Why?"

"Because I wanted to leave as soon as possible."

"Why?"

"Because of their indecent behaviour."

Cranstoun has no further questions. The Court is adjourned until March 27 at 10 A.M.

Lord Meadowbank's Notes on the Testimony of Eliza Stirling, March 26, 1811

Miss Stirling's testimony now places even further doubt on Charlotte Whiffin's role. I am very skeptical about the real history of the maid's communications. But let me believe for a moment that Charlotte Whiffin did tell Miss Stirling certain things. What might she have said? Miss Stirling has testified that the scholars were forbidden by the mistresses to speak with the maid. When they did so, it must have been with some sense of discomfort and hurry. And considering how general the hints must have been which could be uttered by young ladies in asking or answering inquiries about such a delicate subject, there must have been much room for misunderstanding. The young ladies may well have ascribed to venereal improprieties what the maid meant to apply truly to the impropriety of quarrelling.

Miss Stirling remembers hearing "something about the dressing room," but she cannot remember whether it was Charlotte Whiffin or Miss Cumming who told it to her. Nor can she remember who told her the story of the drawing room keyhole. She also admits that her complaints against the mistresses are based solely on the information of others. I am convinced that a darker hand than hers has been guiding all this. But what are the motives?

Lord Robertson's Notes on the Testimony of Eliza Stirling, March 26, 1811

Of the females I have seen thus far, Miss Eliza Stirling strikes me as being the most ingenuous. She also elicits my sympathy where the petulant and more knowing Miss Munro did not. Miss Stirling is a pale, timid little kitten. I have seldom seen a father as solicitous and gentle as hers appears to be, but he sees the mournful position

is placed and perhaps feels that his care can help her
ᴛat a wretched chore she must perform in being forced
ᴛcerning this degradation, and what a heavy burden
ᴛ it. I am greatly disturbed by the horror of our situa-
ose task it is or should be to protect such innocence,
must force it to mouth indecencies it cannot, thank God, understand.

It is clear that Miss Stirling has no knowledge to interpret
what occurred between her mistresses, neither their violent exchanges nor their shameful alliance. She can simply report what
she has observed. But I would count it as being of high significance
that she has corroborated that the young ladies had frequent communication on the subject with the maid Charlotte, who did indeed
appear to understand what passed. I can much more easily believe
Miss Stirling than I can the maid's perjured testimony.

JULY 4, 1982

Meadowbank was guided to the truth by his prejudices, but I think
he was nevertheless right. Jane Cumming's hand does seem to have
directed what passed: it is probable that it was she who told Eliza
Stirling about the dressing room and drawing room. Eliza can remember almost nothing that Charlotte told her directly (notwithstanding what Lord Robertson apparently thought he heard). It
may have all come through the Indian girl.

Ollie thinks that Meadowbank and I are deceived. She says it
is inconceivable that Eliza really did not know what the mistresses
were doing. But I am more and more convinced that they were not
doing anything—at least not in the sense Ollie means it. Their relationship was certainly stormy and intense, and beset with violent
recriminations and just as violent reconciliations. But Jane Pirie
was a stormy and intense person, and within the framework of her
personality, she behaved just the way romantic friends behaved.
Romantic friends held each other and kissed when they reconciled,

and they did the same when they were happy with each other, without the excuse of a reconciliation. Such behavior would not have been unusual since women often acted that way with each other—although they did not often shake the bed, one atop the other.

Ollie insists that many females did shake the bed together, even in Scotland in the early nineteenth century. "Why else would the mistresses have wanted both the dormitory rooms to be supervised at night?" she asks. I would guess that if they feared anything other than all-night talk sessions or bullying of the younger students by the older, it was masturbation, which was supposed to have promoted insanity, epilepsy, and infertility.

I think that Eliza Stirling was probably confused by Jane Cumming's hints. She was told that the mistresses were extremely nasty, that their behavior was improper, but what sense could she make out of that? Her mother asked if a man was involved, and since none was, neither mother nor daughter understood it. And if no man was involved, her mother could see no harm in her staying until the end of the school year, when the paid tuition would run out. Of course had a man been involved, Mrs. Stirling would have known how to interpret the events, but what could be made of two women who happened to be in bed together?

Eliza persisted in describing the women's behavior as "improper," even after reiterating that she was not able to explain of what it consisted. But that was the word she had been taught by Jane Cumming, and she now had a vested interest in the word. She held on to it like a talisman. If their behavior was not "improper," why did she have her mother remove her from the school, and why did she contribute to its ruin? All was explained and justified in that one word. . . .

Ollie has just created what she calls an irreverent scenario with these young innocents at the center. Never mind for now what the mistresses did, she says; look at the girls. Most of them were born into dullness and led totally uneventful lives at home. They were educated to passionlessness, all right—told from the very beginning that good girls had no genitals, except as vessels in which the marriage act would be performed, and out of which would pop one little Britisher after another. But regardless of what the nanny or anyone else told them, they knew the truth, since no child, no matter how well schooled, could be oblivious to the variety of sensations from the lower depths that accompanies childhood and adolescence. Furthermore, their curiosity about those sensations would have been boundless—much greater than that of their counterparts today, because they were told that they were not supposed to have sensations. Then suddenly they were sent away to boarding schools—the distance from their families must have been liberating in itself. And then there were all those other limpid-eyed creatures who had been experiencing the same sensations. It is unimaginable to Ollie that they did not share them with each other, first through talk (and she depicts the surreptitious little circles in which they gathered, titillating each other with fantasies and rumors, giggling and sniggering behind hands, relishing their release from the strictures that made them believe themselves peculiar). Then the group talk was replaced by paired play, little acts that brought nameless little pleasures, furtive at first and then bolder. And having done those things themselves—probably from nine o'clock at night until eleven, when the mistresses came to bed—they could not have failed to recognize the import of those same gestures when the mistresses made them. She thinks that Eliza must have seen because her bed was only a few feet away. She thinks they may have all seen.

But I think we have been convinced in our century that sex is everywhere and behind everything, and that even little children have vast sexual knowledge. I believe it was not always so. I maintain that when Eliza Stirling claimed she had no idea what the women were supposedly doing, she was telling the truth. I doubt there were many sexual experiments between the young ladies. Instead there was panic about suddenly being at a distance from the family, on which they had been much more dependent than we are with our preschools and kindergartens and elementary schools, which force a child to stand on her own feet from the age of three. There was great trepidation about making friends—and in that class-ridden society there was probably family pressure to make friends with those a cut above one's usual social circle. And there was a great desire to please. If the granddaughter of Lady Cumming Gordon told the daughter of John Stirling, Esq.—who had only recently arrived at the school—that she had observed improper behavior, who was Miss Stirling to argue?

* * *

Ollie and I pored over 1811 newspapers in the National Library all this past week. I feel guilty about using up her vacation time this way, especially because I know she needs to get back to revising her own manuscript. But she says that at this point she finds working on my case much more compelling than wading through her "British Jurisprudence as a Shaper of Western Thought" yet again. She assures me that the time away from her manuscript is giving her a fresh perspective on it. She says she is sure it will help.

MARCH 26, 1811, 1:00 P.M.

Lord Justice-Clerk Hope and Lords Meadowbank, Robertson, Newton, and Boyle assemble in the Lord Justice-Clerk's chambers. At the request of the counsel for the plaintiffs, they have agreed to inspect the house at Drumsheugh, lately occupied by the plaintiffs as a boarding school. They are accompanied by counsel for the plaintiffs and the defendant.

They first inspect the drawing room, which seems to be nearly square (Fig. 1). That room is separated from the school room by a wall, about two feet thick, which contains the fireplaces of both rooms. There is an entry from the school room to the drawing room in which there are two doors. One door opens into the school room, the other into the drawing room.

The door of the school room has a lock in which there is a keyhole that goes through the door. But in the door of the drawing room there is a lock that has no keyhole. If the drawing room door was standing open and the door of the school was shut, a person looking through the school-room-door keyhole could see into the drawing room—but, because the walls are so thick, she could see nothing laterally, only straightforward. Only the opposite door of the drawing room would be in her line of vision.

This door, on the other side of the drawing room, has an old-fashioned brass lock: there is a keyhole only on one side, so that no

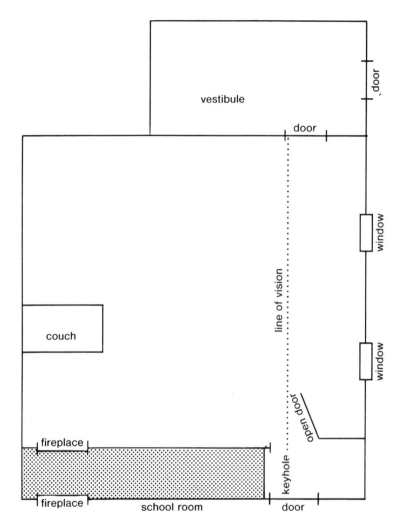

1. The drawing room

one can see into the room through it. The judges do not perceive any other chinks or holes in the door through which a person could peep.

They see the couch standing against a wall, opposite the fireplace. In this position it is invisible from the keyhole of the school

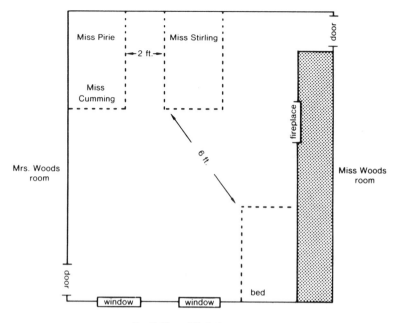

2. Miss Pirie's room

room door. The couch has rubbed against the wall paint, plainly over some period of time. The judges are satisfied that the couch has usually stood in this place.

The judges then examine Miss Pirie's bedroom and the situation of the beds (Fig. 2). Miss Pirie's bed, in which she slept with Miss Cumming, stands with its side to the wall. The bed in which Miss Stirling slept stands approximately two feet from the Pirie and Cumming bed. There is also a third bed in the room, about six feet away from the other two.

Adjoining Miss Pirie's room is a small room in which Mrs. Woods, the aunt, slept. There is no passage from this small room to Miss Woods' bedroom except through Miss Pirie's room.

In Miss Woods' room there are also three beds (Fig. 3). The bed standing across the foot of Miss Woods' bed (where she slept with Miss Munro) is less than one foot away from it. The other bed, alongside the Woods bed, is about three feet away. Next to this room is the small one in which Charlotte allegedly saw the mistresses' improper behavior one morning; it was referred to as the dressing room.

143

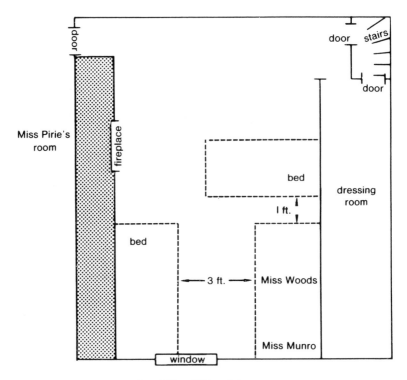

3. Miss Woods' room

LORD JUSTICE-CLERK HOPE'S NOTES, MARCH 26, 1811

The supposed confirmation of the story by what was attributed to the maid has fallen to the ground. If Charlotte had corroborated what Miss Munro had said, and if what Charlotte was supposed to have told her would have been possible, I would have considered it quite probable that the mistresses' conduct had been improper and criminal. But the maid did not corroborate the young lady's statement, and her supposed observation was impossible. We saw this with our own eyes. We who visited and inspected the house saw that the story of the keyhole was an outright lie.

Suppose the maid had sworn that she saw the mistresses

through the keyhole. We would have had to send her to jail immediately for perjury. But she has sworn the reverse. And since the
expected corroboration is totally done away, the failure of it must
affect the rest of the evidence.

In the carriage to Drumsheugh Newton suggested that we
must consider sentencing Whiffin for perjury, and Robertson
agreed. I am happy we waited to inspect the house before expend-
ing any effort on such a deliberation. I can believe that the maid's
testimony is truthful to the letter, although I shudder to think that
young ladies of respectable families might have concocted such a
horrifying story on their own.

March 27, 1811, 10:00 A.M.

Miss Jane Cumming is offered as a witness for the defence. Counsel for the plaintiffs present a challenge: she is the granddaughter
of the defendant, her future is plainly at the mercy of the defendant, and as the originator of the tale she has a vested interest in
proclaiming its truth; therefore, she can not be considered an impartial witness.

Counsel for the defendant claims as precedent *Gumin against
Gumin,* in which a wife suing a husband for separation on account
of maltreatment was permitted to offer their common children as
witnesses; *Cameron against Malcolm,* where the crime of abduction
was alleged and the plaintiff's mother and sister were accepted as
witnesses; and *Boyd against Gibb,* a suit regarding propinquity to a
remote ancestor, in which the plaintiff's aunt was accepted as a
witness because there was a paucity of other testimony available.

The judges repel the objection of the mistresses' counsel to
Jane Cumming as a witness, pointing out that she is not related to
Dame Cumming Gordon by law, but is a natural granddaughter.
However, they order that she be received *cum nota,* reserving ob-
jections to her credibility. She is sworn in. Present are the Lord

145

Justice-Clerk, Lords Meadowbank, Boyle, Robertson, Newton, and Glenlee, counsel for both parties, Marianne Woods, Jane Pirie, and Lady Cumming Gordon. Cranstoun examines her for the defence.

"Miss Cumming," he asks, "what was the first time you were disturbed in the middle of the night by your school mistresses?"

"During the summer holidays, when I went to Portobello with them in July and then when we came back, I was disturbed by them a good deal."

"Did you sleep with Miss Pirie at that time?" Cranstoun asks.

"No. I slept with Miss Pirie before. But when all the young ladies left the school for the summer, and I alone remained, Miss Pirie and Miss Woods slept together. I was made to sleep in a bed at the foot of theirs both when we went to the beach at Portobello and at the school until the others returned from their holiday. I was disturbed very often then, especially early in the morning."

"What kind of disturbance was it, Miss Cumming?"

"They were speaking and kissing and shaking the bed," she says.

"When you returned from Portobello did your mistresses continue to sleep together?"

"Yes, until most of the other scholars returned, about the middle of August. Then I had to sleep with Miss Pirie again. And Miss Woods went into the other room."

"Miss Cumming, during the time you slept with Miss Pirie, did Miss Woods come to your bed?"

"Yes, she certainly did. She came many times."

"On any of these occasions, were you awakened from your sleep?"

"Yes, I was. Many times."

"What was it that awakened you and what did you observe on being so awakened?"

"The first time I only heard them whispering and kissing one another. And that's what I saw when I was awakened."

"When Miss Woods came the next time to your bed, what did you see?"

"She had come different times when I only heard whispering and kissing."

"Now, Miss Cumming, at any time when Miss Woods came to

your bed, did you hear anything more than whispering and kissing?"

"Yes."

"Please tell the court what you heard, Miss Cumming."

She is silent for minutes.

"You must tell, Miss Cumming," Mr. Cranstoun says gently.

"I heard Miss Pirie say one night, 'You are hurting me.' "

"Did you hear anything more?"

She begins to cry.

"I know this is very difficult for you, Miss Cumming," Mr. Cranstoun says, "but you must tell."

"Yes," Miss Cumming says, still sobbing, wiping her tears. "I heard Miss Woods one night ask Miss Pirie if she was hurting her. And Miss Pirie said, 'No.' And another night I heard Miss Pirie say, 'You are in the wrong place.' Then Miss Woods said, 'I know,' and Miss Pirie said, 'Why are you doing it then?' and Miss Woods said, 'For fun.' Then another night I was awakened with a whispering, and I heard Miss Pirie say, 'Oh, do it, darling,' and Miss Woods said, 'Not tonight.' Miss Pirie asked her two or three times, and then Miss Woods said, 'Oh, not tonight for it may waken Miss Cumming and perhaps Miss Stirling.' But Miss Pirie still kept pressing her to come in. So then at last she came in and she lay above Miss Pirie. And then Miss Woods began to move, and she shook the bed, and I heard the same noise I heard on the holidays."

"Miss Cumming," Lord Justice-Clerk Hope says softly, "I must ask you to describe for the Court, as near as possible, the kind of noise you heard."

She stares straight ahead. Then she weeps again into a handkerchief. Then she is silent.

"Miss Cumming," Cranstoun says, "do you think you can try to describe the noise?"

"It was like putting one's finger into the neck of a wet bottle," she whispers. "That's the likest description I can give of it. But there's more to tell. Do you want me to go on?" she asks.

Cranstoun nods.

"Well, I asked Miss Pirie what was shaking the bed so, and she answered, 'Nothing.' But when I asked her that, I felt Miss Woods move over to the other side of the bed. I think that was the same night I heard Miss Woods say, 'I would like better to have somebody above me.' And then I remember another night when I awakened and I heard Miss Woods say, 'Now Jane, will you promise me one thing?' and Miss Pirie answered, 'I don't know, what is it?' So Miss Woods said, 'Now Jane, will you promise not to come to my bed, or take me in your arms until the holidays?' And Miss Pirie said to that, 'Oh, Marianne, don't ask me, for you know I could not keep it if I were to promise.' And then Miss Woods said, 'Oh, do promise, and I'll take care you shall keep it.' But Miss Pirie still would not promise. So then Miss Woods said, just as if Miss Pirie had promised, 'Nor will I take you in my arms, or come to your bed until the holidays, but you may kiss me and I will kiss you.' And then Miss Woods went away." She pauses.

"Do you recollect anything else that happened on this occasion?" Cranstoun asks.

"No, not at that time. But on the other night, when I spoke, I remember that I lay awake a long while, and when I complained that I could not sleep, Miss Pirie told me to turn my face to the wall and try to sleep. But I didn't turn. Instead I just said again that I could not sleep. Then Miss Pirie turned, and she said, 'Now you must turn as I have turned.' Then I heard Miss Woods go out of the room, and when she came to the door Miss Pirie coughed so that I wouldn't hear Miss Woods opening the door. And a little while after Miss Woods was gone, Miss Pirie said to me, 'Have you heard Miss Woods cough tonight?' And I said, 'No.' Then in a little while Miss Woods coughed and Miss Pirie said, 'Oh, there she's coughing, poor soul. I must go and see her.' And she went."

"Miss Cumming," Cranstoun says, "can you tell the Court exactly what happened on that same night when Miss Woods was in your bed, before the mistresses discovered you were awake."

"I felt them both lift up their shifts. And the next morning before breakfast, in the little garden in front of the house, I told it to Miss Munro, and Miss Munro said that the night before Miss Pirie had been in Miss Woods' bed, and she also heard a curious noise. She said she wondered what it was but didn't know. Then after I told her what happened she said she would watch the next night, and she did, and afterwards she told me it was all I had said. Oh ... and something else happened—when we came in from our walk on the same day, Miss Munro and I were talking in the school room, and the maid Charlotte came in, so I told Miss Munro to hold her tongue. But Charlotte said, 'Oh, you need not. It is long since I have known it.' She said she had seen them lying on the sofa as she passed the drawing room. And another day she went to the drawing room, but the doors were locked. Miss Pirie said, 'Who's there?' and Charlotte said, 'It's me,' and Miss Pirie said, 'What do you want?' Charlotte answered, 'I want to get in.' Miss Pirie said, 'You must come back later, we are busy just now.' But Charlotte said she saw them quite well and what they were doing. Oh ... and another thing—on another day Charlotte came to the school room door and called me out and said, 'They are at it just now.' She had been up in the dressing room, where the bed was shaking, and they were making such a noise that they didn't hear her. So Charlotte went to the bed and said, 'It's near nine o'clock, Ma'am.' Then Miss Pirie came out of the bed in a great hurry, with her face quite red, and she said, 'What do you say, Charlotte?' and she went away to dress herself, and Miss Woods hid herself in the bed clothes."

"Miss Cumming," the Lord Justice-Clerk asks, "did the mistresses give any indication that they suspected they had been found out?"

"Sir?"

"Do you think Miss Woods and Miss Pirie knew that you were aware of what they were doing?"

"Oh, yes ... I forgot to say something else that happened. When I asked Miss Pirie what made the bed shake so, on the next day I bid the girls to look at Miss Woods, for I thought she would not speak to me. And then Miss Woods came into the room and went out again, and none of the girls had looked at her. So I told them again to look at her when she came back. Then when she came back all the girls went up and shook hands with her, but when I went up she turned away, with her face quite red, and she didn't speak with me the whole day, until after dinner, when I went up and spoke with her. Then the next day, Miss Munro and I wished to let them know for certain that we knew it, and we said we would speak of it at breakfast time, but we lost courage. But then on that same day when we were out walking, I told Miss Munro that I would wait no more. I would complain of it that afternoon, and I would say that I was tired and could not get sleep.

So I told her to put the question to me, 'Did you not sleep well?' so that I could answer, 'No, I couldn't sleep because the bed was shaking so.' Then when we came in from our walk Miss Pirie was in the room, and Miss Munro and I talked just as we decided we would."

"Did Miss Pirie hear you?" the Lord Justice-Clerk asks.

"Well, of course. She stayed in the room for some time, but when she saw we weren't going to stop talking about it, she left the room with her face quite red. I said to Miss Munro, 'Oh, do you see guilt on her face?' Oh . . . and I remember some other things now. May I say them?"

"About Miss Woods and Miss Pirie?" Cranstoun asks.

"Yes. Several times after Miss Woods had been in our room I heard her say to Miss Pirie, 'Good night, darling, I think I have put you in the way to get a good sleep tonight.' Sometimes Miss Pirie would say, no. And then Miss Woods would do it some more. Other nights Miss Pirie would not say anything, and then Miss Woods went away. And also I've heard the maid Charlotte call them brutes and beasts, and worse than beasts. And I've seen Charlotte put out her tongue at them . . . I think that's all I can remember now."

Mr. Cranstoun says he has concluded his examination.

"Miss Cumming, what did the mistresses do when Charlotte stuck out her tongue?" Lord Robertson asks.

"They weren't present. Charlotte also said, 'They are pretty ladies. I am a better lady myself.' Oh . . . and I also remember something else Miss Munro told me."

"Objection, your honours," John Clerk says. "We have already heard Miss Munro's testimony first hand, as well as the maid's testimony."

"Overruled. Please continue," the Lord Justice-Clerk says.

"Miss Munro said that one night when they were in her bed she awakened with the noise they were making, and Miss Woods had turned, and seeing Miss Munro awake, she said to Miss Pirie in a whisper, 'Good gracious, what should we do, she's awake?' Then Miss Pirie covered herself up with the bed clothes. Then Miss Woods said to Miss Munro, 'How long have you been awake?' and Miss Munro answered, 'A long time.' And then Miss Woods sent her to the dressing room for a glass of water."

"Miss Cumming, will you think a minute," the Lord Justice-Clerk asks. "Can you remember any indications that the other girls, besides Miss Munro, were aware of the mistresses' behaviour?"

"Yes. I remember that Miss Stirling heard Miss Munro and me talking about it, and she said she knew about it too, and she advised us to tell the mistresses that we knew. Then one night when Miss Pirie was out of bed, Miss Stirling and I were talking about it, our beds being so close. Meanwhile, Miss Pirie came in, and when she came to bed she said, 'Oh, if I were rich I would have two beds in summer.' Also, one night before I had seen anything at all between them, I saw Miss Woods and Miss Pirie come into the bedroom, and both of them had nothing on but their night shifts. I sat up in bed, and was quite surprised to see them. Then Miss Woods went to the foot of my bed, as if to hide herself, but I saw her quite plainly since the window was opposite to the foot of the bed. After that Miss Pirie went out of the room, but I don't know what became of Miss Woods because I fell asleep."

"Is there anything else you can think of regarding the other scholars having known about the mistresses?" the Lord Justice-Clerk asks.

"Oh, yes, two more things. Once I had been out at Mr. Forbes', my uncle's, at dinner, and when I came to bed I saw the bed clothes all turned down. Miss Cunynghame was with me, so I said, 'Who can have destroyed all my bed?' And she answered, 'Oh, it will be Miss Woods and Miss Pirie, for they were upstairs together a long time.' Also, I'm certain that all the girls must have seen Miss Pirie sometimes take Miss Woods out of the school room, as if against her consent, into the drawing room when it was dark, and stay there a long time. And then one morning when I went into the dressing room, all the girls were laughing at Miss Pirie coming out of Miss Woods' bed with her stockings on and a red garter. And Miss Edgar has told me many times that she was disturbed with the noise that Miss Woods and Miss Pirie were making in the room. I don't remember anything more."

"In view of the time," Lord Justice-Clerk Hope announces, "let us adjourn until the morrow at ten o'clock rather than calling the counsel for the plaintiffs up for only a few minutes."

Lord Glenlee's Notes on the Testimony of Miss Jane Cumming, March 27, 1811

It is infinitely more probable that the mistresses should have been guilty of the offence charged against them, than that Miss Cumming, even supposing her to have been ever so much corrupted in her morals, should have been able to invent such a story.

Lord Newton's Notes on the Testimony of Miss Jane Cumming, March 27, 1811

The story has now been clearly sworn to by two young ladies. Since these two girls had no passion to gratify by inventing such an abominable tale, I cannot doubt that, however improbable it may appear, it really was so. It is true that Cumming is the grandchild of the defendant, and she has interest in supporting the accusation, since she originally made it, but what possible interest did she have to trump up a story like this in the first place? What could make her say that she had seen certain facts, unless they really had been so? Nothing short of the spirit of the devil could have induced Munro and Cumming to invent this tale and swear to it as they have done, and I do not conceive that they have that spirit.

Lord Meadowbank's Notes on the Testimony of Miss Jane Cumming, March 27, 1811

Miss Cumming is the young person from whom the information of the fatal imputation proceeded. Because of her connection with Lady Cumming Gordon, she has been received *cum nota*. She is wanting in the advantages of legitimacy and a European complexion, and in consequence she is entirely dependent on the favour of her connections. But her testimony is suspect to me for other reasons as well. After we adjourned, Glenlee and Robertson remarked, where could she have gotten such information if she were not telling the truth? That answer is extremely clear to me. It is an historical fact and matter of notoriety that the language of the Hindoo female domestics turns chiefly on the commerce of the sexes. The instructions of Hindoo nurses to their female infants are also frequently on the same subject and are calculated to excite anticipation of its nature, even before the venereal instincts have begun to exist in a girlchild. The seclusion of women in the Zenanas of the more wealthy gives birth to contrivances to supply the absence or neglect of males. In fine, it is impossible to live in Indostan without learning through observation and instruction, by the age of eight or nine, something about venereal intercourse. If my recollection is correct, Miss Cumming had fully attained that time of life before she left Indostan and escaped from the tuition of Hindoo domestics. Certainly her information may have already been adequate to this purpose.

But what were her motives in inventing such a story about her mistresses? After she arrived in Britain, she remained five years at a boarding school of inferior rank in Elgin. She was then taken out of the school and told she would be given the education of a young lady, she would be recognized as belonging to the Cumming Gordon family, and she would be introduced into society. In these circumstances she was placed at the Drumsheugh school. It may reasonably be presumed that she was anxious to hasten the time when she was to become a member of so very respectable a family and perform the part of a young lady of condition. The discipline at the Drumsheugh school is said to have been strict and actively exercised. Miss Munro has testified that she had to endure consid-

153

erable punishment. Perhaps Miss Cumming was also punished often. It is possible that she felt if she were not successful at the school—and frequent punishment might have suggested to her that she was not—all that had been promised to her would be retracted. Perhaps she did not understand what horror such an imputation as she made against the mistresses would raise in Britain. Possibly she thought the only result of her accusations would be her removal from a school that she felt was too rigorous, and her placement in one more to her liking.

July 8, 1982

During the summer, at Drumsheugh and Portobello Miss Woods and Miss Pirie slept together, and Jane Cumming was made to sleep in a bed at the foot of theirs. But why? Ollie thinks that since they had at least six empty beds in the house when they were at the school, their choice to sleep in one bed together proves they were lovers. I agree. They were lovers. I never said they were not. I only said they did not have genital sex. Of course they kissed and caressed as romantic friends did. Romantic friends always shared a bed when they had the opportunity. What puzzles me, however, is why they had Cumming sleep at the foot of their bed. If Ollie is right, if they really had sex together, then they must have been depraved to want a witness to their deeds. Ollie thinks it is conceivable they "got their jollies that way," as she puts it. But I cannot believe that—not along with everything else that is known of them. I think it is more likely that they worried about what exotic, erotic pleasures Jane Cumming could bring to herself in the middle of the night, and so they wanted to keep an eye on her. But surely they would have understood that if they could keep an eye on her, she could keep an eye on them. If they had had sexual intentions, they would have packed her off to another room.

"Perhaps they didn't have such intentions to begin with,"

Ollie says. "But those things happen, you know." We both know.

"What about the wet bottle description?" I ask Ollie. That struck me as being ludicrous. Ollie thinks it accurate and goes into the kitchen to find a bottle, but we have none that is empty and I will not let her empty the vinegar bottle for the experiment, with Edinburgh prices as exorbitant as they are this summer. She wants to know what kind of legal historian I am if I will not make a few sacrifices to learn the truth, but she works her finger in and out of the full vinegar bottle. We agree that the sound might be right.

But there are other parts of Jane Cumming's description that are absurd: if one woman is on top of the other, moving back and forth or up and down over her genitals, what would make that noise? There would be no room for a hand to be squeezed in between. Somewhere the Indian girl must have seen a man and a woman coupling, and she must have heard that two females could couple too—and, in her utter ignorance, she assumed (perhaps not understanding about penetration, perhaps having fantastic notions about female tumescence in passion) that it was done in the same way.

What I can believe is that there were many times when Miss Pirie would take Miss Woods out of the school room "as if against her consent." I think Pirie had no control over her temper, and she must have made awful, hysterical scenes. She would rein in her anger for a while, and it would tug and tug, and finally it would go wild. There are types who exacerbate such fury in an explosive person, and Marianne Woods appears to me to have been such a type. For the last three of the four years I lived with her, Pearl had that effect on me. As much as I thought I loved her, I could not check my rage. It would happen over the silliest things—when she forgot to pay the electricity bill, when I thought she didn't take my part enough in a mild political debate with a friend over dinner, when she came home a half hour later than I expected her. I realize now my rage was always just beneath the surface. A minor incident might raise it up, but it was never really about that incident. It was about my abiding discontent with our lives together. I could never believe she loved me enough. Sometimes it seemed to me that one of us would not get away from the other alive, that I would either kill her or kill myself.

I cannot imagine feeling such violence with Ollie. She has

turned away my wrath, so that now it is hard to remember that I have such anger in me. Woods never knew how to turn away Pirie's wrath. So they would fight, Pirie screaming, Woods hardly answering—and somehow, no matter what the issue was or who was at fault, Pirie would be convinced or would convince herself that maybe it was her own fault after all. She would end by apologizing and promising to do better. Then they would be very loving again for a while and pretend the anger had never erupted. But, of course, all the fury, instead of resolving itself through rational talk, would be bottled up again, and would build and build until the next explosion—when again Pirie would drag Woods out of the school room to say the matter must be settled, once and for all. The cycle must have repeated itself an endless number of times. Just as it did with me, until finally I left Pearl. Pirie never had the chance to leave.

MARCH 28, 1811, 10:00 A.M.

The Lord Justice-Clerk calls the court to order and announces he must examine the witness. Jane Cumming looks at him solemnly. "Do not be afraid of me," he tells her jovially. "I never yet ate a witness, especially not a fine young lady." She does not smile. "Now, then, Miss Cumming," he begins, "when Charlotte said she saw the mistresses quite well and what they were doing, did she mention to you how she saw them?"

"Through the keyhole."

"Now, you did not mention a keyhole the last time, did you?"

"I forgot, and then I thought I would be asked again."

"Were you ever told that there was no keyhole to the drawing rooms doors?"

"No, I don't think I ever was."

"Do you know if there were keyholes to the drawing room doors?"

"No."

"Well, Miss Cumming, will you explain more particularly

what Charlotte said with respect to looking through the keyhole of the drawing room door."

"She said nothing more particular than that she had seen them quite well through the keyhole."

"Did she tell you they were lying on the sofa perhaps?"

"No."

The Lord Justice-Clerk asks if the other Lords have questions at this time. They do not. "Does the counsel for the plaintiffs now wish to examine the witness?" he asks. John Clerk rises.

"Miss Cumming," Clerk asks, "did Charlotte tell you that story about the keyhole more than once?"

"I don't remember."

"Are you perfectly certain that Charlotte told you that story even once?"

She stares at him. She looks to Lord Justice-Clerk Hope who says nothing. "I am quite certain," she says.

"When did she tell you that story?" John Clerk asks.

She says nothing. Minutes pass.

"Miss Cumming, did you hear my question?"

Her eyes are tearful. "Yes," she says.

"You must answer, Miss Cumming," the Lord Justice-Clerk tells her.

"I don't remember, but it was after Miss Munro came to the school. And it was after Miss Munro and I talked about it."

"Do you remember the day of the week when Charlotte told you the story?"

"No."

"At what time of day was it?"

"I don't remember."

"Was it before or after dinner?"

"I don't remember."

"Who was present when Charlotte told the story?"

"I don't remember if there was any person present."

"Miss Cumming, you remembered so much yesterday. How is it that you remember so little today?"

"Objection," Erskine says. "Counsel is intimidating the witness." He is sustained.

Clerk resumes in a softer tone. "Was Miss Munro present?"

"I don't remember."

"Did you ask Charlotte any questions about the story?"

"I don't think so."

"Well, perhaps you will remember more of this incident later, Miss Cumming. Let's pursue another line of inquiry now. Did you have a nanny while you were in India?"

"I don't remember anything that happened while I was there."

"Come now, Miss Cumming, you were almost eight when you left. You must remember. Did you attend school?"

"Yes. I remember I was at school."

"Can you mention anything else?"

"I was at two schools, but I don't know how long."

"Were you acquainted with girls of your own age in India?"

"Yes, with many."

"Who took charge of you?"

"It was a Mr. Palmer, I think, but I boarded at the schools."

"Who were the women who took charge of you?"

"I don't remember any, except the school mistresses."

"Were they natives or European?"

"The first were Europeans," she says. "I don't know whether the second were or not."

"Were the women servants at the school natives or Europeans?"

"I think they must have been natives."

"When you sailed for Britain, who attended you?"

"A maid-servant."

"A native?" Clerk asks.

"Yes, then she went back to India."

"How long did she continue in this country before she went back?"

"I'm not sure. I think about half a year."

Lord Meadowbank wishes to know whether, while she was in India, she ever observed among the children or anyone, the servants perhaps, any such practices as those she described between the plaintiffs.

"Never."

"Did you ever hear conversations about such things?"

"Never."

"Did you ever hear any language in India that, upon recollection, you now think was improper?"

"Never."

"When you arrived in Britain," John Clerk now asks, "who attended you?"

"I think I landed at Greenwich and was taken to London, to the house of Mr. George Cumming, my great uncle. I remained there a week or fortnight. And I and the maid were then brought down to Scotland, by a Mr. Tullock, I think. I remained some time with my grandmama, but I don't remember how long. Then I was sent to the boarding school at Elgin kept by Miss Charles. I think I was there about five years. And then I was sent for, to come here."

"At Miss Charles' boarding school, had you any time allowed you for play?"

"Yes."

"How much time?"

"In the winter we had free time between two and three, and then between five and six. And in the summer, after the writing master went away at seven o'clock, we could walk by ourselves. But we always had to be in before nine o'clock at night."

"Were you ever allowed to walk by yourself, or was the mistress always with you?"

"As I already said, we could walk by ourselves."

"Miss Cumming, did you find the discipline more or less strict at Drumsheugh than at the school at Elgin? Had you more or less time for amusement?"

"It was more strict. We had less time for amusement."

Lord Meadowbank wishes to know if they had no person to take charge of them when they went out to play at Elgin.

"We went out but a very little way, sir," she says. "There was a hill at the back of the house, and we always went there. Sometimes Miss Charles went with us."

"Miss Cumming," John Clerk continues, "did you feel the discipline at the Drumsheugh school harassing or disagreeable compared with that of the Elgin school?"

"I thought it was much more strict. I wouldn't say it was disagreeable."

"Were you frequently exposed to the punishments of the school?"

"Yes, pretty often."

"Didn't you seldom escape a single day without being punished for something or another?"

"No, I was not in punishment every day."

"Do you know what a disgrace book is?"

"No. I remember a disgrace table, but I don't remember a disgrace book."

"Miss Cumming, did you not keep a book in which you wrote down from time to time the punishments you were exposed to?"

"Oh, yes. I think I remember—I did for a short time before I came away."

"Did you keep that book of your own accord?"

"Yes."

"Have you that book still?"

"I think I have."

Lord Justice-Clerk Hope instructs her to find the book and give it to the Clerk of the Court as soon as possible. He asks if she has altered it since leaving Drumsheugh. She has not.

"Miss Cumming," John Clerk resumes, "during the holidays, did you observe anything in the conduct of Miss Woods and Miss Pirie other than what you have already described?"

"No."

"Did you hear that kind of noise like putting one's finger into the neck of a wet bottle oftener than once?"

"Yes."

"How often did you hear it?"

"I don't remember."

"Did you hear it only on one occasion or on different occasions during the holidays?"

"On different occasions."

"Did you always hear that kind of noise when you heard them speaking and kissing?"

"Not always."

"How often did you hear them speaking and kissing during the holidays?"

"I don't remember. It was often."

"Did you hear it every morning during the holidays?"

"No."

"At what time in the morning did you hear it?"

She sits in silence.

"Miss Cumming?"

"I don't know what time. It was early."

"Miss Cumming, you said the noise was a wet noise, is that right?"

"Yes."

"Can you give a better or more particular description of the kind of noise it was?"

"I can't. It was like I said before."

"When you heard the mistresses speaking and kissing and shaking the bed in the mornings during the holidays, did it occur to you that they were doing any improper act?"

"No."

"At this time, did you feel that degree of respect for them as your school mistresses that you think ought to be felt towards people in that situation?"

"Yes."

"Had they always behaved properly, according to the best of your judgements, in other respects?"

"I don't remember if I took any notice of their conduct."

"When did it occur to you that their conduct with each other was wrong?"

"I don't remember. After the holidays they used to quarrel very often."

"Did you think that their quarrelling was wrong?"

"I didn't think it was right. But I don't remember that I thought it was wrong. I only wondered at it because at other times they seemed to be so fond of each other."

"Did you conceive that anything improper, indecent, or criminal was done by the mistresses when in bed in the mornings during the holidays?"

"I think I already said no to that."

"Do you now conceive or believe that anything improper, indecent, or criminal was done between them on those occasions?"

"I think it was very improper and very indecent, but I don't know whether it was criminal."

"Since it did not occur to you at that time that it was improper or indecent, Miss Cumming, when did that first occur to you?"

"When they came into my bed."

"Please recollect as nearly as possible when it was, how long after the holidays, that Miss Woods came into the bed which you shared with Miss Pirie and behaved in such a way as to make you think their conduct improper or indecent."

"I daresay it was about two months after the holidays before I thought there was anything indecent in what they did."

"Do you mean to say that until near the end of September it did not occur to you that their conduct was indecent—that is, until about three weeks after Miss Munro came to school?"

"Yes, I'm certain it was after Miss Munro came to school, but I don't remember exactly when."

"Did the suspicion arise in your mind in consequence of your own reflections, or in consequence of something you heard from another person?"

"I thought of it before I talked to anyone about it."

"When did you become certain of it?"

"That night when Miss Woods came to our bed, and when Miss Pirie asked her to come in and Miss Woods said, 'Not tonight, it would awaken Miss Cumming and perhaps Miss Stirling.'"

"Miss Cumming, do you mean to say that you became certain merely from that conversation?"

"No, but from what happened in bed afterwards. It was the conversation that made me curious to observe what should pass."

"Describe exactly what happened at that meeting that made you certain they were indecent together."

"I think I have described it."

"You are desired to describe it again, Miss Cumming," Lord Justice-Clerk Hope says.

"When Miss Woods came into bed, I felt them both take up their shifts, and I felt Miss Woods move and shake the bed, and Miss Woods was breathing so high and quick. Miss Woods was lying above Miss Pirie at this time. And I heard the same noise I already described. I think it was the same night I heard Miss Woods say she would rather have somebody above her. That's all I recollect at present."

The Lord Justice-Clerk wishes to know how long the noise she described as resembling a finger in a wet bottle lasted.

"I daresay for about five minutes at a time."

"And how many times did it happen during the meeting?" he asks.

"Three or four. I don't remember whether it lasted as long as five minutes each time."

"Miss Cumming," John Clerk asks, "did you ever yourself make any such noise with your finger in a wet bottle? Or did you ever hear any other person make such a noise with their finger in a bottle?"

"No."

"Well then, how came you to describe a noise which you actually heard by being most like to a noise which you never heard?"

She is silent. "Because I thought it would be the same," she says finally.

"Was it anything like the drawing of a cork?" John Clerk says.

"No."

"Was it like a person clapping or patting another on the cheek or shoulders?"

"No."

"Miss Cumming," Lord Robertson asks, "was it perhaps like a person dabbling their hands in water?"

"It was not quite like that, but more like it I think than rubbing or clapping."

"Miss Cumming," Lord Robertson asks again, "have you ever heard a dairy maid making up butter? Was it anything like a dairy maid patting butter?"

"Yes. It was like that. And it was so loud that I heard it during the holidays, though I was in a separate bed."

John Clerk resumes. "Had you ever heard any such noise before or since, except between the mistresses?"

"I don't remember that I ever did."

"Had any person ever told you that such noise took place between persons when they were indecent together?"

"No."

"Miss Cumming, will you say how this noise came to strike you as one of those circumstances which made you certain the mistresses were indecent together?"

She says nothing.

"Shall I repeat the question, Miss Cumming?" John Clerk asks gently.

"It was because I felt Miss Woods put down her hand just before I heard it."

"I will repeat the question, Miss Cumming. How did the noise come to strike you as one of the circumstances that made you certain the mistresses were indecent?"

There is a very long silence. She says finally, "Because I felt Miss Woods put down her hand just before I heard it."

"Is that the only answer you can give, Miss Cumming?"

She looks confused, then begins to cry. "Yes," she says.

"Miss Cumming, when and to whom at the school did you first mention this noise you had heard like a finger in a bottle?"

"I don't think I mentioned it to anyone at the school."

"Would you care to take a few moments to compose your-self?" the Lord Justice-Clerk asks her. She dabs her eyes and tells him she will be all right.

"Miss Cumming," John Clerk continues, "as it was dark at the time, in what manner did you feel them both put down their hands and pull up their shifts?"

There is a long silence. John Clerk repeats the question. Another long silence. He repeats the question again very softly. Finally she says, "With my leg."

"Did you feel both their hands with your leg?"

"I didn't feel their hands."

Erskine objects that counsel for the plaintiffs is purposely confusing the witness. He is overruled. John Clerk continues. "Miss Cumming, if you did not feel their hands, how did you feel them both take up their shifts?"

"I was lying quite close to them and I felt quite well when they took up their shifts."

"Did you distinctly feel them put down their hands?"

"My own arm was covered and I didn't feel their hands, but I felt them move their arms downwards. And with my leg I felt their naked legs."

"Did you feel anything naked higher up than their legs?"

"No."

Lord Meadowbank wishes to know whether she is positive she felt both the mistresses move an arm down in order to lift up their shifts.

"Well, I'm not positive they both moved their arms down, but I'm positive they both lifted up their shifts, because afterwards I felt both their naked legs with my leg."

"Did you feel any other parts of their bodies naked?" Lord Meadowbank asks.

"No, because I was covered everywhere else."

"Miss Cumming," John Clerks asks, "had you drawn up your own shift since your own leg was naked?"

"No, but it had got up."

"Miss Cumming," Clerk asks, "since it was dark, how were you certain that on all occasions Miss Woods was lying uppermost?"

"I wasn't certain. I don't think I said that."

"Was the kissing you heard very loud?" John Clerk asks.

"Not very, but loud enough for me to hear that it was kissing."

"Did they speak in so audible a voice that you are quite sure that you are not mistaken in the conversation you related?"

"Yes."

"And you stated that one of them said to the other, 'Oh, you are in the wrong place'?"

"Yes."

"Are you quite certain that one did not say, 'You are *on* the wrong place'?"

"I am quite certain one said *in* the wrong place," she says emphatically.

"Miss Cumming, how came you to state that Charlotte put out her tongue at the mistresses when they were not present?"

"Not present?"

"Yes."

"Oh . . . I meant that she was speaking so disdainfully of them that it was like putting out her tongue. But now I think of it, on the last day I was at the school, Charlotte did put out her tongue at Miss Woods. Only it was behind her back and she didn't see it."

The Lord Justice-Clerk says they must adjourn. Lord Newton wishes to ask one further question now. "On the occasion when you heard one of them ask the other if she was hurting her, did you hear the noise like a finger in a bottle before or after?"

"I didn't hear it either before or after on that night."

They adjourn until ten o'clock, March 29.

165

Lord Justice-Clerk Hope's Notes on the Testimony of Miss Jane Cumming, March 28, 1811

When I see invention at work in one quarter, I must be prepared to suspect it in another. Who invented the keyhole story? Was it Charlotte? It is likely that she would have observed that one could not look through a keyhole into the drawing room, since she must have had many occasions to call the mistresses from the drawing room. Would Miss Cumming have had occasion to scrutinize the drawing room door? That is less likely. Very possibly she would not have known that one could not look through a keyhole into the drawing room. I would venture to guess that she invented the story.

And there is evidence of another brilliant invention by her, the *curious noise.* How does she describe it? Not by any other noise she ever heard. To suit the occasion she invents a noise which she admits she never heard. There was no hesitation in her answer to the question, though she hesitated often and for very long periods in her answers to simpler questions. She at once said that the likest thing she could think of to the noise was putting her finger in a wet bottle. Is that not an absolute lie? "The likest thing"—it was implied in this that she had tried it. But if not, it was mere invention,—an effort of imagination. There is no difficulty to understand what she meant. It is most significant. I believe she is both more knowing and more ignorant than some of us had imagined. She has read or heard a good deal of the intercourse of the sexes. I believe she is ignorant in that she is innocent in her own person, but she has conceived a pretty accurate idea of the act of copulation, and has imagined that it was attended with a *wet* noise. The chief thing is that this shows invention,—a habit of imagining. She said she heard it even in the next bed. Miss Stirling never heard it; Miss Munro never heard it.

Lord Newton's Notes on the Testimony of Miss Jane Cumming, March 28, 1811

As to the noise, I had supposed that Miss Cumming meant to represent it as the noise previous to penetration. I asked her if it took place always immediately before the motions. She said it did not. Now, this very circumstance tends to support her evidence. If she meant to swear falsely, why should she introduce a circumstance as unintelligible as this? For to me, it is unaccountable, and yet if untrue, introduced needlessly.

Lord Meadowbank's Notes on the Testimony of Miss Jane Cumming, March 28, 1811

Miss Cumming's imperfect knowledge of the subject led her to suppose that acts of copulation were attended with a particular noise, and hence she ascribes a noise to the intercourse of the mistresses—and she compares it to what yields no sound (no more than copulation does): to a finger moving in the neck of a wet bottle.

I must say I think her other stories miserably ill contrived as well. The eternal conversations suit strangely with venereal congress. The "You are hurting me" seems utterly foreign to congress between women of ordinary conformation without the use of tools. And she never mentions tools. The whole description of quick breathings, eternal whisperings, violent agitations, simultaneous gratification of both parties, wet bottle and patting-of-butter noises—all of these seem utterly inconsistent with the venereal congress she imputes to the mistresses. The remark about "in the wrong place for fun" is incompatible with the fury of unnatural lust. The coquettish solicitations for Miss Woods to come into bed, and her declining and at last yielding to them is ridiculous, since she was supposed to have come there in the first place to commit the crime. Miss Woods' alleged bedside conversation attempting to exact a promise from Miss Pirie not to come to her bed until the holidays, and Miss Pirie declining to make a promise because she could not keep it, and their then agreeing to kiss one another in the meantime, is so absurd and nonsensical and unaccountable. Here they were in bed, in dalliance, but Miss Woods is at the bedside, come there on purpose to chatter thus, and so loudly that Miss Cumming should hear it. If such stories do not betray the invention of falsehood, I do not know what can do it.

JULY 11, 1982

Ollie has been reading the transcripts with me in the Signet Library, which adjoins the Scottish Parliament House, where the trial took place. As we read we could look out the window and see the cobblestoned square that they all crossed to get to the courtroom. Ollie says that my mystery must have taken over her subconscious. Last night she dreamed that the mistresses were in a bed next to ours, making love. This morning she woke up and remembered that the room in her dream was one she had not seen in fifteen years, since she separated from Sheila. They had had a one-bedroom apartment with two beds, a double and a single. The room was small and the single was no more than two feet away from the double, but of course neither she nor Sheila ever slept in it. The single was a decoy for display to visiting relatives or straight guests who might ask to use the bathroom, which was connected to the bedroom. One summer, Sheila's sister Denise, who was then sixteen years old, came to spend a few weeks with them. Denise slept in the single bed. After about a week of celibacy, Sheila (who claimed that abstinence gave her headaches) decided that enough was enough. Ollie was terrified, told Sheila she would not be able to live with herself if they traumatized the child, adamantly refused, called Sheila a lunatic. Sheila said that she had listened to the girl snoring nightly for more than ten years and she was certain that nothing short of 8.3 on the Richter scale would wake her up. They made love every night for the next three weeks, and the girl never stirred.

"What if she had?" I ask.

"It was dark in the room, and she couldn't have seen much in any case. And Sheila had already decided that if Denise managed to see any motion at all we would tell her that I (or Sheila) had been suffering from painful kinks in the legs, and that massage helped. We kept the covers on. We weren't overly adventurous during those weeks either. I'm sure that if I'd really thought she could see anything at all, or that there was any possibility that she'd wake up, I wouldn't have taken the risk in the first place. But I guess after the first or second time, when we got away with it, I became as confident as Sheila. I think I remember that we got braver as the nights went by and we weren't caught. Although I'm certain we always kept the covers over us."

I am not too charmed being put in Sheila's bed, even if it is only in a dream. And I don't think Ollie's story proves anything, except that twentieth-century women might behave that way. I doubt that in those pre-Freudian days women believed that abstinence from sex gave them a headache (although the indulgence in it—often unwilling—might have). Without powerful "libidos," such as women today feel compelled to lay claim to, would those women have been so bold, especially when so terribly much was at risk?

Nonetheless, Ollie thinks Jane Cumming's testimony is convincing. I do not. Cumming has the mistresses behaving as human beings never do.

"But I just told you about Sheila and myself," she says.

"It is not that aspect that I am talking about [although I think I have already answered that point], it is this: Jane Cumming first joined the school in December of 1809. From then to the midsummer of 1810 she had never—even in retrospect—observed anything suspect in the women's behavior. It is not likely that people start a sexual relationship with each other only after having been close friends for about eight years. If they were sexual in the summer of 1810, they would have been sexual in the winter of 1809. It is much more likely that physical intimacy would have been a part of their relationship earlier rather than later. If they were not doing it after having known each other for seven and a half years, they would not be doing it six or seven months later."

She concedes that might be a good point. "However," she says, "you don't know that they weren't doing it in the preceding winter and spring."

"But Jane Cumming would have observed them in her bed, just as she did in the fall."

"Not necessarily," Ollie says. "Remember that in winter the school had only four students and six beds. In the spring it had fourteen students, and five of them were day pupils. That meant that only nine slept at the school. There would have been five girls in one room: two pairs of them shared two beds and the fifth slept with one of the mistresses. In the other room there would have been four girls, and they too slept in pairs. The mistress in that room had a bed to herself. The other mistress could have visited her regularly in the middle of the night. The sleep of the girls in the other beds need never have been disturbed, just as it wasn't disturbed in the fall of 1810."

Now I must concede that she has a good point.

"Yes," she says. "And if you're going to use as an argument 'how human beings behave,' human beings don't invent such fantastic stories as the one Jane Cumming is reciting to the Court, unless they have some dark motive. And I agree with Lord Newton, who pointed out in his notes that she had none."

"But she does, she has a half dozen, and they might even have all worked together to compound her bitterness toward the mistresses. First of all, as I have already suggested, she might have seen the mistresses as surrogate parents, and alone with them in Portobello during the summer, she may have become very attached to them: they provided a kind of stability that she did not have from anyone else. Then, when their violent fights resumed after they returned to the school, the situation might have been extremely unsettling to her. She would have known of no effective way to express her fury at having been robbed of this stability other than by inventing an outrageous tale about them. A second possibility is that she resented the harsh discipline that was imposed on her, and she was going to get even. She wanted to hurt them as much as possible, and what better way to hurt an early-nineteenth-century woman than to accuse her of illicit sexuality? Had there been a man around whom she might have said they carried on with, she probably would have chosen to represent their immorality in that way. But since there was no man around, she accused them of carrying on with each other. Now surely that is how a vicious young human being might behave.

"Another possibility was suggested by Meadowbank. Remember that she was one of the oldest girls in the school. She probably saw herself as a woman already, and school was for children. She wanted to be released—she wanted to begin the fashionable life that was coming to her as a recognized member of an illustrious family. She concocted the story, not realizing what explosive power such a tale would have in an antisexual society. The fourth possibility is that she had a crush on one of the mistresses, perhaps her bedfellow, and was deeply wounded when Jane Pirie seemed so repelled by her that she slept so far away as to raise a lump in the mattress, as the maid observed. Another possibility is that she was enamored of Janet Munro. At the moment, this is the explanation I favor. Remember she had asked Janet to be her bedfellow and Janet turned her down. Janet was disturbed enough by the proposition to discuss it with Miss Pirie, perhaps because Jane Cumming had suggested to her that one advantage of such an arrangement would be the opportunity for sexual experimentation. If Janet seemed disgusted, Jane Cumming might have pointed out that everyone was doing it, even the mistresses, and then convinced Janet (who appears not to have been too swift anyway) that when one woman came to rub the other for rheumatism they were really doing what Jane Cumming thought she and Janet ought to do. She might even have convinced herself of it."

"Five," Ollie says, but I think she looks less skeptical.

"And the sixth possibility," I conclude, "is simply that—as you said of Jane Pirie—she was crazy."

The same parties are present. John Clerk resumes the questioning of Miss Jane Cumming for the plaintiffs.

"Miss Cumming, did you commonly lie near to Miss Pirie in bed, or away from her?"

"Near her."

"So near as to touch her?"

"Sometimes—with some parts of our bodies."

"How often was Miss Woods in Miss Pirie's bed?"

"There were four times when she was in bed that I'm quite sure what they were doing. But I know she was much oftener in bed before I thought anything about it."

"Why did it take you so long to suspect they were doing anything indecent, Miss Cumming?"

"I suspected it before, but since I myself didn't know of any such thing, I wasn't willing to allow myself to believe it."

"What was it that you did not know of?"

"I didn't know of any such thing as that which I was made to describe yesterday and the day before."

The Lord Justice-Clerk wishes to know whether before she became sure of their guilt she had read any book or been informed by any person that such vicious things were sometimes practised between women.

"Never."

"Miss Cumming," John Clerk resumes, "you have stated that you told Miss Munro what you observed between the mistresses when you were in the garden with her. Will you tell the court the particulars of what you said."

"I don't remember that I told her any particulars except that Miss Woods had come to our bed and that she lay above Miss Pirie and they were moving, and that it had been going on that way for a long while, but that I didn't know what they were doing. And then she said that the night before Miss Pirie had been in their bed, and that they were going on in such a curious way that she could not think what they were doing."

"Did Miss Munro first mention the subject to you, or were you the one who first mentioned it?"

"I did. Miss Munro was the first person I mentioned it to."

The Lord Justice-Clerk has been shuffling through his notes. "Miss Cumming," he interrupts, "when you felt the legs of both Miss Woods and Miss Pirie, was the one's leg lying directly above the other's?"

"No, not when I felt them."

"How were the two legs lying?"

She pauses.

"Can you remember, Miss Cumming?"

"I'm inclined to think that Miss Woods' leg was lying within Miss Pirie's."

"Do you mean you put your leg over Miss Pirie's so as to feel Miss Woods?"

"No, of course not. But I'm quite sure I felt both legs."

"In what manner was your own leg lying when you felt both legs?" John Clerk pursues.

"I don't remember. I think I was lying half turned on my right side, with my back towards them."

"So you felt Miss Woods come into the bed, lie above Miss Pirie, they took up their shifts—and then how did you feel their legs?"

"I think Miss Pirie moved her leg towards me."

"How were their legs lying with respect to each other after they had taken up their shifts and before Miss Pirie laid her leg out?"

"I can't say, but I'm sure I felt both their legs."

"At what particular moment was it that you felt Miss Woods' leg?"

"Just at the time they took up their shifts. It was then that I felt their skins."

"I believe Miss Cumming has answered that line of questioning as best as she can," the Lord Justice-Clerk interrupts John Clerk. "Kindly go on to another."

"Miss Cumming, do you know whether Miss Pirie had any rheumatic complaint during the space between the end of the holidays and the breaking up of the school?" John Clerk asks, somewhat annoyed.

"She had the rheumatism in her arms."

"Did the rheumatism affect Miss Pirie's back?"

"I never heard her say so."

"Do you know whether Miss Pirie used to have any part of her body rubbed for the rheumatism?"

"I don't know, but once when Miss Stirling was ill and got something from the doctor to rub her back with, Miss Pirie said she got a pain in her back also, and she asked for some of the same stuff. But I don't know of her being rubbed with it."

"Miss Cumming," Lord Meadowbank asks, "were there any occasions such as you recently spoke of when you were doubtful as to what the plaintiffs were doing together?"

"Well, as I said, I didn't become quite sure until the last time of all, when Miss Pirie asked Miss Woods to come into the bed and she wouldn't for fear of waking me and Miss Stirling."

"But when you had suspicions earlier—and obviously they affected your mind so strongly—why did you not mention them to Miss Munro or any other person at that time?" he wishes to know.

"Because I was ashamed, and I never wished to speak of it."

"Miss Cumming," the Lord Justice-Clerk asks, "upon any of the occasions when the mistresses were in bed together, did you feel anything wet in the bed?"

"No."

"The next morning after these occasions, did you ever perceive any stain upon the sheets?"

"No."

John Clerk continues. "When did you first mention to anyone out of school that you suspected or believed that the mistresses had been conducting themselves indecently?"

"It was some days after my grandmama had come home."

"To whom did you mention it?"

"Well, I was going to tell it to one of my aunts, Miss Sophia, but she wouldn't hear it. Then she said that if I had anything bad to tell she didn't want to hear it, but I wouldn't have to go back to school that night, so I could tell it the next morning to my grandmama."

"Did you understand that your aunt Mrs. Forbes had the charge of you in your grandmother's absence?"

"I don't know what charge Mrs. Forbes had over me, but she told me just to consider her house as my home whenever my grandmama was gone."

"Why did you not tell Mrs. Forbes what had happened?" John Clerk asks.

"For one thing, she was nursing at the time. And for another thing, I thought she wouldn't understand what I meant."

"When you told your grandmother what had happened, what did she say?"

"Well, at first she was against my going back to the school. Then afterwards she said I should go back. And a few days later, as soon as she could she brought me home again."

"Miss Cumming, did you ever meet with the maid Charlotte Whiffin after you left the school?"

"Yes. I think it was the next day, but I'm not sure. I was with Miss Dunbar, one of my cousins."

"What did you say to Miss Whiffin?"

"I asked her how she did. And I think I asked her if Miss Stirling and Miss Munro were gone. And I remember she told me that Mrs. Kennedy had come and taken away Miss Hunter in a great hurry. And that there was a coach at the door waiting for the Miss Frasers. Then she asked me what I was taken away for. And I think that I answered—but I'm not quite sure—that it was about the beds."

"What did Charlotte say?"

"Well, she looked surprised. Then she said, 'Don't mention my name and don't tell that you saw me,' or something like that."

"When Charlotte told you that the young ladies were taken away, did you express any joy?"

"I don't remember, but if I did at all it was because Miss Munro was taken away."

"Did you clap your hands, turn round, and say to Miss Dunbar, 'Do you hear, Margaret, they're all gone from the school'?"

"I don't remember doing that, but I will not say that I didn't do it."

"Well, did you feel any joy on the occasion of the other young ladies being taken away?"

"I remember I felt very happy, but it was because Miss Munro was taken away."

"Miss Cumming, did you behave with respect to Miss Woods as long as you continued at the school?"

"I was very fond of her."

"Were you fond of her to the last?"

"I was always fond of her, unless when I thought of that."

"Miss Cumming, did you ever ask to sleep with Miss Woods?"

"Yes. I don't recollect the time, but I think it was one of the days when Miss Munro went home to sleep."

"Didn't Miss Woods complain of your officious attention in handing her bread and tea and such when she did not want them?"

"I remember Miss Woods complained of my handing her bread, but not tea."

"Did Miss Woods not frequently complain of your officious attentions?"

"I don't remember that, but Miss Woods often used to say I was very selfish."

"Were you anxious to be next to Miss Woods in walking?"

"Yes, when I had not my cousins to walk with."

"Did you ever bespeak Miss Woods' arm in walking a day beforehand?"

"I think I recollect I may have done that at some time."

"Didn't you continue anxious to be next to Miss Woods in walking right down to the time you left school?"

"Yes, except when my cousins were with me."

"Did you on any occasion when Miss Woods was angry with you for ill behaviour send Miss Margaret Dunbar to beg that Miss Woods would be reconciled with you?"

"I may have. I don't remember."

"Do you recollect a windy night in October when Miss Pirie was out all night?"

"I remember something of it, but not distinctly."

"You were told that Miss Pirie was in James' Square that night and could not return for the violence of the wind."

"Yes, I think I remember being told so. But not distinctly."

"Did you sleep by yourself that night?"

"The only person I ever slept with at Drumsheugh was Miss Pirie."

"Were you excessively frightened that night?"

"I remember being frightened one night. I think it was that night."

"Did you bang on the partition wall to Miss Woods to come to you?"

View from Princes Street of the Old Town in Edinburgh,
where Jane Pirie grew up (c. 1814)

Leith Harbor from the Pier, near Jane Pirie and Marianne Woods'
Drumsheugh school; colored aquatint by W. Daniell (c. 1822)

Gordonstoun, Lady Cumming Gordon's estate. Today the estate is a school, which Prince Charles attended.

The coat of arms at Gordonstoun—*"Sans Crainte"* (Without Fear)

Lady Cumming Gordon's house at 22 Charlotte Square, Edinburgh (1981)

Typical Charlotte Square art of the early nineteenth century from the Georgian House, 7 Charlotte Square

No portraits of Jane Pirie and Marianne Woods exist today but these popular representations of romantic friendship are typical of the early nineteenth century:

The Duchess of Devonshire and Lady Duncannon, engraving by W. Dickinson after a painting by Angelica Kauffman (1741–1807), detail

The Two Friends, engraving by William Dickinson (1746–1823) after a painting by C. Knight (c. 1800)

Engraving by J. Thomson after a painting by George Henry Harlow (1787–1819). The engraving has the following inscription: "CONGRATULATION. Nay! turn not those dear eyes away. The tender truth is now revealed."

A Lady Painting and Two Figures, oil on canvas, by Matthew William Peters (1741–1814), detail

Mrs. Woods (*left*) in the tragedy *Douglas* during her brief career as an actress; Mrs. Siddons (*center*) was the most beloved British actress of her century. (Kay's *Portraits,* 1784)

Among the judges on the Court of Session:

Charles Hay, Lord Newton: it was claimed he never heard a case without first imbibing six pints of claret. He died soon after rendering his decision in favor of the defendant. (Kay's *Portraits*)

(LEFT) William Baillie, Lord Polkemmet: a member of one of the wealthiest families in Britain, described by a contemporary as a "good man, but huge and brainless" (Kay's *Portraits*)
(RIGHT) William Miller, Lord Glenlee: his son was married to one of Lady Cumming Gordon's daughters. (Kay's *Portraits*)

Charles Hope, Lord Justice-Clerk: he presided over the Second Division of the Court of Session. The record indicates his performance was perhaps not as intelligent as his appearance. (Kay's *Portraits*)

Allan Maconochie, Lord Meadowbank: he was known to be an extremely conscientious judge who was often blinded by pride and prejudice. (Kay's *Portraits*)

"I don't remember."

"Do you remember nothing of Miss Woods staying with you on account of your fears that night?"

"No."

"Are you quite sure, Miss Cumming?"

"Objection, your honours, the witness has already answered that question," Erskine says. The objection is sustained.

"Miss Cumming, didn't you always sit next to Miss Woods at work?"

"Not always, but sometimes when I could I would."

"Didn't you always express a desire to sit next to her at work?"

"No. Sometimes I did."

"Was that on account of the preference you gave Miss Woods before Miss Pirie?"

"Yes."

"Do you remember the quarrel you had with Miss Cunynghame?"

"Yes, it was about the decorum card. I wrote about it in the book my grandmama gave the clerk this morning."

"Did Miss Woods turn you out of the room that evening for behaving ill to Miss Cunynghame?"

"Yes."

"Did you come back desiring to speak to Miss Cunynghame?"

"Yes."

"Did Miss Woods tell you that Miss Cunynghame was too good to speak to you and order you again to leave the room?"

She sobs.

"You must answer the question, Miss Cumming," the Lord Justice-Clerk tells her.

"Yes," she answers.

"Did you have a dispute with Miss Edgar about the decorum card?"

"Very often."

"Do you recollect one occasion in October in which Miss Pirie took Miss Edgar's part in such a dispute?"

"No."

"Do you recollect being provoked at Miss Pirie because of such a dispute?"

"I don't remember that particular dispute at all, so I can't recollect being provoked at Miss Pirie for it."

"Did you have a dispute with your washerwoman at the beginning of November last?"

"I don't remember any quarrel with the washerwoman. But I remember a short time before I left the school Miss Pirie scolding me for having forgot to put some of my things in the dirty bag. And I think the washerwoman was angry at me for having marked more down on my list than there was in the bag. I think I wrote about it in the book the clerk now has."

"Miss Cumming, did Miss Pirie ever censure your feeling or your heart in the presence of the other girls?"

"I don't remember her doing that before the other girls. I do remember her once finding fault. I think it was during the holidays."

John Clerk has no further questions. Lord Meadowbank wishes to know if Miss Pirie did not usually sleep with a bedgown and wrapper and petticoat on.

"Yes, I think she usually did."

"But you said you observed your mistresses in their night shifts."

"I meant in the night things in general."

"Then you meant to say that Miss Pirie lifted up her bedgown and wrapper and petticoat, all in one motion?"

"Yes."

Lord Robertson wishes to know if she perceived any puffs of air come up from between the bed clothes when Miss Woods was in motion above Miss Pirie. She did not.

"Did you observe whether Miss Pirie made any corresponding motion to Miss Woods' motion?" he asks.

"I don't think Miss Pirie moved," she answers.

There are no further questions. The Court is adjourned until the following day.

Lord Robertson's Notes
on the Testimony of Miss Jane Cumming,
March 29, 1811

She is entirely dark and has little trace of British features. One wonders if her mother did not invent a tale for young Mr. Cumming. Yet while I can believe the possibility of her mother's invention in that sort of circumstance, I can less readily believe the possibility of Jane Cumming's invention in this instance. First of all, I am certain that her upbringing, here rather than in India, and careful tutelage of Lady Cumming Gordon herself, must render her different from her female parent—but my incredulity also has to do with the nature of the tale she was supposed to have invented.

What is this story that the plaintiffs claim three girls dreamed up? Not an ordinary offense, such as may be supposed to have fallen under their observation. But rather, if we can believe the plaintiffs, these girls have, from their own imaginations, devised a story of an offence which our honourable Lord Ordinary, a not unworldly man in his sixties, had claimed never to have heard of. It is my opinion that the young ladies have said only what they saw and heard, and that it is impossible that they could have invented these things had they not observed them. Even if I could believe all three of them capable of the greatest mischief—and I can't—I could not believe them capable of such a virtuosity of imagination.

Although I see a considerable amount of confusion in evidence, it is not sufficient as to shake Jane Cumming's credibility as to the main point. Her examination extended over three days, and the cross-examiner was obviously very set on trapping her. Such an ordeal could scarcely fail to produce embarrassment and even some disorientation in the mind of a young girl. She swears to four or five different occasions when the mistresses were in bed together. Since the events often resembled one another, it is to be expected that she would confound what passed at one time with what happened at the others. But she essentially corroborates all that Miss Stirling and Miss Munro have said.

Even were I convinced to doubt Miss Munro and this dark, spurious natural grandchild of Lady Cumming Gordon, and to believe they could have invented such a story on their own, I have the strongest conviction that Miss Stirling is entirely scrupulous. If she is discredited, we must believe that such a gentle-seeming young lady, of the age of innocence, of purity, of candour, had entered into the most abominable conspiracy to ruin the fortunes of two women from whom she has received no injury, and to overwhelm these women with infamy. My mind has difficulty in conceiving of Miss Stirling taking part in such a wilful and deliberate conspiracy to commit perjury.

Lord Justice-Clerk Hope's Notes on the Testimony of Miss Jane Cumming March 29, 1811

I can make nothing of Miss Cumming's testimony with regard to the situation of the legs. But that is nothing compared with the physical improbability she describes. She says that Miss Woods was lying above Miss Pirie, and that she felt them both pull up their shifts. To say nothing of the petticoat (which only came out later), it must be remembered that this relates to women's shifts reaching to their feet and having no opening. Lay two women flat, one above the other, and I venture to say that they cannot then pull up their shifts. Another thing is that if this indecent conduct had been going on, would the shifts not have been up before? In short, the whole circumstances detailed by Miss Cumming appear to me to be grossly incredible.

If I had been sitting as a single judge, listening to her testimony, I should have committed Miss Cumming for prevarication. I felt inclined to move it, and I fear I was swayed by too much respect for the family of Lady Cumming Gordon to do so. Lord Armadale and myself, sitting in the Justiciary Court at Glasgow, sent a woman to the pillory for less prevarication than Miss Cumming was guilty of.

Also, I cannot help observing that any hesitation which she showed in the course of her examination was *never* in the points of *indecency,* but always when she was called on to reconcile her own contradictions. She was *thinking* and *contriving.*

Lord Meadowbank's Notes on the Testimony of Miss Jane Cumming, March 29, 1811

As I suspected, Miss Cumming, as well as Miss Munro, frequently incurred the punishments of the school. Miss Cumming seems to have received very severe rebukes, Such discipline was likely enough to have inspired not only a strong distaste for the school, but strong feelings of resentment towards the mistresses.

It is especially interesting that despite such apparent resentment, Miss Cumming professed great fondness for Miss Woods, to the last of her attendance at the school. And even after all the pretended detections, she admits to having asked to share Miss Woods' bed when Miss Pirie happened to be absent. How is it then that the breaking up of the school and the ruin of the woman on whom she showered affection did not excite the slightest feeling of distress in Miss Cumming? On the contrary, it was a matter of exaltation and joy to her. I detect something inscrutable and disturbing about this child of India.

LORD GLENLEE'S NOTES
ON THE TESTIMONY OF MISS JANE CUMMING,
MARCH 29, 1811

I can discover no contradiction as to the important and fundamental articles in this testimony. Hope afterwards laughed at Miss Cumming's confusion with regard to her leg and in what position it was lying when she felt with it both the mistresses' legs. I must say that, mathematically speaking, I do not know if I could construct the problem. I have never tried and I am sure I never shall: first, because it is a very disgusting subject; and secondly, because I do not conceive it to be at all necessary. If she actually observed them in bed, what earthly motive could she have for inventing a false story to account for how she observed them? When we observe anything, we never notice the process of observation, if it be easy. The process passes so rapidly through the mind that we do not remark the steps of the observation which gives us a certainty of the fact observed. At this moment, I see the two sides of this room. If I am asked how I saw both sides of the room, I would say that I looked first at the one side, and then to the other. In this I know that I am right. But it is by reflection that I know this must have been the process, which passed so rapidly in my mind that I did not notice it at the time. We are not conscious of such operations of the mind. We discover them only by reflection. Now, when a witness is cross examined upon a point of this kind, she is pardonable if she calls in imagination a little to assist her recollection. And if she is led partly by imagination not to give a very intelligible view of her observation, it does not militate against the fact that she actually did observe what she described. In short, as I believe she did feel both legs, it is of no importance *how* she discovered that they were both there.

With regard to the noise, I really do not understand it, and therefore lay it entirely out of view.

As to her hesitation and the different accounts she has given, which Hope is also making much of, it seems to me that all of these are about things that do not require accurate observation at the time. So any contradictions as to such points do not in the least affect me.

July 12, 1982

Eleanor Butler, who lived at about the time of this trial, kept a diary. She was one of the "Llangollen Ladies," the paragons of romantic friendship so admired by Wordsworth and his contemporaries. In the diary, which traced the life she led with her beloved Sarah Ponsonby for over fifty years, she referred often to her dreadful headaches, which allowed her to stay in bed all day with "my Sally, my Tender, my Sweet Love lying beside me holding and supporting my Head," "never leaving me for half a moment the entire day," "reading to me for near two hours," "a day of tenderness and sensibility." Perhaps if people are forced to repress, that repression manifests itself in headaches or in rheumatism, which requires of the other interested party the most intense patting and petting. Ollie points out that I am sounding very Freudian. But what I am referring to is not precisely repressed sexuality. I think what is important to many women today about sex is not just the variety of genital sensations, but rather that the beloved pays absolute, concentrated attention to their person. Ordinary romantic friendship in other centuries would not have allowed such concentrated attention, not to one's *person* at any rate. So I wonder if headaches and rheumatism were not simply a way of guaranteeing one would get that sort of concentrated attention. I have seen one monkey at the zoo pick fleas from the coat of her female monkey friend for more than an hour, both animals rapt by the activity. Perhaps if they had had fleas Eleanor Butler and Jane Pirie would not have had to have headaches or rheumatism.

Marianne Woods massaged Jane Pirie for rheumatism, and maybe in this freezing, rheumatism-inducing Scottish weather (it is the middle of July now and the temperature is 36 degrees Fahrenheit) there were occasions when Pirie had to massage Woods as well. I do not think the Indian girl mistook their massages for other things, since she invented a dialogue to accompany whatever activity she made up. But Janet Munro might have been awakened by one woman vigorously massaging the other. On her own she might have thought nothing of it, or she might have understood it for what it really was. But if Jane Cumming had done the interpreting

191

for her, had told her that the motion she observed was caused by their erotic play, she might have ignored the real and obvious explanation and analyzed all the innocent occurrences through Cumming's tale.

Ollie says the more she studies the court records the more certain she becomes that Jane Cumming was simply describing what she saw. I only become surer of this Indian girl's villainy. But I do not think she was evil. I can easily understand what motivated her even outside of my half-dozen reasons. She was attacked from all sides at the school: Woods told her she was officious, Pirie slept so far away from her that there was a bunting board of a lump between them. Miss Edgar and Miss Cunynghame fought with her. Only her young cousins appear to have tolerated her, and they were probably forced to by their grandmother. When Miss Munro came, perhaps Jane Cumming thought that here was a creature she might control and manipulate. I do not imagine that she wanted to control her out of some evil impulse, but rather because she had been powerless, an outcast of sorts. She had some prestige that she might claim as a relation of Lady Cumming Gordon's; no doubt the mothers of all the girls hoped their daughters would befriend her so that they might get invited to Gordonstoun or Altyre or Charlotte Square. But in fact, in the isolated atmosphere of the school, from which Lady Cumming Gordon was far removed, she was only a dark girl among white girls. She knew that many of these girls' fathers and grandfathers and great-grandfathers had gone to India as members of the conquering race, that her ancestors were the conquered; but what could have reminded her of her connection with the conquerors when she was away from the Cumming Gordon household?

Or even when she was there? How real could her alleged father, George Cumming, have been to her? He died when she was little more than a baby, and while he lived, how much did she see of him? He was himself almost a child—barely in his twenties when she was born. How much patience and affection would he have given to a dark-skinned, illegitimate baby daughter?

What ferocious resentment must have been inside her. Mary Tilford had no cause to hate as Jane Cumming had. Her malice could only be explained as the blind villainy of a bad seed. But Jane Cumming! How miserable she must have been as an eight-year-old child, being carried, without the possibility of resistance, from hot India to frigid Britain—to be brought to gray, palatial Gordonstoun, with its dining room and drawing room each sixty feet long, with its turreted wings and its coats of arms mocking her by their inscription, *sans crainte* (without fear, the gray-haired, stiff white woman who called herself her grandmother would have explained), while she herself had so very much fear, with the grand portraits of courtly white men and haughty white women who had lived generations before, with the acres of trimmed shrubbery and manicured grass, with the private lake on which British swans floated decorously. What had all this to do with her?

Nor would it have made her feel happier to know that the man who supposedly sired her was an eldest son, and had he lived he would have inherited all this. If she believed he would have brought her to the Scottish Highlands one day and recognized her as his daughter, her sense of loss would have been intolerably bitter. But more likely, she understood that had he lived he would have returned to Scotland and left her and her mother behind in Patna. He would have married a white woman and had legitimate children—and Gordonstoun would have been theirs, never hers. She would have been smart enough to understand that she had been brought to Gordonstoun only because young George Cumming had died before he could have any white children, and so she was all of him that was left to his mother. If the old woman could not believe the girl had come out of her eldest son's loins, then she was bereft, with nothing of him left to her.

Jane Cumming would have understood that she was tolerated by the family not for herself but for the sake of the dead man and his mother. When she was sent away to the Elgin school for shopkeepers' daughters it must have been both a relief to leave that cold mansion and a cause for more fury and hatred. How could she have loved any of them?

Whom had she to love in the whole world? When she permitted herself to have a very typical school girl crush on one of her teachers, she was rebuffed even there. I would have been devastated had my Executive Director treated me like that. When she smiled at me or said a kind word I could think of nothing else for days. Once when I came early to the Theatre Arts Showcase I sat in a chair she had occupied, over which her light blue sweater, redolent with her perfume, was still draped. I let my fingers rest on the soft sweater all the while I sat there. I can feel it and smell it to this day. I was in ecstasy. How potent such passions are to the young. And Jane Cumming received nothing but disdain in return for her devotion. The white woman who rebuffed her and the other who was ostensibly favored by her cruel mistress would have been good targets at which to spit out her bitterness at her life and the whole white world. Perhaps she simply did not calculate how far her spittle would fly.

WITNESSES FOR THE PLAINTIFFS

I am surprised that John Clerk seems to have thought it unnecessary to summon many witnesses for Miss Woods and Miss Pirie. Perhaps he believed, with the cockiness for which he was famous, that he had so effectively demolished the defendant's witnesses in his cross-examinations that little was left to be done, and he saw no reason to exert himself more than necessary. Or perhaps after the ineffectual testimony of the first witness he called, Helen Campbell (about which she wrote the Court on March 31, 1811, saying she regretted being so nervous that, she felt, she had not done Jane Pirie justice), he decided that the fewer women required to take the stand for his clients, the better.

Of course he had Mrs. Ann Woods summoned, and he must have been somewhat taken aback when she addressed a long letter to the Court, explaining that she could not come in person. But after reading her letter he must have been relieved by the thought that she might not have to take the stand.

> April 3, 1811
> Honourable Lords of the Court of Session,
> I have been summoned to appear before you, but as my doctors will swear, I have been very ill lately and am still very weakly. Therefore, I hope you will accept my written testimony and not require me to leave my bed. I

will send this letter through my niece's lawyer, and I will swear before him that everything I say is truth, just as it would be if I appeared before you.

As for my first associations with my niece, they date from her childhood, when she came to live with my husband, the actor William Woods, and myself on various occasions. Then, when she was aged fifteen or thereabouts, she came to live in my home permanently. Mr. Woods and I endeavoured to give her as good an education as was in our power and to instil in her the best principles, with a view to enabling her to earn her own bread by her accomplishments and good character. I found her always a well-disposed and well-principled girl.

After she received training from Mr. William Woods, she at first assisted him in teaching. Then, when she came of age, Mr. Woods, thinking her perfectly qualified, made her independent of him, and she began to teach on her own account. Soon after that she went to Camden House Boarding School in London, not with a view to learn anything herself, but as a teacher, and also to see how a large establishment of that kind was conducted.

I believe that some time before my niece went to London she formed an acquaintance with Miss Pirie, and I think it was by attending the same classes in Edinburgh, although my niece is not at home at the moment so I cannot ascertain if my recollection is correct. From their views in life being the same, and perhaps from a favourable opinion of each other's abilities, they appeared to form an attachment to each other. I was not much acquainted with Miss Pirie at the time, but I cannot say that I thought she possessed that polish of manners which my niece had acquired. However, I had no objection to her in a moral or religious view. On the contrary: since I always have known that I might rely on my niece's virtue and discernment, I was quite satisfied that she would not have associated with Miss Pirie unless her morals and principles had been unexceptionable. With regard to Miss Pirie's temper, I knew her so little so as not to be a

judge of it at the time, although I have had many unhappy experiences with it since.

But to get to the major points, my Lords—when the
school at Drumsheugh was set agoing, it was ultimately
agreed that I should take a share in the concern, and I
began with my niece at Whitsunday, 1809. Miss Pirie
joined us at the Martinmas thereafter. I did not know,
until I understood from certain circumstances that happened after Miss Pirie came to the school, that I was to
take no further concern then in the management of the
domestic affairs of the establishment.

During the first half of the year there were few boarders, and we suffered a loss of about £75, although, as I am
sure your Lordships have discovered already from the
records which I kept and have submitted to you through
my niece's lawyer, the school began to grow rapidly
thereafter, and was soon a success.

But to continue on the main point, my Lords—after
Miss Pirie joined us she seemed to be very discontented
and unhappy, and she behaved in a very imperious manner toward me, and indeed also toward my niece, or so I
thought and still believe. She would never express any
specific cause of such discontent, except one which had
arisen out of the circumstances of the school having been
conducted for the first half-year by myself and my niece.
As soon as we heard to what Miss Pirie objected, we rec-
tified it. This cause of complaint was very simple: the
tradesmen's bills for articles furnished to the house were
made out chiefly in my name. Well, Miss Pirie took offence at this. Although, as I say, we attempted to rectify
the misunderstanding with the tradesmen as soon as possible, this did not appear to do away with the differences,
as there continued to be a dissatisfaction and discontent
on the part of Miss Pirie, both toward me and my niece. I
certainly thought Miss Pirie behaved ill to me and my
niece, particularly since everything was done to satisfy
her, and all our efforts met with no success.

I can swear that my niece complained to me often of
Miss Pirie's conduct, and she told Miss Pirie, in my pres-

ence, that she thought Miss Pirie tried to make the scholars treat her with disrespect, and that though she had put up with this for some time, if Miss Pirie persisted in it, she might depend upon it, she would expose her before the scholars. I said nothing at all in the midst of this since I hoped their own good sense would make them see the impropriety of this.

It was about this time that my niece told me in private that she was exceedingly unhappy and that she had thoughts of leaving the house without even telling Miss Pirie. I of course was very alarmed lest she should do this, and I remonstrated with her against leaving me alone with Miss Pirie. I believe this happened about six months before the school broke up.

I know they had many other quarrels, which I did not see directly. But from the little I did see, and from my niece's appearance and expressions of unhappiness, I think their differences rather increased, most particularly during the last three months that the school continued.

I should explain the reason I did not see many of their quarrels directly during the past months. During the spring, I believe it was, Miss Pirie and I had so particular a difference regarding her behaviour to my niece, and she insulted me so much, that I took a final determination to leave the house and not associate with Miss Pirie anymore for as long as I must continue in the house. After that I always took my meals in my own room, which were sent up to me from the schoolroom. I should also say that on the occasion of this very bitter quarrel that I just mentioned my niece and I left the schoolroom, and my niece told me that she herself would never again go to the schoolroom except for the purpose of teaching. After this quarrel my niece constantly supped with me in my room.

I wish to say finally that my niece never was on the stage as an actress at all, but once she danced a minuet for a benefit in honour of my late husband, William Woods, and once for the benefit of Mr. Aldridge's family, which was at the time in distress, when her parents permitted her to dance a minuet with Mr. Aldridge's son. She was then a very little girl, not more than ten or eleven years old. Mr. William Woods did not permit her to frequent the theatre, although he did occasionally allow her to go see the play on a Saturday when her studies were over.

My Lords, I have now written everything I know about this unhappy affair, and I pray it will suffice, as I have been and still am ill and very weakly and would find it a great hardship if I must appear before you to reiterate all that I have already said.

With my prayers that you will accept the above
as my full testimony, I am your humble servant,
Ann Quelch Woods, widow of the late William
Woods, Comedian of the Theatre Royal for
thirty years

I wish to add, my Lords, that despite my weak condition I have made every attempt to find work in order to support myself and my poor niece since the school was broken up, and I have been entirely unsuccessful in finding any suitable position. I attribute this to the horrid slander which appears to have blackened my name as well as my niece's. I am sure your Lordships will have sympathy with me for this woeful plight, which has affected not only my physical well-being, but my state of mind also.

John Clerk also asked that Dame Mary Cunynghame be summoned. She was the one parent who did not immediately withdraw her daughter from the school on hearing the rumor of the mistresses' conduct. She testified on April 4, 1811.

April 4, 1811, 1:00 p.m.

Dame Mary Cunynghame, spouse of Sir William Augustus Cunynghame, Baronet, aged fifty and upwards, is solemnly sworn and purged of malice and partial counsel. Present are Lord Justice-Clerk Hope, Lords Meadowbank, Newton, and Robertson, counsel, Jane Pirie, and Marianne Woods. John Clerk questions Dame Cunynghame for the plaintiffs.

"Lady Cunynghame, how did you come to know the plaintiffs?" he asks.

"My eldest daughter was a pupil at their school."

"How did you first become acquainted with the school?"

"Well, when Monsieur Turreau, who had been fourteen years in my family, was going to leave us, he was extremely anxious that my daughter should be put under the charge of a person who would take proper care of her, and he undertook to make inquiry. He reported to me that he had received the highest character of Miss Woods. But at that time Miss Woods' house was not ready. And so, since I also received a very high character of a Miss Weston, I placed my daughter with her, and probably would have had her continue there if Miss Weston had not gone to England. It was on Miss Weston's going to England that I sent my daughter to Miss Woods' school."

"Had you inquired from anyone else about the character of the school once it was opened?" John Clerk asks.

"Yes, I made a great many inquiries."

"Will you say from whom, Lady Cunynghame."

"Well, I cannot recollect. I made so many. I believe I remember in particular dining one day at Mr. Walker's at Dalry, where Lady Cumming Gordon was, and knowing that she had some young friends at the school, I inquired of her what was her opinion of it. Lady Cumming Gordon gave it the highest character. Also, one day, I remember I was accidentally in company with Miss Erskine of Cardross who I also understood had a young friend there. So I made similar inquiries at her, and I received the same satisfactory account. And then I also remember making similar inquiries at Mrs. Professor Dalzell, since I had many years before known that Miss Woods taught in that family, and I had heard the

Professor talk of her in high terms and recommend her to me in case I ever had occasion for a person in her line. But I cannot recall which of all these recommendations came first, after the one from Monsieur Turreau, I mean."

"Once your daughter became a boarder at the school," John Clerk asks, "did she ever make any complaint to you of anything she had observed there?"

"No, on the contrary. I was highly satisfied with the progress my daughter made. I took her away only because of the reports which began to be then in circulation to the school's disadvantage."

"Had you considered taking her away before?"

"Certainly not. On the contrary."

"Lady Cunynghame, how had you first heard the reports which you mentioned?"

"I received a letter from Lady Cumming Gordon."

She is shown the letter dated "Thursday morning" (November 15, 1810), and she affirms that it is the letter to which she just referred.

"After I received it," she continues, "I called on Lady Cumming Gordon to thank her for having stated to me that she had objections to the school. Then I asked her please to tell me exactly what those objections were. But her Ladyship said she did not wish to state them."

"So she never told you why she wrote to you suggesting that you remove your daughter from the school as soon as possible?"

"Yes, she finally did. I asked her a second time, and I mentioned that I did not wish to take my daughter from the school on a mere report of objections without knowing what those objections were. But Lady Cumming Gordon added then only that she was not at liberty to tell them. So then I asked her if all the parents had taken their children from the school on a general report from her Ladyship, without knowing the reason. I believe that Lady Cumming Gordon felt the force of this observation. She went out of the room, saying she would let me know in a few minutes whether she was at liberty to tell me or not. Then she returned shortly after and she said she did not feel herself at liberty. So I told her that I most certainly should not take away my child from the school without knowing the reason—but that since there was so much mystery about it, I would go myself to Miss Woods and state to her the manner in which I was desired to take my daughter from the school. Her Ladyship then said that if I would call again in two hours she would obtain leave to tell me."

"Did you do as she requested?" John Clerk asks.

"Well, I told her that it appeared to me to be very extraordinary that her Ladyship should find it necessary to obtain permission to tell the reason to me, the parent of the child, but since it was so, I would do what she requested, with pleasure."

"When you returned after two hours, what did Lady Cumming Gordon tell you?" Mr. Clerk asks.

"I didn't return after two hours, it was close to four hours. In the interim I went home and I found waiting for me a lady who asked, 'What have you done with Mary?'—that is my eldest daughter's name. I replied, 'She is at Drumsheugh.' And the lady answered, 'Then you must not lose a moment in taking her away, for I have just taken away my two daughters.' I asked her what was the matter, and she replied that she did not know. So then it occurred to me that it might be the scarlet fever, of which I am in great dread. But the lady said, 'No, no, it is not that, but all the young ladies were already gone, except for one or two.' I said, 'Well, well, my daughter has been so long there that there can be no harm in her staying a day longer, until I inquire further about the matter.' Upon this the lady rose to her feet and said in great earnestness, 'Lady Cunynghame, if you are not particularly engaged you had better drive to Drumsheugh and take your daughter away immediately.' "

"Did you follow her admonishment?" John Clerk asks.

"Certainly not. I now thought it even more prudent to make further inquiries. Since it was not yet the time when Lady Cumming Gordon would see me again I drove to Mrs. Dalzell's and I said, 'What is this, Mrs. Dalzell, that has been going on at Miss Woods' school? I understand all the children are taken away, and they are making a sad piece of work.' Mrs. Dalzell said, 'I do not know, but I suppose your Ladyship has received a letter from Lady Cumming Gordon.' She knew that several parents had. So we decided to drive to Drumsheugh and call for Miss Woods, whom we saw. I said to Miss Woods immediately, 'I suppose you know the purpose of my coming here?' And Miss Woods replied, 'I too well judge it.' Then I said to her, 'Miss Woods, I don't know what has happened, but I am grateful to you for the kindness and attention you have always shown to my daughter. There are only Mrs. Dalzell, myself, and you present. If you have done anything imprudent and will disclose it confidentially to me, you may rely on my advice and assistance to the utmost of my power to extricate you from the scrape, if possible, whatever it may be.' Miss Woods was much affected and with great emotion she thanked me for my kindness, but, she said, 'I cannot avail myself of it, for I am myself utterly ignorant of what was laid to my charge and I am not conscious of anything.' "

Lady Cunynghame is silent for a moment, and then she weeps. John Clerk suggests to the judges that it may be proper here to insert in the transcripts that Lady Cunynghame was herself much affected when she narrated these circumstances. Lord Justice-Clerk Hope assents. Lady Cunynghame continues.

"I'm sorry," she says. "Then Miss Woods, in great agitation, threw her arms around Mrs. Dalzell and earnestly entreated her and me to endeavour to find out of what the school was accused."

"Did you take your daughter from the school then?" Mr. Clerk asks.

"No, not then. I was so extremely affected with Miss Woods' behaviour that I said to her that I could not bring myself to take my daughter from her under such circumstances, and that I would at least delay until the next day. Then Miss Woods herself said to me that as all the chief scholars were already gone she thought it was better that I should also take my daughter. But I still persisted and I left my daughter with her at that time. She expressed herself to be very grateful to me for my kindness in being the first person during that ordeal who entered the house or spoke a word to her on the subject. The others all sent for the girls without any kind of communication."

"When did you finally remove your daughter, Lady Cunynghame?"

"Well, after seeing Miss Woods I returned to Lady Cumming Gordon's house, and at that time she told me those particulars which had induced her to take away her grandchildren from the school. When I heard her story I said, 'Bless me, Ma'am, are you sure of it?' and Lady Cumming Gordon answered, 'O yes, you may rely upon it, there is no doubt at all about the matter.' "

"Will you tell the Court exactly what Lady Cumming Gordon told you," John Clerk asks.

She pauses a long while. "I would rather not," she says. "Is it not already known? Why must I repeat it?"

Lord Justice-Clerk Hope rules that she need not repeat what she was told.

"Was it at this point that you sent for your daughter?" John Clerk asks.

"Yes. I then thought it improper to show any more patronage to Miss Woods. I have not seen her since. I wish to add also that I then sent my daughter to Miss Weston, who had returned to Edinburgh in September. Well, Miss Weston finally accepted my daughter, but she told me that she had very great difficulty in taking her into the school because some of the parents objected. I understand from what Miss Weston said that if my girl had been examined as a witness in this case she would have had to leave Miss Weston's school. Miss Weston told me also that she positively refused to take two other young ladies on account of their having been with Misses Woods and Pirie."

Mr. Clerk says he has no further questions. Mr. Cranstoun rises.

"I have only one question, your Ladyship," he says. "Upon the second occasion when you called on Lady Cumming Gordon and she told you the particulars you alluded to, did she swear you to secrecy?"

"Yes. She cautioned me not to mention it to a single individual, not even to Sir William, my husband."

Lord Meadowbank wishes to know if she ever learned that Miss Cunynghame had received any information at the school or heard any surmise there of those improprieties about which Lady Cumming Gordon told her.

"Not in the least," she replies.

LORD JUSTICE-CLERK HOPE'S NOTES, APRIL 4, 1811

On April 3, 1811, at 4 P.M., the Court received from Mrs. Ann Quelch Woods, in response to a summons delivered to her April 2, 1811, a letter declaring that she is ill and begging to be excused from an appearance before the Court. Counsel for the plaintiffs requested that the letter be included in the Court record and serve in lieu of an appearance by Mrs. Woods. Counsel for the defence expressed no objection. Approved.

Mrs. Woods and Miss Pirie seem to have been slashing at each other like game cocks from the very beginning of their association. I surmise that it was Mrs. Woods who exacerbated the conflict between the two mistresses and kept it ever fresh. But the source of the conflict is at this point immaterial. What is significant is the evidence that shows that the mistresses fought incessantly, and no one can convince me that two females who are perpetually fighting and appear to despise each other can feel in the slightest degree lust toward one another. I may believe that a man can feel lust toward a woman whom he despises, but women are not so constituted from my observations.

Lady Cunynghame's appearance before the Court this afternoon has left a deep impression on me. It is regrettable that all the parents (not to mention Lady Cumming Gordon herself) did not respond as did Lady Cunynghame before they accepted hearsay evidence and acted in so drastic a manner . . . although in the presence of Lady Cumming Gordon's horrendous accusations even Lady Cunynghame's admirable circumspection collapsed and she did not continue her valiant efforts to uncover the truth of the matter.

There is no question but that it was Lady Cumming Gordon who spread the rumour of the mistresses' unnatural escapades, and she was thus responsible for the removal of all the children from the school. She appears to have acted in the most high-handed manner, without consciousness of the slightest obligation to explain to the parents whom she contacted of what she suspected the mistresses. But even more troublesome is her seeming oblivion to what was her duty to ascertain personally the truth of her suspicions before she had acted on them.

She would be vindicated in her actions only if it were certain that the mistresses truly did behave with unnatural impropriety. What I have been convinced of from the very beginning of my sad acquaintance with this case is that such manner of impropriety is inconsonant with all else that is known of the mistresses. What I witnessed in the courtroom today, as indirect a piece of evidence as it may be, confirms what I have felt from the start. I count it as exceedingly significant that Lady Cunynghame should have crumbled into tears when telling of the mistresses' plight. That the two mistresses had managed to win the trust and sympathy of this good lady, who appears to me to be a paragon of sound judgement, wisdom and modesty, speaks more in their favour, perhaps, than any piece of evidence I have yet heard.

WRITTEN TESTIMONY FOR THE PLAINTIFFS

John Clerk either saw no reason to or was not able to procure other witnesses to appear in court. However he did have the mistresses gather written testimony in their behalf.

Mrs. Hamilton, who had been Jane Pirie's confidante in the fall of 1809 and to whom Jane Pirie had written so feelingly, just before the disaster struck, of her love for and disappointment in Marianne Woods, sent a letter describing Jane Pirie as "a very conscientious, well principled young woman, rather irritable in her temper, but very ardent in the discharge of her duty; not of the most polished manners, but of great propriety in her moral conduct." She referred specifically to Jane Pirie's rheumatism, which was often so bad that Miss Pirie could not bathe or go out with her pupil. "I remember the more particularly," Mrs. Hamilton wrote, "since I was obliged to send out my own maid with the young lady." She also emphasized Miss Pirie's piety and how shocked Miss Pirie was when she discovered that one of the students at the school, who was very deficient in religious instruction, was going to be taken by her family to receive the sacrament. "She was extremely anxious to do everything in her power to prepare the young lady for it in a suitable manner. She asked my advice as to what books I would recommend to be put into the young lady's hands for that purpose." Finally, she alluded to Jane Pirie's complaints about Marianne Woods over the subject of Mrs. Woods and Jane's plea for advice in the matter. It is apparent that John Clerk coached Mrs. Hamilton on what points she must emphasize in the letter, which he would then incorporate into his argument.

John Clerk had Mrs. Dirom, Jane Pirie's first employer, emphasize similar points: "I can declare that I always considered Miss Pirie a very religious, sincere, good Christian, and the most indefatigable teacher I ever met with. I felt positively convinced that my girls were safe in her hands from all evil whatever, and that they were made to attend to their education. . . . The impression she gave them of a future state of the soul will, I hope, remain with them throughout their lives. . . . My only criticism of Miss Pirie," she added, "was that she had too great a warmth of feeling, such as proceeds from an ardent temper. On this point we differed often." That would explain to the Court why Miss Pirie's expressions of affection might have seemed excessive to a student or two, and it would corroborate that her emotional eruptions had nothing to do with Eros. Mrs. Dirom also emphasized the very moral nature of the mistresses' attachment. Jane Pirie "thought a residence with Miss Woods was to make her a much wiser and a better woman, and she told me so in a letter I still possess in which she informed me of the opening of the school."

An Episcopalian minister, Simon Reid, stated in his letter that he was called in at the start of November by Mrs. Woods, who thought herself ill used, to bring about an amicable separation between herself and Miss Pirie. Perhaps John Clerk hoped to confirm by Reid's letter that the conflict between the women was most intense just at the time when, according to the girls, they were supposed to have made loving night visits to one another.

I am surprised that Marianne Woods did not produce any substantive written testimony on her behalf. All that exists is a card from the Episcopalian Bishop Sandford, dated the preceding year, April 5, 1810, in which he requests that her students who are to be confirmed be brought to his house during the following week. At the end of the card he adds a thanks for the attention Miss Woods and Miss Pirie have given to his daughter's improvement: "Of that improvement the Bishop and Mrs. Sandford are daily more sensible. Their daughter speaks of her kind friends in terms of respect and gratitude, which, to the great satisfaction of her parents, show her to be a 'good scholar' in the best sense of the term."

The only other testimony for Miss Woods came from a George Thomson, the Principal Clerk to the Board of Trustees for Manufacturers, who had been a friend of her uncle, William Woods, and, as a frequent visitor to the actor's house, had had "opportunities of conversing with Miss Woods at table." John Clerk must have asked Marianne to solicit this note in order to assure the Court that although her uncle was an actor, she was never contaminated by the loose morals that, according to popular belief of the day, were ubiquitous among actresses. Thomson states: "I am certain that while in her uncle's family she was not allowed to associate with the ordinary female players. Although he was a professional actor, he brought to his home few theatrical people and often quipped to me that he preferred businessmen as being more down to earth, honest, and respectable. The few performers he associated with were of the greatest respectability. I know it was his earnest desire that Miss Woods should be educated in the most virtuous principles."

JULY 18, 1982

This weekend Ollie and I drove to Gordonstoun, which is in the north, not far from Elgin and the Highlands. In the village of Gordonstoun we stopped to ask directions to the estate from a muscular man of about forty, with rolled-up sleeves, who was pushing a wheelbarrow. I imagined him to look just like his ancestor, who probably tugged on a forelock before Lady Cumming Gordon. The mansion has been made into a private school for children of the fabulously wealthy. Our landlady here tells me that Prince Charles went to school there when he was a boy. Now many of the students are dark-skinned, the sons and daughters of Arab oil sheiks and African princes and Indian statesmen. So the dark-skinned have inherited Gordonstoun after all. Wonderful irony. It is a boarding school, and perhaps in Lady Cumming Gordon's very own bedroom such things go on as once made her blue blood pound with indignation.

The students, all dressed in white, were playing cricket in the field. On the main stairs that led to what must once have been the drawing room we passed another couple, a man and woman, who were probably the parents of one of the students. Ollie said hello to them as though we belonged there. There seemed to be no one else in the building so we were able to wander around alone. Perhaps the two or three adults on the field who must have seen us walk in assumed we were parents and had come to inspect our children's quarters. Ollie wanted to find the headmaster to see what he knew of the history of the place. But it is enough for me to know that the Cumming Gordon family had to relinquish this mansion. I was happy that I did not have to explain why we were there.

Although one of the gardens has been changed into a playing field, I think the rest of the grounds and the outside of the building remain the same. The coat of arms is still impressed on one side of the building. I knew what Gordonstoun would look like from the peerage books I had read, but I could not guess what it would feel like to me, being there. I am confirmed, I believe, in what I had in-tuited about Jane Cumming, how grand and terrifying this place must have been to her eight-year-old Indian eyes. But I also think that having seen Gordonstoun I understand Lady Cumming Gordon more than I had before.

With my American middle-class notion of luxury I could have had no idea how vast this place was. The small village outside Gordonstoun once belonged to the estate, and probably those who lived there labored in industries that were largely under the juris-diction of the Baronet of Gordonstoun. Between the village and the mansion there are perhaps two miles of parklike path, all once belonging to the estate. All around the mansion there are lush, green acres, and there is the lake on which the British swans still float. Lady Cumming Gordon was mistress of all she surveyed—

not only here but in Altyre as well, where now only a heap of old stones and five or six graves stand to mark the site of that palatial home.

What a terrible effect such power must have had on one who was not born kind and gracious. It must have felt insulating. Who might come near her, who could touch her, who dared to question her? She was a law unto herself. Hundreds were at her mercy: perhaps she did not have the power to declare life or death over them, but she had power over their livelihood, which was almost as prodigious a power as the other. As long as she sat in her mansion in Gordonstoun, in those days when the inefficiency of transportation limited visits from the world outside, she was Yertle, the Turtle Queen, and no one she could see, except perhaps her husband (who was anyway often absent with his legislative duties), was as high as she.

She would have taken that conception of herself wherever she went, even to Edinburgh, where she must have come in contact with many other Yertles. But knowing that Gordonstoun was home would have insulated her from any intimidation by their wealth or power. Except for an occasional Duchess she might meet, how could anyone be grander than she?

So, when she was outraged by the rumor of the mistresses' behavior, it would not have occurred to her that she needed to check the facts before she acted. Just as she had *made* the mistresses, virtually on a whim, she could *break* them, virtually on a whim. To whom was she accountable?

No, I must be more fair. Three days ago I found in the *Edinburgh Advertiser* for Tuesday, November 20, 1810, a short announcement: "The Lady of Sir Archibald Dunbar of Northfield, Bart. gave birth to a daughter last week." The child must have been born between November 10 and November 17. It was on November 11 that Jane Cumming told the shocking story to her grandmother. It was on November 14 that Lady Cumming Gordon sent a servant to fetch Jane and the two Dunbar girls from the school. On November 14 and 15 she wrote the letters telling the other parents that their children should be removed from the school immediately. Her daughter, Lady Helen Dunbar, her namesake and favorite, was in her mid-thirties. All Lady Dunbar's other children had been born in the previous century and she had thought that her childbearing days were over. She was old to be having another child. Many women died in childbirth in those days, and a woman's chances for survival were lessened when she was past the optimum age for giving birth. Even if Lady Cumming Gordon had not been the imperious curmudgeon I suspect she was, under these anxious circumstances, would she—or anyone—have exercised more care before sounding the alarm? As Ollie reminds me, she did not willingly repeat the infamous tale. She merely informed the parents that she had removed her grandchildren for serious reason and suggested they might wish to do the same.

But even if she did not accuse them of impropriety or immorality, she was nevertheless responsible for casting suspicion on those two women, who may well have been innocent under any nineteenth-century scrutiny of the matter. Regardless of whether she did it with all her senses about her or when she was distracted with cares for her daughter, Miss Woods and Miss Pirie were ruined.

JULY 23, 1982

We read in the Signet Library again today. While I was trying to locate the speeches of the attorneys and ploughing through one inconsequential memorandum after another, Ollie sat at a back table, reading from a loose, yellowed stack. She looked amused. Once she actually chortled, and in that vast, empty room the sound was absolutely booming. The librarian and the only other reader looked up at her, and I thought the librarian was deliberating about whether to ask her to leave. But Ollie assumed a more serious expression and the librarian kept her place.

I tiptoed over to her. "What's going on?" I whispered.

"I'll tell you later," she whispered back, without looking up.

I took the chair next to her and began reading from the pile she had finished. This is what she found:

MEMORANDUM ADDRESSED UNTO THE RIGHT HONOUR-
ABLE THE LORDS OF COUNCIL AND SESSION, FROM
GEORGE CRANSTOUN, SENIOR COUNSEL FOR THE DEFEN-
DANT IN MISSES WOODS AND PIRIE AGAINST DAME
HELEN CUMMING GORDON:

Because the Lord Ordinary in hearing had expressed
doubt of the existence of the vice in question, the defendant begs leave to provide proof of the Authorities with
regard to the practice of tribadism.

I. *Divines*

1. Paul, *Romans,* I, 26

"For this cause God gave them up unto vile affections:
for even their women did change the natural use into that
which is against nature."

2. Macknight

Dr. Macknight gives this commentary of the above
verse and subjoins the following note:

"For even the women changed the natural use of their
bodies into that which is contrary to nature, burning with
lust towards one another.

Note: 'For even their women changed the natural
use . . . '—The women of Lesbos are said, by the ancient
authors, to have been, many of them, guilty of this vice.
They were called Tribades. Martial inscribes the 90th
Epigram of his first book to a woman of that character,
named *Bassa.* See also Levit. xviii, 23. *Macknight on the
Epistles,* vol. 1, p. 158."

See also Hugonis Grotii, *Annotationes,* iv, 14 and
Mathew Poole, *Commentary on Epist. ad Romanos,* v.

II. *Law Writers*

1. Lord Royston

Lord Royston, in his notes on Sir George Mackenzie's
Criminal Law, on the Chapter of Sodomy and Bestiality,
thus writes:

"The Spanish authors, both Lawyers and Divines,
state many cases of those execrable crimes of sodomy and

bestiality, not fit to be named by Christians, and, I hope, never to be known amongst us. But in case such questions should come before a criminal Judge, as they deserve condign punishment, it is fit he should not be ignorant of the opinions of lawyers, and the practice of other nations in punishing them.

Gomez, Comment ad. Ll. Taur. leg. 80, states a great many cases and treats them with great learning, related to acts of women with women against nature. He mentions many different ways in which these abominations are committed, which must needs offend chaste ears.

These detestable crimes are treated of by the French Lawyers under the title of 'Luxure abominable,' see Paponius, where he cites many decisions, both as to bestiality and the unnatural pollution of women with women."

See also Julius Clarus, L.v. n. 29.
Conradus, Tit. de Sodomia, n. 4.
Petrus Caballus, Resolutiones, 19, n. 14.
Simon Van Lewen, Censura Forensis, L. v. c. 28.
Petrus Gregorius, L. 36. Syntaq. c. 14. n. 2.
Paponius, Corpus Juris Francici, L. xxll.

III. *Miscellaneous Authors*
See Juvenal, Sat. VI.
Ovid, Epist. Sappho ad Phaon.
Martial, passim.
Phaedrus, IV. 14. 1.
And the following:
    1. Lucian
A Dialogue between Cleonarium and Leaena:
"*Cleonarium:* I've heard strange rumours about you, Leaena. They say Megilla, that rich lady from Lesbos, caresses you as a man would. How is it, for God's sake? Tell me, is it true?
Leaena: Yes, it's true. But I'm ashamed because I know it's unnatural . . . although Megilla is terribly like a man.
Cleonarium: What do you mean? Is she the sort of woman who likes ladies? I hear that in Lesbos there are many women like that. They have faces like men, and

they do not like men. They wish to consort only with women, as though they were themselves men.

Leaena: Yes, that's right, I believe. . . .

Cleonarium: But how did it come about with you and Megilla?

Leaena: Well, . . . Megilla and another wealthy woman, Demonassa, from Corinth, had organized a revelry, and they hired me to provide the music. I played until late, and then it was time to go to bed. Well, they were drunk, and Megilla said to me, 'come Leaena, it's bedtime. You sleep between Demonassa and me. . . .' At first they only kissed me, like a man would do, not only touching my lips with theirs but opening their mouths and fondling me and pressing my breasts. Demonassa even bit me as she kissed me, and I didn't know what to think. Finally Megilla, who was by now rather heated, told me . . . that although she didn't have what a man has, she didn't need it at all. She said she had a much pleasanter method of her own . . . She said though she was born a woman like the rest of us, she has the mind and desires and everything that a man has. When I asked if she found those desires enough, she said, 'why don't you let me show you? If you give me a chance I will prove to you that I am as good as any man. I have a substitute of my own. . . .' Well, Cleonarium, I did, because she begged me so much and then she gave me an expensive necklace and a beautiful linen dress. So then I put my arms around her as though she were a man, and she did her job, kissing me, and panting, and obviously really enjoying herself.

Cleonarium: But what did she do? How did she do it? That's what I really want to hear.

Leaena: Oh, don't ask about the details. They're not very nice. So, by the goddess of love, I won't tell you."

2. Brantome

Lives of Gallant Ladies: "I once knew a courtesan of Rome. She was old and wily and her name was Isabella de Luna, a Spanish woman. She had this sort of friendship with another courtesan, who was called Pandera.

This Pandera eventually married a butler in the Cardinal d'Armaignac's household, but she never left her profession. Now, she was the mistress of the same Isabella, and because Isabella was so rowdy in her speech, she said many times, in my hearing, that she caused Pandera to give her husband more horns than all the wild fellows she ever had. I do not know exactly what she meant by this, unless her meaning was like that of Martial's Epigram: 'a strange thing that in the absence of a man, adultery might anyway be done.' "

3. Massinger

The Bondman, Act 2, scene 2:
"Corsica: Fie on these warres,
　I am starv'd for want of action, not a gamester left
　To keep a woman play; if this world last
　A little longer with us, Ladyes must studie
　Some new found Mistery, to coole one another,
　Wee shall burne to cinders else; I have heard there
　　have been
　Such arts in long vacation; would they were
　Reveal'd to mee."

4. Diderot

The Nun: "The Mother Superior kissed and hugged me. Then she sat me on her knee ... She lowered her eyes and tightened her hand that was around me even more. She squeezed my knee harder with her other hand. Then she pulled me to her, until my face was on hers. Then she sighed and fell back into her chair, shaking all over ... In a while she raised her collar and placed one of my hands on her breast. She said nothing and neither did I. She seemed to be feeling the most wonderful sensations. She asked me to kiss her forehead, cheeks, eyes, mouth, and I did as she bid me. I didn't think there was anything wrong in it. And since it made her pleasure increase even more, I was only too glad to add to her happiness in an innocent way. I kissed her everywhere on her face again. The hand that she had had on my knee now wandered all over my body, from my feet to my girdle, pressing me everywhere. Then she gasped, and she asked me in an odd, soft voice to kiss her more, and I did. Finally a moment came, I cannot say if it was of pleasure or of pain, when she turned as pale as death, closed her eyes, and her whole body stiffened suddenly. Her lips pressed together, and then they parted and became wet with a sort of foam. With a deep sigh, she seemed to expire."

See also Bayle, article *Sappho* and the authors quoted by him. *Confessions of a Young Girl* in *The English Spy*, vol. I, p. 197. *Paris as it was and is,* Vol. II, p. 214, London, 1803. Mirabeau's *Secret History of the Court of Berlin,* letter 47.

My own discoveries of the day were somewhat less amusing. The first was a document dated May 10, 1811, in which counsel for both the defendant and the plaintiffs beg the Lord Justice-Clerk to print enough copies of the transcripts so that they and all the judges might be able to peruse them. "Without this," counsel complained, "we must confess that we do not see how your Lordships can be enabled to pay attention to the details of the case, nor how the counsel in their pleading can do it the justice which it requires, owing to the length of the testimony to which references must be made." Apparently the Court continued to be concerned that word of the nature of the proceedings would reach the public and corrupt morals, and they hoped to lessen that possibility by not duplicating the transcripts.

In this document the lawyers assure the judges that they understand why the Court has been reluctant to print copies, but, they plead, secrecy regarding the case can be maintained if proper precautions are taken: "A person on whose secrecy we can depend may be procured to undertake the printing, the number of copies may be limited to whatever your Lordships shall think sufficient for the Court and the counsel, and at the conclusion of the case the copies may be destroyed or otherwise disposed of under the authority of your Lordships—so that any further disclosure than what has already taken place could only be to a very trifling degree."

In a document dated May 17, 1811, the Lords of Session agree that twenty copies of the testimony may be printed under the limitations suggested in the note, "with the additional proviso that all copies shall be lodged under seal with the clerk, at the disposal of the Court, the counsel being sworn to the faithful implementation of the regulations suggested."

Was it their intention to destroy all copies of the transcripts after the case was settled and pretend it had never happened?

The Speech of John Clerk, Counsel for the Plaintiffs, to the Lords of Session, May 22, 1811, 10:00 a.m.

My Lords, Miss Marianne Woods and Miss Jane Pirie are both children of respectable parents. From their infancy, they were educated in the strictest principles of religion and morality. They were taught to reverence and to practise all the duties and the restraints which Christianity enjoins. The past years of their lives have been spent in one continuous exertion to fill their minds with the knowledge which elevates the human character. They have laboured to cultivate by the propriety of their manner and by sober industry the friendship and the esteem of the wise and the good.

Years ago, my Lords, they had determined, each for herself, to devote themselves to an honourable and useful profession,—a profession which, above all others, demanded the most careful attention to the honour of the female character. Their studies, their habits, their employments, and their feelings all taught them to abhor anything even approaching to indelicacy in the mind or manners of a woman. And under the calamity of the weight which has fallen upon them, it is (next to the consciousness of their innocence) the greatest consolation that in all their efforts to become useful members of society their conduct has been above reproach.

The plaintiffs first became acquainted with each other about nine years ago. They met at a drawing school and soon formed a close friendship. Their pursuits being of the same nature, they assisted one another in them. Their friendship gradually increased into a settled and very sincere intimacy. They little thought that the mutual regard which springs from the finest and purest feelings of the human heart, and can only exist in pure and virtuous breasts, should be the source of the foulest condemnation and the means of imputing to them the blackest and most disgusting atrocity.

It is certainly true that the plaintiffs formed a friendship for one another of the strongest and warmest nature, which subsisted without alloy for many years. During a great part of this time they were much separated from one another. But their friendship continued unabated, and they pleased themselves with the idea of forming a school together.

In November 1809, Miss Pirie, who had scrupulously been labouring to fulfill a previous commitment, joined Miss Woods in their newly opened school. After this, the school gradually filled. In December 1809, Miss Jane Cumming, a native of India, by a woman of colour, and who had lived in India till the age of about eight years, was offered as a scholar by Lady Cumming Gordon, whose natural granddaughter she was. There was a hesitation in receiving her, my Lords, but in consideration of the respectability of the family, and by the influence of Lady Cumming Gordon, the mistresses were induced to accept Miss Cumming into the school.

The excellence of the school was soon established. In everything the plaintiffs consulted only the interests of the young persons entrusted to them. It is in evidence that during the whole day there was scarcely a moment in which one or the other of the mistresses was not employed in superintending the education or the conduct of their scholars. They attended strictly to the moral habits of the children in the most minute particulars. They taught them the regular practice of religious duties and took pains to instruct them in the principles of religion as well. They devised punishments for their faults which were calculated to correct and improve them. They laboured to cultivate their minds, both by useful knowledge and the habits of virtue.

But in the meantime, Miss Woods and Miss Pirie were (during the last six months at least) themselves passing their lives in the utmost misery. Because some misapprehension had occurred between Mrs. Woods and the tradesmen before Miss Pirie joined the school, Miss Pirie thought herself to have been degraded— represented as a governess in the school instead of one of its mistresses. Having once taken this idea, she could not divest herself of it. Despite the sincerity and warmth of her regard for Miss Woods, circumstances constantly occurred which she considered to be affronting to her. They led to frequent quarrels for many months before the school broke up. And it is *quite clearly proved* that these disputes were *at their very height* from the *end of August* to the middle or end of *October*—a fact of exceedingly great importance in this case.

But amidst all these disputes, though they found their friendship broken by distrust, they retained a great portion of that virtuous affection for one another that they had so long cherished. It is clearly in evidence by their conduct and their communication to others at the time. They struggled with the recollection and remains of past confidence and long cherished regard on the one hand, and with their jealousy, suspicion, disappointment, and wounded pride on the other.

As I have already observed, my Lords, their differences were at the greatest height from the end of August to the middle or end of October. Even then, being in a perpetual state of constraint during the whole day, they had little opportunity of seeing or talking to one another until the scholars were in bed.

As the plaintiffs readily informed you, my Lords, one of them almost always passed through the room of the other after she was in bed. On a few occasions they stopped and conversed, either standing by the side of the bed or sitting or reclining on the edge of it. They spoke in a low tone of voice, being anxious not to disturb the young ladies and to prevent them from hearing the subject of the conversation. The plaintiffs also inform your Lordships, without reserve, that in one instance Miss Pirie was in a state of great anxiety from a quarrel which had happened that day and on which she had had no opportunity of explanation. She went from her own bed to the bedroom of Miss Woods, and she sat down or reclined by the side of the bed while she conversed with her, certainly in as low a tone as the state of her feeling would permit. Also, though Miss Woods was never in the bed of Miss Pirie, on one occasion she had sat with her aunt until day broke, and Miss Pirie (who had been kept awake by hearing their conversation through a lath partition of two inches) called to Miss Woods as she passed through the room, and a conversation of mutual kindness and forgiveness followed.

However, despite such attempts at reconciliation, their unhappiness remained. Finally it was determined that Mrs. Woods should leave the family. Although Miss Woods felt severely the injury in separation from her aunt, she submitted to it as a matter of necessity. And the plaintiffs both hoped that the school might be conducted with more peace and cordiality in the future.

This was the state of affairs in November 1810: the quarrels had abated, the school continued prosperous and eminent, and there was no hint of dissatisfaction with the mistresses' conduct. Then, on the 14th day of November 1810, Miss Woods and Miss Pirie were, without notice, without inquiry, and without any communication, at once, by the acts of Dame Helen Cumming Gordon, involved in irretrievable ruin. Upon the Saturday preceding, Miss Cumming had gone home to her grandmother's on leave. She stayed the weekend, but returned *to the school* on Monday. It appears that she had in the meantime told the whole of the infamous story which she has since dared or attempted to detail.

After her return to school she was taken away again on the 14th, two days later. It was then that Lady Cumming Gordon wrote a note to the plaintiffs in which, without assigning any reason, she desired that Miss Cumming, together with her possessions and the possessions of the two Miss Dunbars, be sent home. Upon the same day and the next, all the scholars were taken away, one after another, without any cause whatever being assigned. It turned out that all this proceeded on the instigation of Lady Cumming Gordon, acting, as her counsel expressed it in the hearing, on the testimony of Jane Cumming, "a simple, innocent, veracious girl." It has become clear through cross-examination how simple and innocent and veracious this young lady, the inventor and disseminator of the tale, is. In the same way, her motives—her resentment of the strict discipline of the school and of the mistresses who did not favour her—have become clear.

Finally, by dark and distant hints, to their astonishment the plaintiffs learned that they were accused of an atrocity of which neither their knowledge nor their imaginations could give them any idea. And how then did they conduct themselves in this trying situation? Did they take guilt to themselves and fly from the place which had been the scene of their iniquity, fly from the country? Did they submit in silence to the ruin which had thus been brought on them? Were they content to escape the punishment which might be inflicted on such infamy? That is uniformly the conduct of those who are guilty of unnatural crimes and see that they have been detected. But very different was their conduct, my Lords. They asserted their innocence in the face of the world.

The plaintiffs complain then of an injury by which they lost their all: their all in fortune, but still more, their all in character, which they valued above everything else, and on which their very existence in society depended.

And can your Lordships imagine how the plaintiffs must have felt when they discovered what the defendant imputed to them? How entirely puzzled and outraged and sickened they were! She accused them of a sort of lewdness which is altogether unknown and unheard of. It is something that was never under the eye of a court of justice in the whole history of the world until this instant.

Now we do not wish to be misunderstood on this point. It was never denied that women might abuse their bodies with one another. Digitation or the use of instruments no doubt have been practised among females. And it is from the last of these practices that the women referred to by the ancient writers as Tribades derived their name and character. But as the ancients point out, those women committed their infamous acts with one another by the use of a *penis coriaceus,* an artificial object designed to resemble the male instrument of procreation. The defendant has never suggested that an artificial instrument was employed by the plaintiffs, nor has she been able to show any sufficient authority who states the act may be committed in any other manner. The defendant's counsel has referred to obscene books, but it is well known that in such books the human imagination is put to the rack to invent modes of gratifying the venereal passion which have no existence in real life.

But the defendant's counsel also alleged that this crime was mentioned in the New Testament. And if they were right it is the only one of all their authorities entitled to the slightest regard. The New Testament passage which the defendant's counsel refers to is in the first chapter of the Romans, "For this cause God gave them up into vile affections; for even their women did change the natural use into that which is against nature." It is very evident that even supposing this passage had referred to some infamous congress between two women, the proper inference would be that it was by the use of an instrument. But it appears quite clear that the practice referred to was that of *sodomy* between a woman and a man. Thus this text has been understood by the best commentators such as David Pareus, a German Professor of Theology, and Mathew Poole, an English Divine.

We humbly submit now that even the facts as alleged do not describe with any certainty venereal congress. Without previously assuming the veneral propensity, what is there criminal or improper in one woman coming into the bed of her friend? Or what is there wonderful in two women who were upon such intimate habits, and undoubtedly in a state of great excitation with regard to one another, conversing together in whispers when there were five or six young persons asleep in the room? And if the recollection of former friendships, the regrets for unrestrained passions, the contending feelings of pride, jealousy, and affection, all called forth strong emotions, would it be wonderful that some accidental motion of the bed should take place? Nay, even the pulling up of the shifts, *utterly false as it is,* would conclude nothing. They might be pulled up by accident. Miss Cumming herself was forced to admit that her own shift had got up without any particular reason. And certainly if one woman was in pain with rheumatism, and her friend kindly rubbed her for it, that would account for both the motion of the bed and a pulling up of a shift. What the defendant must prove is the plaintiffs' intention to commit venereal congress—and that she cannot.

If a man and a woman are in bed together, venereal congress would be presumed. And perhaps even if a man and a man are in bed together without necessity, an unnatural intention may be inferred. But a woman being in bed with a woman cannot even give a probability to such an inference. It is the order of nature and of society in its present state. If a woman embraces a woman, it infers nothing.

And therefore, in order to convict two women of unnatural behaviour, there must be facts concluding the intention, without the aid of any assumption or inference, and excluding every other supposition. Dame Cumming Gordon has been able to produce no such facts whatsoever.

May it therefore please your Lordships to decree in terms of the libel, and to find expenses due.

July 24, 1982

Knowing what I do of him, I could have guessed that John Clerk would not have neglected to take advantage of the prejudices of the day in his *argumentum ad puellam:* Jane Cumming is not a reliable witness because she is illegitimate, a native of India, and colored.

Ollie thinks that most of Clerk's major arguments adhered to one or another of his day's prejudices. "First of all," she says, "he claims the mistresses could not have done the shocking things of which they had been accused because they were religious, sober, and industrious; and unconventional sexuality is not consonant with those virtues. Secondly, he takes advantage of the simplistic clichés about romantic friendship by depicting the women's relationship as one that only those who are truly moral can form, a 'mutual regard which springs from the finest and purest feelings of the human heart, and can only exist in pure and virtuous breasts.' Then he also insists they could not have been lovers during the last months of the school's existence because that was the period during which their conflict over Mrs. Woods was the greatest, as though love and hate cannot coexist." Ollie points out that John Clerk had no interest at all in scrupulously depicting "how human beings behave." "Obviously everything he says about the mistresses might have been true, and they might still have had a sexual relationship," she insists.

"Had they lived today, yes," I say. "The psyche of our century has a great tolerance for contradiction."

"But it's not contradiction. It's how human beings really behave," she insists. "And anyway, I think the human psyche has always been full of contradictions, whether tolerated or not."

As I examine the striking contradictions in John Clerk's speech, I wonder if perhaps she is right. But did Clerk really believe what he said? I cannot make out whether his naïveté was feigned or genuine. Nor are his feelings clear about what he is claiming to be incredulous over. He acknowledges that women might "abuse" their bodies together, provided of course that they use a phallic substitute such as fingers or a dildo. But he ends by maintaining that on seeing two women in bed together, embracing, one can infer nothing. Is he saying one can infer nothing until one knows if they have brought a dildo along to bed (even though they always have their fingers with them)? Or can one infer "nothing" because women in his day were *permitted* all manner of passionate embraces with each other and such embraces were to all intents and purposes insignificant in the male view?

"Maybe he's implying that anything short of penetration is 'nothing,' " Ollie says. She likes that interpretation. She continues to insist that romantic friends were almost always sexual together, but they didn't call it sexual because everyone believed, as Brantôme said in the days of Henry II of France, "there is a great difference betwixt throwing water in a vessel and merely watering about it and round the rim." Sex in the nineteenth century meant—only and always—filling the vessel. Whatever women did, as long as it did not involve penetration, was not the real thing, either in their view or in men's view.

I cannot quite believe that. Surely if men thought that women brought each other to orgasm through cunnilingus or clitoral manipulation, they would be as maddened at that as at the notion of women's bringing each other to vaginal orgasm.

"But that's the point," Ollie says. "Men did not believe in the possibility of anything but vaginal orgasm, and women were intimidated into silence about how their bodies worked. I think most men believed one of two things: either, as you say, good women were not carnal enough to seek out erotic pleasures—or, if women were, without penetration nothing happened. So although Clerk finally concedes that women may abuse their bodies with each other, he can't admit any other possibility than penetration. That's why, without any evidence at all, he claims it is 'evident' that if Saint Paul was talking about lesbianism in that Romans passage, 'the proper inference would be that it was by the use of an instrument.' Women knew better, of course."

Perhaps. But I think I see something more complex at work here. It isn't simply a question of whether or not men thought that good women would seek out sexual pleasure, or whether or not men thought that sexual pleasure was possible without penetration. I suppose that on some level they understood that both were possible. But I think Clerk's patent self-contradiction shows something of how the male mind worked with regard to female sexuality in his day. He cannot believe what he knows is true. He *knows* that women can pleasure each other sexually, but he refuses to infer they are doing that, even if he should see them in a bed together, embracing.

Ollie's mother is an avid reader of "the best writers." She has told me that she read Hemingway's *Moveable Feast* and Roth's *Portnoy's Complaint*, so I know she can't have escaped from the knowledge that lesbianism exists, nor from the most graphic descriptions of women being sexual together. Ollie and I have no phony sleeping arrangements in our home as Ollie did when she lived with Sheila. Ollie's mother knows we share a bedroom and the one double bed in that room. Once she said to us, "It's really too bad you two can't marry; you would save so much money in income taxes." I was mute the rest of the evening. But Ollie swore her mother did not mean it as I took it. She was being her usual sweet, serious, helpful self, and any innuendo in such a remark would be completely beyond her. But what did she think Hemingway was talking about when he described his revulsion at hearing Gertrude Stein tell Alice B. Toklas, "I'll do anything, pussy"? Did she skip over the scene in which Portnoy is in bed with The Monkey and the prostitute?

"She understands that lesbians exist, and she knows what they do in bed," Ollie said. "But she cannot bring herself to make the connection between that and you and Sheila and all our friends and me—because these are women she admires and loves. Of course she knows deep down that we are like Gertrude and Alice, and that we do what The Monkey and the prostitute did, without Portnoy yet. But that knowledge is never turned into words, not even in her mind. She knows, and yet she does not admit even to herself that she knows."

Perhaps that was true of Clerk also. Men knew that women could reach orgasm through masturbation. Surely they did not believe that women always availed themselves of a candle. And what a woman could do to herself, she could do to another woman—with much more variation. Yet how could men admit what did not accord with their phallocentric views? Sex was for the purpose of pleasing men and bringing children into the world. How could sex that did not conform to those purposes exist? They knew it did—

but how could it? How much more comfortable to them it was to deny what they knew.

"Then you believe that Marianne and Jane really did have sex together?" Ollie asks.

No, I'm not saying that at all. I only think that sophisticated, well-read men then (just like Ollie's mother today) knew the possibilities, but dared not articulate what they knew, not even to themselves. And I suppose that was true of most nineteenth-century women as well. They must have known what they could do to each other. But to have admitted that into verbal consciousness would have denied all the dicta they had been so carefully taught about female passionlessness and "decency." So, like Ollie's mother, everyone knew and did not know at once. There was open agreement that if a woman were in bed with another woman, embracing, one could infer nothing. But everyone knew privately that one might infer a great deal.

THE SPEECH OF GEORGE CRANSTOUN, SENIOR COUNSEL FOR THE DEFENDANT, TO THE LORDS OF SESSION, MAY 24, 1811, 10:00 A.M.

The plaintiffs, through the eloquent pleading of their counsel, have described the calamity which has befallen them and the distress which they have endured on account of it. The magnitude of that calamity, supposing it to exist in the full extent that they have chosen to represent it, is but too apparent, and his heart must be callous indeed who can reflect upon it without emotion. That two young and unprotected females, born of creditable parents, possessing unblemished characters, and looking forward to an honourable and independent place in society, should be compelled to relinquish their employment, have their fairest prospects blasted, and their respectability forever destroyed, is an event calculated to inspire the deepest regret and commiseration. Besides, the offence laid to their charge is of such a nature that the mind turns from its contemplation in disgust. It is painful to imagine that a practice so injurious to the honour of the female sex should have existed in a respectable walk of life, and in a society pre-eminent for correctness of manners. It is scarcely possible to suppress the desire of believing the story to be a malicious fabrication, and not to experience some resentment against the individual who asserts its truth, whatever may be the occasion or motive.

But the defendant knows that your Lordships will not be so misled. You are too well acquainted with your duty and too conscientious in its discharge to allow your opinions to be warped by feelings which arise from narrow and imperfect views. Much as you may pity the situation of the plaintiffs, and much as you may regret the existence of practices like those which have been imputed to them, you will not confine your attention to that side of the picture exclusively. You will not forget that the defendant also has claims to assert, less specious and affecting perhaps than those of her opponents, but nevertheless of deep importance, to herself, to her family, and to the public.

She was at one time the most active of the plaintiffs' friends. She exerted all her influence to serve them and gave three of her grandchildren into their care. If they have been guilty of the misconduct which has been laid to their charge, consider how great an injury they have committed against her and against her family. In violation of a sacred trust, they have endangered the purity of Miss Cumming's mind. They have inflicted upon her the certain misfortune of having witnessed their indecencies, and of being conscious that the world knows she witnessed them. They have held up the defendant as a rash and malicious calumniator. They have dragged her into a painful and disgusting lawsuit. They have coupled her name with a subject offensive to every delicate ear. They have compelled her, in her justification, to wound the feelings of the innocent young women brought forward in evidence, and of their respectable relations and friends.

But let us look more directly at the events which preceded their suit. In the month of November, Lady Cumming Gordon returned to her home in Charlotte Square after a sojourn with one of her children. She was visited by her granddaughter who remained with her during the evening. Miss Cumming had been early taught to unbosom every thought of her heart to her grandmother, and in the course of conversation she mentioned the practices she had witnessed, the improprieties and indecencies, although she could only be an inadequate judge of the full extent of their criminality. The defendant was lost in confusion and horror. It was a story not of reports which Miss Cumming had heard, not of ambiguous circumstances which could be explained or where there was the smallest possible room for misunderstanding: it was a minute detail of obscenities, acted and spoken in her bed.

She determined without an instant's hesitation to remove her granddaughter from the school, but she felt desirous of advice with regard to the mode of proceeding. Miss Cumming was kept at home that night, but next morning the defendant allowed her to return to school, knowing that there was little to worry about in the daytime. That evening, however, a family emergency prevented the defendant from calling for Miss Cumming. But in the meantime she had spoken of the matter to one of her daughters, Mrs. Forbes, on whose judgment she had the most perfect reliance. Miss Cumming was then sent for and minutely interrogated a second time with regard to what had taken place, and she gave precisely the same account that she had before. That account was then confirmed by one of her cousins, Miss Margaret Dunbar, who offered to give testimony in this court but was challenged as a witness by the plaintiffs' counsel, since she is Lady Cumming Gordon's legitimate granddaughter. Although Miss Dunbar had seen nothing herself, as she informed Lady Cumming Gordon and Mrs. Forbes, she had heard the stories of Miss Munro and Charlotte Whiffin. Thus the defendant had obtained the testimony of two witnesses with regard to the fact. If a doubt could have existed in her mind after such information she must have been skeptical indeed. Miss Cumming was accordingly brought home at the first possible moment that Lady Cumming Gordon could have her sent for, the morning of November 14, 1810, and the plaintiffs were informed that she was not to return.

The defendant and her family had recommended the school to two individuals whose children had afterwards been sent there: to Lady Cunynghame directly, and to Mrs. Anstruther through her sister-in-law. Under the circumstances, the defendant believed it to

227

be her duty to mention to those two ladies that she had reason to be dissatisfied with the school, and the opinion of her daughter Mrs. Forbes completely coincided with her own.

Accordingly, she wrote to Mrs. Anstruther on the evening of Wednesday, the 14th of November, the day on which she had had her own grandchildren removed, mentioning that she had done so and that she would state to Mrs. Anstruther the reason. Next day she wrote in similar terms to Lady Cunynghame, advising her also to bring home Miss Cunynghame. With the exception of her daughter, Mrs. Forbes, whose confidential advice she considered of great importance in such a distressing emergency, and of Mrs. Anstruther and Lady Cunynghame, to whom she finally related the circumstances only as part of her indispensable duty, the defendant mentioned the subject to no one whatsoever. Miss Munro and Miss Stirling were removed from the school only because of the information that they themselves had communicated to their parents.

But although Lady Cumming Gordon is not responsible for the circulation of the story, since she told it to none but those to whom, whether true or false, she was bound to disclose it, it could not be long concealed. The remaining boarders were thus soon taken from the school by their families. The plaintiffs, now reduced to the necessity either of acknowledging that they were guilty and abiding the consequences, or of boldly asserting that the whole report was a malicious falsehood, fabricated to accomplish their ruin, adopted the latter alternative.

When the case appeared before the Lord Ordinary, he expressed at once a decided opinion, not only that the whole story was a fiction, but that it was so incredible and absurd that it ought not be made the subject of testimony. However, as has been shown, the existence of the propensity and the prevalence of its indulgence in women who were not hermaphrodites have been recorded by writers of every age and nation, by historians, moralists, physicians, and lawyers. And there is scarcely a licentious work in which it is not treated of at large.

On the physical possibility of venereal gratification being obtained by the congress of two women and the known existence of such practices, counsel for the plaintiffs now has wonderfully little to say—though at the hearing before the Lord Ordinary he said a good deal to suggest that such venereal gratification is impossible. Now he says he never denied that women might abuse their bodies with each other if one had a preternatural conformation or if they used instruments or digitation. This concession is of itself enough for the defendant's case on the point of physical possibility. There is nothing in the facts set forth to exclude the use of instruments or of digitation. In fact, there are some circumstances which strongly indicate that digitation was used, perhaps not constantly, but to a certain degree and sufficiently to produce the intended effect. There is even nothing to exclude preternatural conformation, though that is the least probable case of the three.

Leaving the question of physical possibility, we turn to that of moral improbability. The plaintiffs point to their previous good character, in evidence of which they have called witnesses and produced documents, particularly of a correspondence between themselves and letters of some of Miss Pirie's female friends who have praised her in very warm terms.

But your Lordships are entreated to consider how little weight any presumption arising from general character can have against the direct testimony of credible witnesses, swearing to facts which fell under their own immediate observation—facts regarding what they heard, felt, and saw. In addition to such direct testimony, we appeal to the experience of every one of your Lordships: have you not known persons of the most engaging character, impressed with a strong sense of virtue and religion, and zealous in the discharge of their duties, who have fallen a sacrifice to sensual indulgence, undeterred by the inevitable prospect of their own ruin and the ruin of all they held dear upon earth?

Furthermore, your Lordships, it is a well known fact that in every well-regulated nunnery on the Continent, precautions used to be taken against such practices, and in some of them, notwithstanding, those practices are said to have prevailed to a very great degree. The situation of the plaintiffs in their boarding school was in some respects similar to that of nuns in a cloister. Supposing, therefore, that either of them possessed an unfortunate temperament, or had been previously addicted to solitary indulgence: your Lordships will easily see how peculiarly exposed these women were to temptation. Their early intimacy, their rapturous friendship, and the practice of sleeping together in the same bed during holidays (when, by the way, there was not the least occasion for it) afforded excitement and opportunity. And there is nothing in the smallest degree inconsistent nor improbable in the union of such feelings with every good quality which their most partial friends ascribe to them.

But let the evidence with regard to their character be a little more minutely considered. As to Miss Woods, there is very little information. It seems rather strange that Miss Woods, who has resided so long in this city and neighborhood, should not have been able to call forth a single witness to her character except one who has seldom seen her in recent years and another who has been a partner and is a relative.

With regard to Miss Pirie, there is a great deal more evidence. She seems, by the testimony of all her acquaintances, to have possessed many valuable and excellent qualities. But there is one feature of this lady's mind, so fully brought out by all the witnesses and the letters she has produced, that your Lordships cannot overlook on the present occasion. We allude to an overheated imagination and a morbid irritability of feeling, which made her liable to perpetual excitation and subject to the influence of erroneous and exaggerated impressions.

Feelings like these may be compatible with many amiable qualities, but they are not favourable to the practice of virtue. They are liable to give place in a moment to propensities of an opposite but no less powerful tendency. The romance of friendship or rapture of devotion easily alternates in such a person with the gratification of lowest sensuality. Wherever there is an habitual indulgence of violent but unsteady passions, nothing is more likely than a transition to vice on the one hand, or insanity on the other.

It is curious to observe how the plaintiffs point to the warmth of their love and the bitterness of their enmity almost in one breath—they claim they are both equally conclusive to show they are innocent of what they have been accused. But when you find their quarrels and reconciliations alternately occurred in perpetual succession, from the period of their meeting to that of their separation, you can regard their friendship as nothing but the effervescence of impassioned and ill regulated minds, and the intervals of returning fondness as fitted for the indulgence of habits to which minds of that unfortunate description would most easily fall prey.

We are certain that the simple truth of this reasoning has been all too apparent to your Lordships, and that you will find Lady Helen Cumming Gordon not guilty of the charge brought against her by the plaintiffs for damages.

JULY 26, 1982

These interminable speeches, recapping the horrors that the plaintiffs and the defendant had lived through and had already been forced to hear about again and again! If it were you being discussed, what punishment for body and soul, to have to sit in that cold courtroom and listen! How would it have felt to the two mistresses? It would have been no easier if they were innocent of the accusations than if they were guilty. To hear the length of your clitoris publicly speculated on by strange men, and whether or not you used fingers or dildos; to hear yourself being accused of having neither moral nor intellectual control (the qualities you valued most in yourself), and of seeking "gratification of lowest sensuality"; to hear it said that yours is a personality type that must lead either to vice or insanity. How can the self survive such an assault?

But I know that Lady Cumming Gordon, foolish and pompous as she might have been, also suffered as she sat in the courtroom and heard over and over the details of this horrendous affair in which she (of all persons, she must have thought, she who loved delicacy and was so private) had become involved only because, as she would have seen it, she was too giving, too responsible, too concerned.

Had she always expected some disaster to befall her over the Indian girl whom she had taken into her family against warnings from everyone she loved? Did it seem to her now that through all the past years she had been merely waiting for the other shoe to drop?

I think she must have been furious with Jane Cumming for placing her in a position where her lofty name was dragged through the courts and she was forced to speak the unspeakable. I think she must have cursed the girl's dark skin and dark soul for bringing her to this—whether she continued to believe Jane Cumming or not. And if there were moments when she did not believe her story, how difficult it must have been for the Lady to accept the idea that her ward had enough sexual knowledge to make up such a tale. What a terrible sense of failure and neglect of her most stringent responsibility she would have felt if the girl knew of such things and could invent those stories by herself. Of course Lady Cumming Gordon would rather have believed the women guilty.

But in any case, having found herself inextricably involved in this trouble, I think she must have considered it a judgment upon her for her son's transgressions and lamented that not only are the father's sins visited on the son, but the son's sins are also visited on the mother.

With the conclusion of Cranstoun's speech, the Court was adjourned and the judges met in the chamber of Lord Justice-Clerk Hope. The counsel for the plaintiffs had pleaded with the judges to come to a speedy decision, since neither of the mistresses had been able to obtain employment in Edinburgh after their school was broken up, and Miss Woods desired to leave the country in hopes of finding a position where her good name had not been destroyed.

The judges agreed that they must have at least one month to deliberate. They would meet again on *Miss Woods and Miss Pirie against Dame Cumming Gordon* on June 25, 1811.

Speeches of the Judges, June 25, 1811, 10:15 a.m.

Lord Justice-Clerk Hope: I believe we are all in agreement regarding the painful nature of this proceeding. I never saw a case so disgusting, view it in either light. But unlike some of my Brethren, judging from their occasional remarks, I have not one doubt in my mind. I have no more suspicion of the guilt of the plaintiffs than I have of my own wife.

I will lay out of my view the question of the physical impossibility of the thing charged, although I admit that I have great doubts about an act such as the one described being possible. It is as if I were told that a person heard thunder playing the tune of "God Save the King." If you say the plaintiffs have committed a crime, I could believe it, if it were stated to have been committed with a man. If you accuse them of gross indecency, I may be able to believe either of them capable of it, but not if you say they committed that indecency under circumstances that are incredible. The circumstances that have been described are, to speak directly to the point, simply incredible.

These Ladies were accused of gross immorality and shameful indecency. The description of their behaviour was so gross, brutish, beastly, and absurd that I could not give it the slightest credit. But still, I would be forced to believe it if well proved. However the evidence supplied came from two girls, who spoke regarding facts which they did not understand, and which were supposed to be corroborated by the maidservant, who might be thought to understand a little more about the matter. How great would have been the corroboration if Charlotte had confirmed their statement, especially if what she was said to have told them had been possible. But the thing was impossible. We who visited the house saw with our own eyes that even the keyhole story was impossible. And Charlotte has positively sworn the reverse of what the young ladies said. So the expected corroboration is totally done away, and the failure of it must affect the rest of the evidence.

Now this thing is stated to have been committed under circumstances of absolute improbability. Miss Woods comes from the dressing room. This was not necessary. Why didn't she stay there and have Miss Pirie join her? Again, where was the necessity for interchanging beds? Or why should they have gone to one another's beds at all when they had two hours before bedtime, after the scholars were asleep? We have them quite aware of the danger of discovery. We have a dialogue: One is invited to come in. She answers, "No, because we might awake her, etc." And we are told that all this was so audible that Miss Cumming could directly distinguish between the words *in* and *on*.

233

Well, I must touch on the physical impossibility since it is so absurd. Miss Cumming says she felt both the Ladies pull up their shifts—and Miss Pirie must have pulled up her petticoat as well, since she always wore one. Now ladies' shifts reach to their feet. They have no opening. If you lay two women, flat above one another, how can they pull up their shifts? And if they had gone to bed for the purpose alleged, would their shifts not have been up before?

But enough of such physical impossibilities. It would be sufficient to regard the moral impossibilities alone to find these Ladies innocent. Their character has been proved. With such character is it likely that they of all women could have committed the crime in question? Is there even a prostitute so blasted as these Ladies are described by Miss Cumming? She makes the one say to the other, "You are *putting it into the wrong place.*" I hope never to see such evidence again. I am not one who believes "he seldom errs who thinks the worst he can of womankind." I never saw a prostitute who did not prefer to be treated with decency. Then also remember that Miss Cumming was asked whether she was sure of the words *"in* the wrong place"—whether it might not be *"on* the wrong place," such as one might say if she were being rubbed for rheumatism. I recollect the decision, the teeth and bitterness with which she said, "I am quite sure it was *in.*" Now here is another physical impossibility. If such a thing had been said there would have been no emphasis on the word *in* such as to enable a person in those circumstances to swear that it was *in* and not *on.* Speaking audibly in this Court, if I use the expression in a common way, you probably cannot tell with a certainty which word I pronounce—but if I speak it in a whisper, who could tell or pretend to swear to it?

Another part of the conversation, according to Miss Cumming, is that one says to the other, "What are you doing it for?" and the other answers, "For fun." We are called upon to believe this, as spoken *audibly,* by persons described as afraid of detection, and in the same bed with a girl watching.

Now, with regard to her motives—I am not sure if she was aware of all the consequences, or if she intended at first that it should go as far as it did. Even to get out of the school would be a motive to a girl like her. This motive I can see. Another motive would be the love of tittle-tattle—to have something to say against her mistresses. There is also the motive of sneaking conversation with the maid just because it has been forbidden.

Well, I would rather believe Miss Cumming, and even Lady Cumming Gordon herself perjured, than I would believe the statement about *the wrong place* to be true, especially with regard to women of good character. This is stated with regard to women alive to all the fine feelings of Christian morality—women who are real Christians, if there can be evidence of private belief: just look at Miss Pirie's letter to Mrs. Hamilton! And to commit sodomy with another woman,—a double unnatural crime! Can it be believed of such persons? Is character, and such character, to be of no weight here?

So now what might have been the real circumstances here? I believe the plaintiffs did come to one another's beds—but for good reason, to talk of the business of the school and on some occasions to help each other by rubbing for the rheumatism. But we all know that there is no end to the influence of mere suspicion when it is taken up without knowing the whole circumstances. I can recollect myself to have been in situations which, if seen by a third person without knowing the real cause, might easily have been worked into a source of very extraordinary suspicions. Are there not circumstances here to explain everything? If the Ladies had denied that they were ever in one another's rooms we might have been able to discredit their statements. But when they account for the circumstances, is it not material? Is the admission to be turned against them? Take the case of a man with his hands bloody, found beside a murdered man. It can be accounted for by the fact that he was the first who came to the dead man's assistance. But a distorted imagination will find other explanations for the suspicious circumstance. A person with such an imagination will work himself up to be certain of a fact which never existed at all. I think the same is to be said of Miss Munro. If we suppose the Ladies came to one another's bed for the purpose of conversation, they could not find room without leaning over one another. Miss Munro even admits that on one occasion she is not sure whether Miss Pirie was in the bed or not. And if they came to rub or be rubbed for the rheumatism, of course they would lean over one another.

But even putting these explanations aside, I would say further that according to the known habits of women in this country, there is no indecency in one woman going to bed with another.

But what has happened as a result of the preposterous allegations of indecency? The Ladies have been ruined, but they do not suffer alone. On account of the general contamination, Miss Weston, for this reason only, refused to admit into her house two girls who had been in the school. I doubt if Lady Cumming Gordon, even if she believed all that she says, could have done a greater injury by leaving them all there.

Many other things occurred to me which I could not bring my mind to put down in notes. But I am very clear that the defence is not made out and the defendant must be ordered to recompense the plaintiffs.

JULY 27, 1982

When we woke this morning the wind was shaking the windows and the door. Then the rain came down, and then, despite the season, the hail. We decided we had earned a day off, and that we would stay in the flat and not get dressed. We had coffee in front of the grate of the gas heater, staring at its red flame as though it were a burning log in a fireplace. Then we made love. . . . Ollie says I should have written, "Then we had a headache," just as Eleanor Butler did in the eighteenth century.

Afterward I wondered if we could be arrested for our headache under present Scottish law. Ollie whipped out a book I had not yet seen, which she had purchased on her peregrinations last month, before she started working with me on the research. It was a 1957 report of the Committee on Homosexual Offences and Prostitution, published by the Scottish Home Department. It came out at the same time as the Wolfenden Report, which had been ordered by the Home Secretary in England. Both reports favored liberalizing the laws regarding homosexual activity between consenting adults, but their focus was almost exclusively on males. The Scottish report is an indication that views regarding sexual love between women had not changed much in 150 years. In 1957 the Scots still could not quite believe it existed—even though they knew it did.

The report argues that *male* homosexuality should not be punishable on the grounds that it breaks up families, because "we have had no reasons shown to us which would lead us to believe that homosexual behaviour between males inflicts any greater damage on family life than adultery, fornication, or lesbian behaviour. . . . Where adultery, fornication, and lesbian behaviour are not criminal offences there seems to us to be no valid ground, on the basis of damage to the family, for so regarding homosexual behaviour between men." This suggests that the committee acknowledged the existence of lesbianism and that it was not punishable by law.

However, in a "List of Homosexual Offences" is the category "Indecent assault on a female by a female," and that was punishable by three months' imprisonment ("Indecent assault on a male by a male" drew two years in Scotland; in England the punishments were two years and ten years, respectively).

Ollie speculates that by "indecent assault" they must have meant rape, but as we read further it seems that the phrase could refer to any sort of sexual activity. The report states, "An act amounting in law to an indecent assault does not necessarily involve any violence toward the victim; indeed, we have evidence that offenders frequently approach their victims with gentleness." So lesbianism was acknowledged by Scottish law?

No! A further paragraph, labeled "Indecent assaults by females on females," clarifies the Scottish view:

> Since an indecent assault by one female on another could take the form of a homosexual act, we have included indecent assaults by females on females in the list of homosexual offenses in paragraph 77 above. We have, however, found no case in which a female has been convicted of an act with another female which exhibits the libidinous features that characterise sexual acts between males. We are aware that the criminal statistics occasionally show females as having been convicted of indecent assaults on females; but on inquiry we find that this is

due in the main to the practice of including in the figures relating to any particular offence not only those convicted of the offence itself, but also those convicted of aiding and abetting the commission of the offence. Thus a woman convicted of aiding and abetting a man to commit an indecent assault on a female would be shown in the statistics as having herself committed such an assault.

So, what does it all mean?

"That we don't exist in this country," says Ollie. "Just as we did not exist here in the early nineteenth century. That what we just did is as possible as a person hearing thunder play the tune of 'God Save the King.' "

JUNE 25, 1811, 1:30 P.M.

LORD BOYLE: This case is certainly one of a most singular and unparalleled nature, and one which imposes a most painful duty on all who are compelled to judge of it. I will fairly confess that I have found it attended with very considerable difficulty, and I will not be at all surprised if a diversity of opinion should prevail among your Lordships, acknowledging as I do that different impressions as to the general result of the case have been in my mind at different times in the course of my consideration of it.

The evidence, when viewed in all its bearings, and with the most minute attention, ought alone to guide our judgement in this case. The very extraordinary, and not withstanding the authorities referred to, the hitherto, in this country, almost unheard of nature of the imputation against the plaintiffs,—the no less extraordinary manner in which these acts of criminality are stated to have been committed,—their previous good character and irreproachable conduct,—the excellent system of education practised by them,—their utter absence of all consciousness of guilt,—and their instantaneous and fearless institution of this action, seem to establish so strong a moral impossibility of the justice of the charge against them, as to render it indispensable that their turpitude should be proved by the most decisive evidence.

But what evidence has been presented? The principal and leading witness for the defendant is, unquestionably, Miss Cumming. She is the natural granddaughter of the defendant, and from her, confessedly, the defendant's information as to the action of the plaintiffs was originally derived. This young woman was born in India, her mother being a native of that country, and is now sixteen years of age, having been brought to Britain when between seven and eight years old. She was at first placed at a boarding school at Elgin, and afterwards was removed to that of the plaintiffs, the discipline of which appears, from her own testimony, to have been considerably more strict than that of the Elgin school. Here in itself is a motive for her prevarications: she wished to be released from a disagreeable situation.

Let me say, also, with regard to the crime she claims to have witnessed, that one cannot but help be sensitive to the fact that however well known the crime here charged may be amongst Eastern nations, this is the first instance on record of such an accusation having ever been made in this country.

But most decisive, as far as I am concerned, are the various contradictions on the fact of her testimony, as well as on comparing it with those of Miss Munro and Miss Stirling, two other witnesses for the defendant. The statement as to seeing both of the plaintiffs "in their shifts" cannot be viewed as a loose or inadvertent expression, the witness having sworn about Miss Woods that she saw her quite plainly, as the window was opposite to the foot of the bed. The tardy attempt at qualification of this pointed averment, when she states that she meant "night things in general" must therefore be held as a contradiction of it. She had indeed been previously compelled to swear that Miss Pirie usually slept with a bedgown, a wrapper, a petticoat, and stockings on—a statement not quite consistent with another part of her testimony, as to her feeling them lifting up their shifts on one occasion.

But independently of my minute observations that might be much further extended, let it be considered if the main body of Miss Cumming's testimony is of a credible nature. She states certain particulars which are in their nature hardly within the bounds of possibility, into the enumeration of which, however, it is disgusting to enter at any length. I allude, particularly, to the extraordinary noise stated to have been heard by her during the holidays, though situated at the time in a different part of the room, and the position she describes herself to have been in when she made the discovery of one of the instances of the plaintiffs being in her bed.

But it has been asked whether such statements as those that are contained in Miss Cumming's evidence could have been invented. One thing is beyond all doubt certain: that in the progress of this case there have been some of the most manifest inventions resorted to with regard to the plaintiffs. For example, when the case was originally stated to the Lord Ordinary it appears to have been averred on behalf of the defendant that the mistresses' misconduct was so notorious that they were hooted at by the washerwomen when walking at the Water of Leith. But of a fact of so pointed a nature not one vestige of evidence is now to be found in the testimony. So far from it, there is the clearest evidence that the scholars contested with each other for the privilege of walking arm in arm with the plaintiffs when they went abroad. If there is the strongest ground, then, to conclude that such a statement can have been derived only from Miss Cumming, it is not too much for the plaintiffs to maintain that other inventions sprung from the same source.

It is also to be remembered that the story of seeing through the keyhole of the drawing room door was manifestly an invention, either by the maidservant or someone else, of what is confessedly a physical impossibility, for the express purpose of injuring the plaintiffs.

I wish to turn briefly to Miss Munro, who seems indeed from the beginning to have been very much under the influence of Miss Cumming and to have derived her unfavourable impression of the plaintiffs in a great measure from her; and during the latter period of her stay at the school to have become in reality the dupe of Miss Cumming's superior sagacity. It is to be observed that previous to Miss Cumming's communication, Miss Munro had awoke in a fright, having supposed somebody was in the bed. It is therefore impossible to doubt that such an extraordinary account as Miss Cumming had given, coming from an informer *quite certain,* must have made a very strong impression on the mind of Miss Munro, who was totally *ignorant* on the subject.

Indeed, Miss Munro has herself afforded the clearest evidence that Miss Pirie might be and actually was in Miss Woods' room and even sitting on her bedside on more occasions than one, for purposes perfectly laudable or innocent. Once she heard them conversing about Miss Stirling and Miss Pirie's brother-in-law. And another time, as she swears, Miss Pirie sat down on the bed and rubbed Miss Woods for the rheumatism. Another time Miss Pirie came into the room before Miss Woods got up and made her a present of a Bible.

With regard to the testimony of Mary Brown, it amounts to no more than the hearsay of Miss Munro, who, as I have said, appears to have laboured under the strongest influence of prejudice, created in her mind by the representations of Miss Cumming.

Miss Stirling, who was the oldest in the school, and is a most unexceptionable witness, has testified of her own knowledge to nothing whatever to the prejudice of the plaintiffs. Although she was no doubt sufficiently instructed by the information of Miss Cumming and Miss Munro, Miss Stirling's testimony is in reality to be considered as in favour of the plaintiffs, unless the accounts she gives of the loose conversations and disrespectful language of Charlotte Whiffin, the maidservant, can be held as evidence. Her communications with Miss Cumming seem, however, to have been much more frequent than with the maid, with whom, indeed, she says that she "had very little conversation." When it is recollected that Miss Stirling had almost the same opportunity of observing the conduct of the plaintiffs as Miss Cumming, and that she positively swears she observed no instance of impropriety, it seems impossible to deny that her testimony is entitled to the greatest weight in this case.

It does not appear to me that either party can build much upon the testimony of Charlotte Whiffin. She is certainly not free from suspicion, as she evidently had endeavoured to conceal her having spoken in disrespectful and contemptuous language of her mistresses. I believe her tales must have begun after she observed the inclination of Miss Cumming and Miss Munro, the latter of whom positively states that Charlotte the maid never made any remarks to her as to any improprieties in the plaintiffs' conduct until she mentioned to Charlotte that she had been disturbed on the morning after the second occasion. It was by no means surprising, therefore, that, adopting their statements, Charlotte may have chosen to encourage them by detailing and exaggerating circumstances in no degree inconsistent with innocence.

The counsel for the defendant has indeed referred to certain melancholy instances of human depravity which have appeared amongst persons who previously enjoyed irreproachable characters. There exists, however, between the kinds of cases referred to and the present case the most marked distinction. In the former the guilt was in fact confessed by the accused having instantly abandoned their families, their friends, and their country. But has any such consciousness of crime been discoverable in the behaviour of the plaintiffs? Is it in the scene so impressively described by Lady Cunynghame? Is it in the emphatic language of the note addressed by Miss Pirie to the defendant's daughter? Is it in the plaintiffs' instantaneous institution of a law suit for the vindication of their characters that we are to find such indications of guilt as in the cases referred to?

It has, however, been maintained that even if the defendant fails in proving that the mistresses behaved indecently together, she was nevertheless entitled in the discharge of her duties to act the way she did. This part of the case appears to me to be attended with some difficulty. While I acquit the defendant of all malicious purpose, when I consider the nature of the information she had received, that it came from a solitary informer, unless we count her other granddaughter, Margaret Dunbar, who never claimed to witness the improprieties, and that the inevitable consequence of her acting as she did was to produce the ruin of the plaintiffs, I must hesitate a good deal more than I do at present before I can deny reparation to those against whom a charge of such enormity has not been proved by satisfactory evidence. It can never be forgotten that in reference to their situation in life, no greater crime could be imputed to the plaintiffs. Had the defendant merely withdrawn her own grandchildren from the school, she was unquestionably entitled to do so. But I cannot think that on such information as she had, she was entitled without inquiry, or any demand of explanation, to put down their school, and thereby annihilate the future prospects of the plaintiffs. She put her case upon the authority of Miss Cumming, and on its weight, and the rest of the evidence she has adduced, she must now stand. It does not, however, appear to me, that the defence has been made out by such evidence so that it ought to be sustained. I find Lady Cumming Gordon guilty of destroying the good name and livelihood of the plaintiffs, without justifiable cause.

JULY 30, 1982

What a difference in the styles of Lord Justice-Clerk Hope and Lord Boyle! Lord Justice-Clerk Hope, who headed this court and later became Lord Justice-General, danced around in circles with his preconceptions and ended where he began. Could his style really have passed for judicial analysis in his day? Lord Boyle, on the other hand, made a genuine attempt to grapple with the evidence and, I think, arrived at the only reasonable conclusions.

Ollie, however, is not convinced. She says that Boyle's prose style was clearly smoother than Hope's, but his objectivity was equally specious: beneath his arguments was his inability to believe that respectable, middle-class women were capable of illicit sexuality. While he appeared to be struggling with the evidence, she says, he gave himself away at the beginning of his speech when he referred to lesbianism as "the very extraordinary and . . . hitherto, in this country, almost unheard of nature of the imputation." Lady Cumming Gordon was guilty of libel because there were no lesbians in Britain: therefore, the two women could not have been performing lesbian acts.

Ollie and I spend hours talking about what must have really happened. She thinks we cannot agree because, like the judges, we come to this case with our own preconceptions about behavior. In the twentieth century, she says, most people would not share the prejudices of the judges' day, but we all have our own blood beliefs about how human beings act, and only the starkest evidence can overturn those beliefs for us.

I point out that if she is right, if in the absence of irrefutable evidence all judgments are made on the basis of blood beliefs, then there is no hope of receiving justice in a court of law. The outcome of one's case is dependent on whether or not one is lucky enough to have a judge and a jury with the right preconceptions.

"That's a truism," she says. "But, of course, it is the job of the lawyer to convince the judge and jury that they are rendering a decision in favor of his client not because of their prejudices but because of evidence. He must convince them that all evidence in support of his client is the starkest evidence."

We agree that in the Woods and Pirie case there was no irrefutable evidence. I suppose Ollie is right when she says that what we believe about this case depends as much on who we are as did what the judges believed in 1811.

This is what I believe:

Almost everything Jane Cumming and Janet Munro described had its counterpart in a gesture or remark that was entirely innocuous. Where there was no innocent counterpart it was because Jane Cumming invented that particular detail from a stock of misinformation and half-understood images. These she had gathered from one or two girls at the Elgin school, shopkeepers' daughters who had been out in the world before they were sent to learn a trade.

Of course Miss Woods and Miss Pirie would have slept together during the holiday at Portobello. And they would have continued to sleep together for as long as they could when they returned from the holiday. That was how romantic friends behaved: if no duties or circumstances interfered, why would they want to sleep apart? Here is what Charles Brockden Brown had Sophie say about herself and Constantia, the heroine of his novel *Ormond,* written ten years before the mistresses opened their school: "The appetite for sleep and for food were confounded and lost amidst the impetuosities of a master passion. To look and to talk to each other afforded enchanting occupation for every moment. I would not part from her side, but ate and slept, walked and mused and read, with my arm linked in hers, and with her breath fanning my cheek. . . . O precious inebriation of the heart! O pre-eminent love! What pleasure of reason or of sense can stand in competition with those attendant upon thee?" Marianne Woods and Jane Pirie shared such an inebriation of the heart, which was, as Sophie implies, outside the pleasure of the senses.

Before they started the school they had slept together whenever they could. But once the school began, they heeded their duty over their hearts: the rooms in which the students slept must be supervised, and they themselves must be the supervisors. At Portobello in the summer of 1810 they were relieved to have no such duties to separate them, only one student, and they could exercise their vigilance over her if she slept at the foot of their bed. They had only one room in a seaside lodging house. After Jane Cumming went to bed at nine o'clock, what was there for them to do? They would have loved to walk on the sand, but they were reluctant to leave the girl alone in a strange house. They did not allow themselves to read in the room or do other work by candlelight for fear of waking her. So they were happy enough to get in their bed. They whispered for a while, and fell asleep, and then woke up very early because they were not used to long-protracted sleep. In the early morning, in bed, they would chat in whispers, until it was the hour to get up, or until they saw that Jane Cumming was awake so that they might all dress. They kissed often, out of sheer rapturous joy at being almost alone together, away from the heaviest of their responsibilities and from what had divided them for more than half a year.

When they returned to the school at the start of August, they found themselves with the problem of Marianne's aunt again, although until the scholars began to arrive they had leisure for each other, and the worst of their tensions could be smoothed out by their time together. But once the scholars returned they went back to their separate supervisory posts, and their obligations permitted them few opportunities for undisturbed proximity.

From September to November they came to each other's beds more than a dozen times to talk—about the school, about their feelings, about relatives, and especially about Marianne Woods' most difficult relative. Sometimes they came to argue, in subdued tones—but the strength of their emotion was so powerful that if it could not find vent through the voice, it would be expressed through the body: they might shake each other or pound the pillow or tear at the bedclothes. Sometimes they sobbed, breathing high and fast.

It is cold in Edinburgh now, at the end of July. We have the gas heat on all the time, despite the absurd amount of money we pay for it. In September and October and November it must have been a good deal colder, and they would have had no heat in their rooms. When they came to talk, or even to cry, if they were not too furious with each other they would have gotten under the covers together.

They both suffered from rheumatism, Miss Pirie more than Miss Woods, and the cold weather would have exacerbated it. In October Miss Pirie's rheumatism would have been bad. Sometimes, when they were on good terms, Miss Woods would have gone to Miss Pirie's bed to massage her friend's back. When Miss Pirie's muscles were very tender she would have complained of pain while Miss Woods massaged, though the overall effect of the rubbing was to alleviate the pain. The conversations Jane Cumming heard probably took place during the massaging: "Am I hurting you?" "You are on [or even *in* might be used to describe an area of muscle] the wrong place." "I think I have put you in the way to get a good sleep." Once, when they were lighthearted, perhaps around October 10 or 11, and Miss Pirie was not in great pain with her rheumatism, I think Miss Woods tickled her neck or waist in the course of the massage, and Miss Pirie lightly asked what she thought she was doing, and Miss Woods as lightly responded, "Having fun." Sometimes Miss Pirie suffered so greatly from rheumatism that she asked Miss Woods to give her a massage during the day, and Jane Cumming would have found her bed disordered when she went up to her room in the evening.

I do not think one ever said to the other, "Oh, do it, darling." I do not think one said, "I would like better to have someone above me," although perhaps Miss Woods asked if Miss Pirie would massage her too. I do not think one ever made the other promise not to come to her bed until the holiday. All that comes from a shopkeeper's daughter, or perhaps a pornographic novel that had been smuggled into the Elgin school.

They loved each other, but Miss Pirie, who had no one to help her find her way in the world, who had worked since she was seventeen to cut out a decent niche for herself, who got, or believed she got, little thanks for all her arduous labors in life, loved respectability and position even more than she loved her friend. When Mrs. Woods appeared to want to rob her of respectability, position, her honor in the community, the trappings of her hard-won success—when Mrs. Woods seemed to be scheming to present her as a governess in the school rather than its chief proprietor, then her love was dwarfed by her fury. One master passion superseded the other. But the other, her love, was not dead—and so, after their worst fights, Miss Pirie, torn by ambivalence and grief, would give herself up to hysteria, screaming and praying in the middle of the night, "O Lord Jesus Christ, O Lord Jesus Christ," not caring who heard.

Ollie's version:

They became lovers—not in the romantic friendship sense, but as we would use that word today—shortly after they met, eight or nine years before the breakup of the school. They could not live together because each had her living to earn, and Jane Pirie knew nothing else to do except to be a live-in governess. But they slept together—meaning they made love—whenever they could. Throughout all those years there must have been ebbs and flows in their passion. By 1809 it would not have had the urgency of their earliest years together. For that reason they believed when they opened the school that they could restrain themselves. In fact, they decided in the beginning that it would be preferable, less risky, to do without if they were to make a success of their venture. Perhaps at that time their passion was at a low, and the decision did not seem like a great sacrifice.

With their first anxieties about getting the school established and with Miss Pirie's anger toward the aunt, neither of them felt very erotic. But then they went for the summer to Portobello. Today Portobello is a filthy little seaside town, but then it was clean and somewhat fashionable, and it was where young Edinburgh lovers went when they wanted to leave the smoky city. It was romantic. They were feeling relaxed and happy and almost carefree. They found rekindled in themselves some of the easy affection and maybe the sweet recklessness they had felt together years ago.

And there they were in bed together. They had not been in bed together for over a year perhaps, maybe longer. Miss Cumming snored loudly. They had not intended to, but they found themselves making love. The long abstinence, and the necessity to be covert, the risk, all together made it more exciting than it had ever been. Since Miss Cumming never mentioned a word about it

247

all that month (they had made up a plausible enough story for her should she have alluded to it), they assumed she knew nothing. She would start snoring almost as soon as she got into her bed, and they would reach for each other. Then they would wake early, and she would always seem to be sleeping soundly, so they would reach for each other again.

They intended to stop as soon as they returned to the school. But once at the school they saw that there was no reason to stop immediately: they could still sleep together and Miss Cumming could snore away in another bed in the room, just as she had done at Portobello. There would be no reason to stop until the other scholars came back.

When they began to arrive, the mistresses returned to their old sleeping arrangements. It was understood that they would forgo what they had rediscovered in July, at least until Christmastime, when most of the scholars would leave for the holidays.

But then the anger between the aunt and Miss Pirie raged again, and Miss Pirie would have fits of temper and guilt, and she would drag Miss Woods out of the school room to yell at her. Then Miss Woods would cry, and Miss Pirie would tell her please not to cry, and she would caress her and kiss her. Once, in the dark drawing room, while the girls were doing their lessons in the school room, Miss Pirie kissed Miss Woods to comfort her and one thing led to the next, and they made love—with the door open even. But who would spy on them?

Often these fights would last all day, and then one or the other could not bear to go to sleep with such bitterness between them. So she would come to her friend's bed to make up. But one night their kisses led to more. They hadn't intended to, but they couldn't help themselves. They were terrified; they were ashamed. They were as quiet as could be, and after all it was a big bed. Miss Cumming slept all the way over on the other side of it, near the wall. She did not wake up. But they swore never to repeat it. It had been insanity—they both knew that.

However, a few days later they fought again and could not make up during the day. Again Miss Woods came to Miss Pirie, and it happened again. They did not want it to, but it did. They were so quiet, and Miss Cumming snored so loudly, and it was so dark in the room that they could not see the other girls, and they knew no one could see them. Afterward they thought there had been no reason to be so very quiet even, but they were pleased that they were sane enough to have prudence in their folly.

Each time it happened, they never meant for it to. And it did not happen often—in almost three months perhaps half a dozen times in Miss Pirie's bed, only two or three times in Miss Woods' bed. They knew there was some danger—remote, but nevertheless possible. They knew how much they had to lose, and they did not wish to take chances. They felt guilty too. But it was so good, so comforting. One day Miss Woods made Miss Pirie promise that they would stop. Miss Pirie said she could not promise. Miss Woods said she would be strong for both of them. She would not permit them to visit each other. They would stay apart until the holidays. But they would not forgo everything. They could kiss each other at least. No one would be suspicious of that.

Now, for what perplexed the judges so much—how did they do it? They might have done anything. Miss Cumming said one lay on top of the other, but that might have been only one thing they did, a minor part of the whole. If they were quiet enough she could not have known what else they did, all the way over on the other side of a large bed.

"Well," I say, "I simply can't believe it. I can't believe that two serious, moral, intelligent women would have taken such stupid chances."

We both smile. Ollie says, "I know you can't have forgotten that time, twelve years ago or so, before we lived together. In my office, with Al Barker's voice coming so clearly from the next office. I remember everything he talked about for those two hours—the Davidson briefs that the law library lost, and the Chrysler he was going to buy, and whether he ought to resign from the Martinez case."

No, of course I remember.

"So, what's the difference?" she asks. "If we had been caught, if someone had been peeping through the keyhole or over the transom, that would have been the end of us. I had enemies in that division. Who knows who might have taken it into his head to spy on us? Or what if the janitor had come in? Or Jackson's secretary, to get some papers off my desk? We took a risk. We hadn't intended to, but it ran away with us. What would you have done if someone had seen us?"

"Probably said that he was hallucinating. Acted outraged," I say.

"What would you have done if he told everyone in the building what he saw?"

"Why, I'd sue him for libel, of course," I say.

Yet I still think there is a difference. We are twentieth-century women, and we cannot escape from our sexuality. It has been foisted on us through our culture. In our day women are encouraged to think of themselves as sexual, and we are inescapably a product of our society. Women in 1810 received precisely the opposite indoctrination. We would feel as uncomfortable today being asexual as they would have felt being sexual.

JUNE 26, 1811, 10:00 A.M.

LORD ROBERTSON: In giving my opinion on this extraordinary and distressing case I feel that it is the most painful duty I have ever been called on to perform. No case ever interested my feelings or fixed my attention so powerfully. And after all the pains I have bestowed to get at the truth, I find it extremely difficult to come to any conclusion which is perfectly satisfactory to my own mind. I feel this difficulty the more because the opinion which I have formed differs so widely in almost every particular from that of the two learned Judges who spoke yesterday.

I am unwilling to consume your time or pollute your ears by quoting much of the transcripts. With the details of the transcripts your Lordships are now quite familiar, and I think it appears clear that the plaintiffs went to bed to each other, that they toyed with each other, and kissed each other, that the one lay above the other on several occasions, that while in that situation their bodies were agitated and moving, and that one or both were breathing quick and high. Upon the most attentive consideration of the testimony, I am satisfied that all these things have been shown to be true by Miss Cumming and Miss Munro, and the testimony of Miss Munro was confirmed by that of Mary Brown to whom she communicated the circumstances as they happened. Miss Cumming and Miss Munro have also sworn to frequent communication with the maid, Charlotte, on the subject; and Miss Stirling, a witness above all exception, does the same. Charlotte, to be sure, denies all this, but I have no hesitation in saying that I give no credit to her testimony as it opposes Miss Stirling's.

Counsel for the plaintiffs has argued, and my two learned Brethren have accepted that argument in their speeches, that it is morally improbable that the plaintiffs should have behaved in such a manner of gross indecency. I will respond that I cannot shut my eyes to the moral improbability which stares me in the face on the other side. If the defendant's witnesses are discredited, we must believe that young girls of sixteen, the age of innocence, of purity and of candour, have entered into a most abominable conspiracy, and all to ruin the fortunes of two women who have never injured them.

I have yet to hear a motive that might account for their acting so diabolical a part, and the piddling motives that have been suggested do not begin to account for these young girls' accusations if they are not true. Are we seriously called on to believe that girls of sixteen have, for such insignificant motives, entered into one of the most abominable conspiracies that ever disgraced the most profligate and abandoned of mankind, and have added to their crime of conspiracy the most deliberate perjury?

But I wish now to turn to another point, a major point. Counsel for the plaintiffs has dwelt much on the great improbability of their being engaged in a criminal intercourse at the very time when, it was proven, they were living in a state of hostility and enmity with each other. I would feel the force of this argument if their enmity were of the kind to produce coldness and reserve and distrust. But no such thing appears. At this very time Miss Pirie entertained the warmest and even the most enthusiastic affection for Miss Woods. Of this they themselves have furnished the most decisive evidence: the note that accompanied the Bible which Miss Pirie presented to Miss Woods on October 12, 1810. This is not the language of enmity or alienation; it is the language of strong, warm, and unextinguished affection. That the strength of this passion continued unabated despite turmoil is further corroborated in Miss Pirie's letter to Mrs. Hamilton of November 5, 1810, in which she declares that she can never conquer her feelings for Miss Woods, even should Miss Woods prove to be her enemy. This is the language and these are the sentiments of a most impassioned and undisciplined person.

The plaintiffs have admitted that they frequently went, in the night time, when the scholars were asleep, to each other's bedsides to converse. They account for this by saying that they were so fully occupied that they had no other time for conversing about their differences. This is very lame. It must be asked, was the time of the plaintiffs more occupied than in other boarding schools? Could they find no fitter season for discussing matters of so much importance? Miss Pirie was in the habit of sitting up late. Could they not have found an hour after supper for conversing before they went to bed?

Before concluding, I must take notice of one circumstance which makes a strong impression on my mind: why have the plaintiffs failed to bring evidence which contradicts the defendant's witnesses? Miss Munro says that on one occasion Miss Edgar must have seen Miss Pirie go out of the room and that Miss Edgar laughed. Why is Miss Edgar not brought forward to contradict this statement? Miss Cumming refers to Miss Cunynghame. Why is she not brought forward? It is true that Lady Cunynghame says that her daughter knew nothing, but why was not Miss Cunynghame brought to contradict Miss Cumming? If she had done so, this would have been material. The plaintiffs knew well of what importance it would be to their case if the credibility of Miss Cumming and Miss Munro could be shaken; but they were also aware that a confirmation of their testimony would be ruinous.

For these reasons, my Lords, I find the defendant not guilty.

LORD GLENLEE: Since I came into court today my feelings are very much changed, and are much more at ease than they were. For I had formed an opinion in all respects so like that of Lord Robertson, and was prepared to deliver it in a language so nearly the same, that I might refer to his Lordship's speech for all my sentiments on this case.

The defence, as stated by Lord Robertson, leads me to believe that the defendant did what she is charged with because the plaintiffs were guilty of practices which rendered it unfit that the young ladies should continue in their charge. At first, I admit, I was apprehensive that the young ladies were in conspiracy against their mistresses. But I am now clear that supposition is entirely without foundation. Nor can I see any perjury at work here. To argue that the story the young ladies tell is improbable is not enough.

Of Miss Munro, it has been suggested that she was under the influence of prejudice. It is conceivable certainly that prejudice may lead one to misinterpret a dubious fact—but, can any mere misconception arising from prejudice make Miss Munro suppose that Miss Pirie was on the top of Miss Woods if she was not? No prejudice could make a person *see* that if it were not so.

As to Miss Cumming, she has said that she was disturbed by the mistresses in her bed and that she spoke to them. The counsel for the plaintiffs has explained that Miss Woods had been sitting up late with her aunt and that when she was going to her own bed, Miss Pirie observed she had been in tears. Thus, Counsel said, she kissed Miss Woods, endeavouring to compose her—which is quite innocent indeed if this be true. Then, Counsel suggests, it so happens that a fit of rheumatism comes on at this time, and the rubbing takes place—which shakes the bed. Miss Cumming started out of bed and asked what was shaking the bed. This conduct of hers must have surprised the mistresses at the time, but they did not think of offering any explanation for it or accounting for it. Now, this is quite out of nature: when they saw the poor creature so frightened as to start out of bed, they should, in common humanity, have said something to tranquilize her. They might have chid her for being so frightened, but they should have said something. Since it is so out of nature not to do so under innocent cir-cumstances, it is highly likely that the circumstances were not in-nocent—that they said nothing because they were startled, having been caught in guilty circumstances.

As to the moral improbability, undoubtedly it is great, but much more has been said upon this than sound reason justifies. The indecent practice may have arisen in the holidays when the mistresses were relatively free of observation. It was then repeated, perhaps fearfully and reluctantly even, when they resumed their separate beds. To be sure, it was a more risky thing to do it in bed with another girl present—but this happened only seldom: during two months only five times in Miss Cumming's bed and three in Miss Munro's. It is not even necessary to suppose that they always went, even on these few occasions, with a deliberate, preconceived purpose. Perhaps at first they were simply carried away by a lust which was suddenly inflamed. And it is not unreasonable to sup-pose that once they found they could do it safely, and that the girl did not awake, they were tempted to repeat it. This is often the way with the indulgence of a natural sensual passion—and even the horrible nature of a passion similar to this, that between men, does not always prevent people from doing it in such an open manner as to make detection almost guaranteed. In the present case, I see no evidence of their having continued the practice after they must have known they were discovered.

As to the argument derived from the frequency of their quar-rels, I would agree that hatred and fondness at the same time are impossible. But the plaintiffs have themselves, through the evi-dence they furnished, shown that there were occasional relaxations of their enmities in which they displayed great fits of affection. They say themselves that Miss Pirie kisses Miss Woods because she is in tears, and that such a kiss is quite innocent. But if there is not enough enmity to prevent a kiss in that way, why should it be suffi-cient to prevent kissing in the other way? For these reasons I find the defendant not guilty of having slandered Miss Woods and Miss Pirie without cause.

I do not think the judges exaggerated when they said repeatedly that this was the most painful case on which they ever deliberated. They were exposed to evidence that revealed an aspect of female sexuality that was not supposed to have existed, and however they might decide the case, the implications would be distressing: if these admirable school mistresses were indeed guilty of carnal knowledge of each other, if they had a sexual drive so overwhelming as to seek out gratification without men, what did this say about the most commonly held beliefs regarding females of their class? Proper women were not supposed to have an autonomous sexual drive, and these two women surely appeared to have been trained in properness. If it could not be assumed that women of so many demonstrable virtues such as Miss Woods and Miss Pirie were passionless, how should any woman, even the wife of the Lord Justice-Clerk, be free from suspicion? How could men leave their wives to share a bed with a close woman friend on any occasion (and wives often shared beds with close women friends when husbands were absent), if women were indeed capable of the sort of behavior imputed to the mistresses?

The sexologists who wrote at the end of that century and the beginning of the next were a blessing to mankind, but they came along much too late to be of any help to the judges. They told men—at a time when men needed a great deal of assurance, because women had become so independent—that a female such as the wife of the Lord Justice-Clerk would never be in danger of the temptation to seek carnal knowledge of her female friend: only women who were congenital inverts or whose fathers had been seductive toward them in their adolescence were capable of such twisted behavior. However, since the judges had no sexologists to come to their assistance in 1811, what could they make of Miss Woods and Miss Pirie?

The problem was most sticky because the judges seemed to believe that despite their attempt to maintain secrecy, what they decided in this courtroom would have implications for society's view of women far beyond this case.

But there was no way that the comfortable clichés about female innocence could emerge unscathed here. If they found the mistresses not guilty of indecent behavior, what did that imply about the girls? How could those pure young things have gotten knowledge of the existence of such a vice? And if the daughters of these fine families made up stories about women lying on top of each other, how could the Lord Justice-Clerk be sure that his own daughter did not host such tales in the secret corners of her brain, and that when she was giggling with her young friends it was not a fiction such as this one that had tickled their imaginations?

What I think most bizarre, though, is this room full of men deliberating on what they could know so little about, female sexuality as it is experienced inside women, female sexuality without a male presence. If they were honest with themselves they must have admitted their terror at being forced to wander in this baffling, foreign realm, exploring caves and crevices and lifting rocks to find what they would have preferred not to know about. What had this maleless realm to do with them? How much easier to deny that it even existed.

I think they were frightened, and probably embarrassed, and probably aroused. I have always thought droll those stories about censorship groups reading through 425 sex books in order to identify the extent of the evil in the works. In this I share Ollie's opinion of human nature: I cannot believe that anyone can be exposed to graphic sexual depictions and have no erotic response whatsoever. The response may wear off when the novelty goes, but initially there must be some arousal. What must the judges have felt when they heard stories about wet noises and beseechings to "do it, darling"? Did they really listen without lascivious fascination? Did the stories never come back to them with a vividness, welcome or unwelcome, when they were riding home or eating their dinners or making love to their wives? When they discussed the testimony with each other, or thought about it in their chambers, did no wild images flash though their minds? And how hard it must be to have lascivious pictures in your mind when you are wearing a formidable wig and robe and you probably assume, since sexuality was not as easily discussed 170 years ago as it is today, that none of your other bewigged and berobed brethren are bothered by such images. Of course they would call this case disgusting and painful.

I imagine the class issue caused them pain too. Everyone was supposed to be equal before the law, but in a society which still saw the universe as a great chain of being, did a Lady Cumming Gordon really not have the slightest edge, at least in the minds of some of the judges, over two school mistresses? Is it only coincidence that Robertson and Glenlee, who found in favor of Lady Cumming Gordon, were the staunchest of Tories? Was a Lady of their own class simply not more credible to them than women of the middle class? And then her husband had been a Member of Parliament, and both her surviving sons, Sir William and Charles, were Members of Parliament; her daughter Louisa was married to John Hay Forbes, a judge in the First Division of the Court of Session, and her daughter Edwina was married to Thomas Miller of Glenlee, the son of Sir William Miller, Lord Glenlee, who now sat in this court and deliberated on her case.

But there was still more to complicate matters: while the judges' natural inclinations might perhaps have made them believe Lady Cumming Gordon over the school mistresses, in what direction would those same narrow preconceptions have sent them when they compared the two Scottish school mistresses with an illegitimate dark-skinned girl? If they were ruled by predilection, no course would have been satisfactory. No matter what they decided, some of their most sacred prejudices about females, class, and race would be violated.

JUNE 27, 1811, 10:00 A.M.

LORD MEADOWBANK: No case was ever more extraordinary or required a more grave and mature consideration. The plaintiffs are two women of irreproachable character who have been brought to ruin by communications about their conduct which, however confidential, could not fail to ruin them. The defendant is an honourable Scottish Matron, who thought herself called upon, by strong moral duties, to save her own grandchildren from contamination, and to warn the relatives of the other scholars, who had, as she thought, been placed in the school because of her recommendation, that she now had serious reasons to withdraw her recommendation. There are also the young persons to be taken into account, or at least one young person, from whom the information originally came—one, unfortunately wanting in the advantages of legitimacy and of a European complexion, and therefore all the more dependent on the favour of her protector.

And, in my mind, there is a fourth party whose interest is deeply at stake: I mean the public—for the virtues, the comforts, and the freedom of domestic intercourse mainly depend on the purity of female manners, and that again on their habits of intercourse remaining as they have hitherto been, free from suspicion. It was because I dreaded the baleful effects on domestic morals, which even surmises of a case such as this one must produce, that I so strongly urged when the parties first came before me as Lord Ordinary, that they be certain of the grounds in justice, prudence, and expediency before they proceeded further. And when they did proceed, your Lordships, impressed with similar apprehensions, took every precaution within your power, though with small hopes of success, to confine this case to the walls of the Court, and to keep its subject unknown in general society. If it should become widely known, regardless of who wins or who loses in this litigation, the public will lose in terms of innocence, purity, and the happiness which accompanies those states.

But let me turn to the evidence itself. The extraordinary nature of the imputation is thought by some of my colleagues to guarantee its truth and to preclude the possibility of invention on the part of the young ladies. They argue too that the nature of the imputation sanctions every measure of impetuosity and harshness that the defendant took. It is apparent that such an imputation operates upon the moral feelings as the imputation of witchcraft did upon the religious feelings of our ancestors: to them too the charge was the evidence of its own truth—and all the nonsense and the extravagance and the palpable falsehood which often accompanied the charge escaped the observation of the intelligent and religious, but very enthusiastic minds of the prosecutors and judges.

Because this is so dangerous a case, I have spared no pains to make myself thoroughly acquainted with it before rendering a decision. And though I now see that there have been omissions in the investigation, which less inexperience in cases of such a complexion would have prevented, I have no hesitation to avow to your Lordships that my opinion has no shade of doubt in it: that the criminal imputation against the plaintiffs is false and groundless, and that Dame Helen Cumming Gordon, therefore, is guilty of libel and must be made to pay damages.

I must acknowledge that with respect to the crime I continue to labour under a high degree of incredulity. I have yet heard nothing to shake the observations that I made to your Lordships in my original report of the case when it came to me as the Lord Ordinary. I am not at all appalled that I have been accused of ignorance and the like by the defendant's counsel. I shall never dread obloquy for thinking freely and endeavouring to reason soundly and rationally. On the contrary, I shall refer your Lordships to two Hindoo laws, from the collection of the ordinances of Menu, published in Calcutta, which are certainly worth all the authorities quoted by the defendant's counsel put together. Upon reading them we are left with no sort of doubt that women with a peculiar conformation—an elongation of the clitoris—are capable both of giving and receiving pleasure in intercourse with other women.

I daresay it is also true enough that as a provocative to the use of the male, women have been employed to kindle each other's lewd appetites. Nor would I dispute that by means of tools women might artificially accomplish the venereal gratification. But in this case, the use of tools is excluded from the defendant's evidence, such as it is: please note that Miss Pirie is said to have declared that she could not promise to refrain from visiting Miss Woods in bed until the winter holidays; but it is also said that when she came to Miss Woods' bed she always performed the function of the male, which surely could have given her no venereal gratification if performed only by means of tools—how, then, could she have been so driven that she could not promise to refrain even for a few months from her indulgence!

But if tools and unnatural conformation are out of the question, then I state as the ground of my incredulity the important fact that the imputed vice has been hitherto unknown in Britain. Neither the pruriency of corrupt imaginations has brought it forward in works of obscenity, nor has the wantonness of satire ever ventured to suggest it as a ground of obloquy. Nor was it a crime known to the most corrupt of the ancients: it must be seriously noted that in Lucian's *Dialogues,* no matter how much the woman is questioned as to the means of pretended gratification, he as the writer was plainly unable to give the smallest satisfaction. So that, although Lucian was utterly insensible to claims of modesty or decorum, all he can do is make the woman swear by Venus that she won't tell. Your Lordships, then, will judge of the probability of two Scotch women, of admitted intelligence, educated as Miss Woods and Miss Pirie were, and undertaking such a profession as they did undertake, discovering a venereal gratification which not even Lucian was able to describe, and rushing into a vice which, hitherto, even the most corrupt imaginations in this country had not so much as fancied. And what is perhaps equally extraordinary, that they should have dared to disclose to each other the secret of such depraved inclinations!

Secondly, as to the circumstances in which this supposed crime is said to have been committed: your Lordships cannot suppose that these women were not perfectly aware that the slightest suspicion of lewdness or indecency in their manner or deportment would be absolute ruin to them. You must also be aware that they were in charge of the arrangement of their household, and under the unsuspected state of female intercourse and habits in this country, they would have had no difficulty, if they wished, to have given themselves ample opportunity for indulgence without any suspicion of impropriety. But by the defendant's evidence we are asked to believe that every night in the world, after their pupils went to bed, between eight and nine o'clock, and though the plaintiffs had as many hours as they pleased to meet in solitude, in a drawing room furnished with a sofa, away from the observation of every human being—they chose instead to visit each other in a bed, occupied by a third person, with four or five others very near.

And now, we come to consider, in the third place, the situation and character of the witnesses. They are young females of sixteen years of age. Young persons are naturally curious about venereal intercourse, although they are anxiously excluded from knowledge of it by all the contrivances of civilized life. Hence, if they see action between two persons which they do not perfectly understand the meaning of, and any suggestion is furnished to them that such action is connected with venereal indulgence, they have gotten a hypothesis by which they will solve the phenomenon of the mysterious action.

It appears to me, however, that copulation without penetration of the female, or the gratification of wild and unnatural lust committed in sport, is much like charging a rape as committed *en gaieté du coeur,* and in the course of small talk. By way of illustration I will mention at present (though the transcripts are rife with such illustration) that both Miss Munro and Miss Cumming concur in saying that the plaintiffs whispered unceasingly during their suspected venereal interviews. Is such whispering while one is trying to gratify a furious lust credible?

But there is more that is still more incredible. For example, Miss Cumming's imperfect knowledge of the subject led her to suppose that acts of copulation were accompanied by a particular noise, and hence she describes a noise in the interviews of the mistresses and compares it to what yields no sound, no more than copulation does—a finger moving in the neck of a wet bottle.

I know your Lordships will all recognize the extreme facility with which credit is given in all schools (but particularly female boarding schools) to whatever is there circulated or surmised. Perhaps this is especially so in the boarding schools of girls because their deportment is completely tramelled and their conversations are a subject of constant control; thus the credulity of the nursery is but little diminished. It may be held as a matter of absolute certainty that a young girl at a boarding school gives implicit credit, without inquiry or discussion, to whatever is told her by her companions, unless something has occurred to make her question it; and that the tales of domestics are adopted with nearly equal facility. This will explain how the absurd interpretations of what occurred spread from Miss Cumming to Miss Munro to Miss Stirling and perhaps to others.

The perfect innocence of female habits in the intercourse of women with one another is universally accepted and believed in this country. The plaintiffs thus had every reason to think that their innocent interviews could never suggest a suspicion of lewdness or indecency. They therefore can in no respect be blamable for suspicions fastened on them which were so foreign to them, and so far beyond the calculations of even extraordinary prudence to calcu-

261

late or foresee. Those who were base enough, corrupt enough, extravagant enough, or foolish enough to form such suspicions, convert them into imputations, and then communicate them, must be answerable for the consequences.

AUGUST 3, 1982

The judges were all guilty of selective perception, whether they found for Lady Cumming Gordon or the mistresses. Meadowbank's selectivity, however, is particularly intriguing. He prided himself on his historical knowledge and, to bedazzle his brethren, even furnished abstruse references to ancient Hindu law that corroborated the existence of lesbianism in heathen lands. Yet he could claim that "the imputed vice has been hitherto unknown in Britain," and that "neither the pruriency of corrupt imaginations has brought it forward in works of obscenity, nor has the wantonness of satire ever ventured to suggest it as a ground of obloquy." Could he really have been so ignorant not only of British legal history, but also of pornography and satire in his day and in the preceding century? In addition to the two trials of British transvestite women in the middle and late eighteenth century, I have been able to find numerous references to British lesbians of all classes, in satire and pornography and moral tracts and health handbooks. For example:

In 1713, Anthony Hamilton's *Memoirs of the Count de Gramont: An Amorous History of the English Court Under the Reign of Charles II,* in which Miss Hobart, a maid of honor in the Restoration Court, is made the butt of satire when she is accused of seducing her maid and every other woman she can entrap.

In 1736, *The Toast,* a satire by William King, who accuses Lady Frances Brudenell of unrestrained lasciviousness with both males and females and depicts in graphic terms her wanton behavior with her favorite woman lover.

In 1740, a popular handbook entitled *The Ladies Dispensa-*

tory; or Every Woman Her Own Physician, with a section on a young lady who was indoctrinated into mutual masturbation by her mother's chambermaid, "with whom she continued to practice it seven years, they trying all means to pleasure each other and heighten the titillation."

In 1745, Robert James' *Medicinal Dictionary,* in which he observes that in some women (ostensibly British women as well as others) the clitoris is so far prominent "that they make attempts to converse in criminal manner with other women, rubbing their partners and receiving as well as giving satisfaction."

In 1749, John Cleland's erotic *Memoirs of a Woman of Pleasure,* in which Fanny Hill is initiated into sex by the prostitute Phoebe, who employs digital-vaginal stimulation.

Also in 1749, an anonymous work, *Satan's Harvest Home,* in which the puritanical author complains of seeing often in public "two ladies kissing and slopping each other, in a lascivious manner," and expresses his fear that such behavior might lead to criminal amorousness.

It is curious that an individual as widely read as Meadowbank, with such a fund of arcane knowledge, had no familiarity with these works, which would have been much more accessible to him than the Hindu laws of Menu.

JUNE 27, 1811, 2:00 P.M.

LORD NEWTON: I have taken more pains in this case and have had more difficulty in making up my opinion than in any other which ever came before me as a Judge. On the one hand, I see two women of respectable character accused of a crime. On the other hand, I see two young ladies swearing distinctly and pointedly, whom I must believe unless I charge them with wilful and corrupt perjury. I have no other alternative.

It seems to me that the defendant has no occasion to prove that the mistresses used any machinery or that there was an extraordinary conformation of their parts. It is quite sufficient that there are indecencies which render them unfit for the superintendence of young ladies. If you believe that they were in each other's beds, lying above each other, and that there were motions and shakings of the bed, this is quite enough to convict them of indecencies. Whether or not they were both gratified, or could be gratified by such an act, is irrelevant to our concerns.

The monstrous improbability stuck with me, not of their being guilty of such offences, but that they should choose such a scene for it, and doing it in the way they did, in the bed with a young lady, instead of getting a bed to themselves. This in my mind is not solved by the answer that it is always the custom for one of the mistresses to sleep in the room with the scholars, for I cannot help thinking they might have got the better of this etiquette. However, they might, as has been said, have been hurried away at first by a sudden fit of lust without having intended to be. And having once gotten away with it, they might have thought they could repeat it with impunity. Such a possibility will go a long way toward explaining what at first seems improbable.

But besides, when I recollect that the story is clearly sworn to by two young ladies, and that these two girls had no passion to gratify by inventing such an abominable tale, I cannot doubt that however improbable it may appear, it was really so. It is true that one of the witnesses, Miss Cumming, is a grandchild of the defendant, and that she had an interest in supporting the accusation after it was made, but what possible interest had she to trump up this story in the first place? What could make her say that she had seen certain facts unless they really had been so? I conceive that nothing short of the spirit of the devil could have induced Miss Munro and Miss Cumming to invent this story and to swear to it as they have done.

If the plaintiffs were being tried for this crime, I might probably, if called upon to decide, return a verdict of Not Proven. But in the present shape of the question, I think enough has been established to justify Lady Cumming Gordon for everything she has done.

2:40 P.M.

THE LORD JUSTICE-CLERK TURNS TO LORD POLKEMMET: This case now comes to your Lordship's vote. Is your Lordship prepared to give your opinion now, or—since you were unable to be present at the testimony and just yesterday you received the printed transcripts—had you not better take some time to consider the case?

LORD POLKEMMET: My Lord, I have formed an opinion in this case, and I am now ready to deliver it. My opinion is to find the defendant, Lady Cumming Gordon, not guilty.

AUGUST 4, 1982

And so the case was decided in favor of Lady Cumming Gordon on the basis of a swing vote delivered by a judge who was not present for a single day of the testimony. But if Ollie is right, it would not have mattered had he attended every session faithfully. Because the mistresses could not offer irrefutable evidence in their cause, he would anyway have found Lady Cumming Gordon, whose husband and son had served with Polkemmet's father and brother in Parliament, innocent of libel.

I spent a frustrating week trying to find out what became of Miss Munro and Miss Stirling after the trial. They were listed in none of the postal directories I could locate. Both of them probably married a few years later, but I could find no trace of that in the marriage records for Edinburgh or Kippenross, Miss Stirling's home, and I have no idea where else they might have gone. Since I do not know their married names, I cannot find their death certificates. And they were not highborn enough to have been listed in any of the peerage books.

But what I would most like to know about them could not be found in any official record anyway. For the rest of their lives after this trial, how did they regard romantic friendship between women? Most women of their class seem to have had loving female friends. It was not unusual for women to tell each other, as Lady Mary Montagu told Anne Wortley in the previous century, "Your friendship is the only happiness of my life; and should I lose it I would have nothing to do but to take one of my garters and search for a convenient beam," or as Mme. de Staël told Mme. Récamier, about the time Miss Munro and Miss Stirling were in school, "I love you with a love surpassing that of friendship. I go down on my knees to embrace you with all my heart." Such effusions were normal between romantic friends.

But most romantic friends probably did not understand the potential inherent in such intense passions. Miss Munro and Miss Stirling, however, could never again escape from their wisdom. I believe that because of that wisdom, which was so horrifying in an antisexual age, they would have felt compelled to cut out of their lives all manifestations of love for their own sex, just as most women of our own sophisticated century have. What other women of their day would have seen as a delightful fascination or a happy refuge from the lovelessness of a sexually dichotomized world, they now saw as leprous.

Ollie believes there is an inverse relationship between the amount of social independence a woman has in a society and the latitude she is given to express affection for another woman. "In the United States, where women are freest in all other areas of their lives," she says, "they don't dare walk down the street arm in arm. In western Europe, where they aren't quite so free, there are no taboos about women walking together with arms linked. And in eastern Europe and the Orient they can even walk together holding hands." She claims an anthropologist friend once told her that among the Cubeo Indians of the northwest Amazon, where young females had no autonomy whatsoever, they were used to expressing affection for other girls with strokes and kisses on the breasts and even on the nipples. "There was virtually no possibility that they would run off with each other. They were the property of the patriarchs, so that men could allow them all manner of expression and still not feel threatened."

I think she is partly right. What women do together becomes far more threatening to men if women are socially and economically independent. They can reject marriage and the family as dependent females never could. They can cleave to each other as women are expected to cleave to men. But there is more to it: women cannot be romantic friends in our century because of Freud and the other sexologists. Now everyone knows about the "mental aberration of lesbianism." A hundred or two hundred years ago, almost no one did.

I remember reading in the early 1970s a newspaper article about two California high school girls who were enrolled in a course on social behavior. For their term project they chose to study the limits of proximity between friends. During three weeks they behaved as romantic friends always had in other centuries: they held hands when they walked together, they sat with their arms around each other, they exchanged kisses on the cheek when they parted. They did no more. Their classmates, products of twentieth-century wisdom, who knew a "perverted" impulse when they saw it, or thought they saw it, called them lezzies and threatened to beat them up.

Forever after their experience with this trial, Miss Munro and Miss Stirling would know that woman's love for other women might be construed as a perversion. I would venture to guess that they were very careful not to hold hands or link arms or kiss their female friends, if they dared to have female friends again.

Although the party for whom Miss Munro and Miss Stirling testified was victorious in the June 27, 1811, decision of the Court, the girls must have heard that verdict with some ambivalence. Lady Cumming Gordon's victory meant that it was believed that they had indeed witnessed indecencies, and while it would have been dreadful for them had the judges thought they made up such a tale, this was barely better. They must have felt that now they were marked in everyone's mind, cast beyond innocence prematurely and forever.

The next turn of events, which showed them they were not going to be allowed simply to put the case behind them, must have added to their discomfort. According to Scottish law of the early nineteenth century, if strong doubt and hesitation had been expressed by those lordships who concurred in the judgment, the losing party could petition the Court to review its decision. On October 10, 1811, John Clerk prepared such a petition for his clients. The petition was granted on November 22, 1811.

PART III

The Review
and Appeal

In the Court of Session, Again

Lord Newton died on October 19, 1811, nine days after the petition for a review was submitted to the Court. He was replaced by Adam Gillies, a staunch Whig and an outspoken opponent of the party in power. That Gillies should have been elevated to the bench in 1811, during the height of Tory strength and animosity toward political rivals, was a marked tribute to his legal talents.

On November 25, 1811, Charles Hope, who had been Lord Justice-Clerk of the Second Division, was made President of the Court of Session. His approval of John Clerk's petition was his last act as head of the Second Division. Charles Hope's rise continued until, at the death of the Duke of Montrose in 1836, he became Lord Justice-General, which was the highest official position in Scotland. Hope's role as the Lord Justice-Clerk of the Second Division was taken by Lord Boyle. Hope requested Alexander Fraser Tytler, Lord Woodhouselee, of the First Division to assume on *Woods and Pirie against Dame Cumming Gordon* the spot he himself had vacated to become Lord President.

Woodhouselee had been on the bench since 1805. Twenty-five years earlier he had become a professor of universal history at the University of Edinburgh, and history remained his first love, but in 1790 he was urged to accept the office of Judge Advocate of Scotland. It is said that he pleaded often, too often in the judgment of some, for a mitigation of punishment where the sentence of the Courts-martial appeared to him unnecessarily severe. His liberalism made him a number of enemies.

Before the year 1811 was at an end, Lord Polkemmet decided, to everyone's great relief, including his own, to resign his gown and retire to his country estate. He was replaced by Robert Craigie, whose ability, many said, was as good a match to Polkemmet's as could be found.

Therefore, when the Court of Session came to review *Woods and Pirie against Dame Cumming Gordon* in January 1812 the Second Division was constituted in this way: Lord Boyle (Lord Justice-Clerk), Lord Meadowbank, Lord Robertson, Lord Glenlee, Lord Gillies, Lord Woodhouselee, Lord Craigie. In the 1811 decision Lords Boyle and Meadowbank had found in favor of the plaintiffs; Lords Robertson and Glenlee had found in favor of the defendant. The 1812 decisions of all four were essentially the same as their earlier pronouncements.

FEBRUARY 25, 1812, 10:00 A.M.

LORD WOODHOUSELEE: This is the most painful question on which I have ever been called to form an opinion since I have sat as a Judge of this court. When the case came to be decided by your Lordships in a former stage of the proceedings, I sincerely congratulated myself that I was relieved from that disagreeable job. I most earnestly wish it were still in my power to escape from a duty so truly painful to the mind as that which my being transferred to this Division of the Court, in order to replace our Lord President Hope, has now imposed on me. But as that is impossible, I must prepare to discharge my duty in the best manner I can.

I believe that I have conscientiously tried to arrive at a sound and mature judgement in this case before us—and I am happy at least to think that the opinion I have formed is free from all manner of doubt, however much I may regret the consequence of that opinion to a person whom I sincerely esteem and value. She is a person whose worth I know, and with whose family and connections I myself and mine have been united by the bonds of friendship and personal regard for more than a generation.

If that respectable matron to whom I allude, and on whose side all my natural prejudices (if I were conscious of any in this case) must have lain,—if she erred, as I think she has grievously erred in this one unlucky exercise of her judgement, I am sure it was a virtuous error. It was an error proceeding from a worthy principle, and though it cannot be deemed venial, since its consequences were of so severe and cruel a nature, it had at least its origin in a mistaken sense of duty and in an earnest desire to do what she felt to be a moral obligation.

But, Gentlemen, I do not doubt that she did err, for, after examining everything that was placed at my disposal, it became painfully clear to me that it was the tainted imagination of Miss Cumming that furnished the shocking interpretation of events. It was her warm imagination, speculating on things upon which she had thought a great deal, and perhaps talked a great deal, without having distinct ideas about them. It was her fancy that first raised that phantom of an unnatural commerce, known perhaps in that Eastern climate from which she came, and talked of probably among the women whose discourse she had been accustomed to hear, but which in this part of the world is a thing unheard of,—a thing perhaps impossible. That this young woman's mind was contaminated, that she was no stranger to those impure ideas which she had imbibed partly from her Eastern education, and partly perhaps from that precocity of temperament which she owed to an Eastern constitution,—that her mind, I say, was familiar to such ideas, we have proof from her own mouth, when she declares that the suspicion of some criminal intercourse between her mistresses *arose from her own reflections,* before she conversed with anybody on the subject. This was in answer to a shrewd question put to her, according to the transcripts, and it is apparent that she did not herself understand the significance of her response, or else we would not expect such an honest answer. The inference, however, is clear: her mind and imagination were familiar to such matters; the idea, which would never occur to a pure and uninstructed mind, occurs to her. It would never have occurred to such a mind as Miss Stirling's. It had never occurred even to Miss Munro until Miss Cumming suggested it to her. To this young woman it occurred, as she admits herself, *from her own reflections.* And once having conceived this abominable idea, she construes everything she sees, every word she hears, every equivocal incident in those mysterious night visits (for mysterious they certainly must have been if the reason of them was unknown)—she construes everything, I say, into so many proofs of this shocking supposition which had entered her mind.

She probably had wrought herself into something like a belief in the criminality of her mistresses. She *had* reason, and a *good reason too,* for bearing them ill will. She had experienced little indulgence from them, because they did not think her conduct deserved it. She had been more frequently at fault, and more frequently disgraced and censured than any girl at school. She had had severe things said to her, things that were likely to stick and rankle in her mind. She, therefore, did not like her mistresses. She was tired of the school and was earnestly desirous of getting home to her grandmother's, and of associating with her family, and of having her share in fashionable amusements with them. The bondage of the school was irksome to her. The discipline was too rigid for her. In one word, the mistresses had no high opinion of her, and she did not like them. This is human nature.

But still, I do not think so ill of her as to believe that she would have brought this horrid charge against them to her grandmother if she were conscious that it was altogether a falsehood of her own contrivance. And here I will state what I believe to have been the progress of Miss Cumming's mind upon the subject. Counsel for the defense argues with great plausibility when he says that it is a most revolting supposition to conceive that a young girl of sixteen should invent such a diabolical plan as to bring about the utter ruin of two innocent women by means of a horrid fiction—and one which could not fail to bring herself and her family into the most distressing situation from that inquiry to which the charge would lead—an inquiry in which there was every probability that her own malice and falsehood would be fully detected, her own character destroyed, her grandmother's favour forfeited, and which, in short, must lead to her own ruin. The answer to all this is, in the first place, that to Miss Cumming's mind, the fact of such a lascivious commerce between persons of the same sex did not carry with it either the idea of impossibility or of that shocking criminality which it would have excited in the breast of a young girl born and educated in this country. And the mysterious circumstances which she observed may have actually led to *a pretty strong suspicion* that the fact with which she meant to charge them had some ground in reality.

But in the second place, Miss Cumming's original intention was neither of so black and diabolical a nature as has been supposed, nor did she fear any of the dangers and consequences that I have mentioned. She neither meant to ruin these two poor women, nor did she in the least fear that she was to bring herself and her family into any distress by the scheme which she had formed. Her purpose and her plan (wicked enough as they were) went not one whit further than to accomplish her removal from the school that she so disliked, and to procure her the liberty and gratifications of fashionable life, which she longed to partake of. These, I firmly believe, were the sole objects she had in view.

But the greatest blame, Gentlemen, I must, to my very great regret, lay on Lady Cumming. Her motive, no doubt, was virtuous, and I give her all the credit that can be allowed her on the score. But her conduct was rash, inconsiderate, and cruel to these unhappy women. Lady Cumming may have acted in good faith. I doubt not she did. She believed what she was told. But she took no means to ascertain the truth of her information. Here, therefore, her conduct was negligent in the extreme. She scorned all idea of questioning the truth of her granddaughter's story, however incredible, however shocking in itself, and however fatal in its consequence to those women of whose character she had thought so highly, and had had the best reasons for thinking so.

They were sacrificed at once, and their ruin sealed, without her even attempting to hear them in their own defence, without even acquainting them of their crime. If there was not malice in this conduct, there was a precipitancy and a culpable negligence, for which it is impossible to find excuse.

It is with the utmost pain, the most sincere regret, that I must add my opinion to those of your Lordships who are in favour of finding damages due, though I am not prepared to say to what extent the recompense should be. That must be matter for future consideration.

AUGUST 5, 1982

Woodhouselee, liberal as he allegedly was throughout his judicial career, obviously felt no need to hide his prejudice in this case. He knew that it would be shared by other respected members of the Court, that assumptions about the corruption of other races were acceptable bases for arriving at a verdict: the mistresses were innocent because in his part of the world lesbianism was "a thing unheard of,—a thing perhaps impossible." Jane Cumming was undoubtedly the culprit, because it was "in that Eastern climate from which she came" that she must have learned of such "unnatural commerce" between women. It was through her "Eastern education" and her "Eastern constitution" that her mind was contaminated with impure ideas. Miss Munro and Miss Stirling would never have come to such conclusions without her. It was also her inferior moral heritage that made her unhesitant to tell such outrageous lies for the slight reason of wishing to be taken out of school. That she was supposedly one-half white and of the Scottish aristocracy, and that she had received the greatest part of her education on the Cumming Gordon estate and at a boarding school in Elgin, Woodhouselee overlooked.

"How convenient that Woodhouselee had a dark-skinned girl to explain how the specter of lesbianism could have emerged in this Scottish school for young ladies," Ollie points out. "But what would we have done if it had been one of Lady Cumming Gordon's legitimate, white granddaughters who made the accusations against the women?"

After several days in which I could locate nothing material to this case, I finally met with some success. Today I found a sketch of Mrs. Woods at the National Library. When we first arrived in Edinburgh I had hopes of locating pictures of all the principals, certainly of Dame Cumming Gordon and her grandchildren and the other wellborn young ladies at the school, since there was such an active enterprise in portrait painting of the wealthy in the early nineteenth century. But their likenesses all seem to have vanished. Aside from sketches of the judges and the lawyers, I could find nothing, until today.

The picture is a treasure: it is a 1784 sketch with the most famous actress of her day, Mrs. Siddons, at the center. Mrs. Siddons is in costume, on stage, in the play *Douglas*. On her right is the actor Mr. Sutherland; on her left, the actress Ann Woods, looking exactly as I had imagined her to look. She is very posed. She is also tiny compared to the majestic Mrs. Siddons. Perhaps her size in this picture only reflects the artist's notion of the unimportance of her role, but I always thought of her as being just that small and just that artificially theatrical despite her small stature. Her face, I am sure, is captured faithfully. Her chin recedes, as it should in a caricature of a weak personality, and her forehead is round and large and stubborn: a passive-aggressive type. Her eyes are veiled. Perhaps I see in this sketch a secret sensuality and self-indulgence only because of what I already know of her, but I think she could not look otherwise and play the role she has in my drama.

I wish I understood Marianne's attachment to her better than I do. I can imagine how very little Jane Pirie must have understood it. Jane must have looked at Mrs. Woods and seen only a selfish and grasping old woman. To Marianne, her aunt may have been the only spot of warmth in her adolescence, her Executive Director, perhaps—and as a young woman with a strong, if not rigid, sense of responsibility, Marianne could probably not allow herself now to neglect what she saw as just payment on her debt. If Mrs. Woods had no place to go and no means of support, of course Marianne would have to take her in, and not only provide for her, but help her to a respectable occupation if she desired one—just as Mrs. Woods and her husband once did for Marianne. Jane Pirie, never having labored under a debt of gratitude (since she always envisioned herself as embattled and unbefriended by anyone but her God—and perhaps Marianne), could not bear Marianne's solicitude toward her aunt.

"Has it occurred to you that maybe Marianne and her aunt set Jane Pirie up?" my ever cynical love asks.

I confess it has occurred to me, since I am as paranoid as Jane no doubt was. I am reminded that paranoids have enemies too.

Ollie has already worked out "what probably happened": Mrs. Woods could never approve of the friendship between Jane and Marianne, and she told her niece so. Miss Pirie was crass in her manners, cross in her disposition, not a proper lady at all. Mrs. Woods also told her niece that she considered Marianne's intention to form a partnership with that creature sheer lunacy. But Marianne demonstrated that she knew what she was doing.

A short while before Jane's proposal, Marianne had lost two students in one week. It had become hard going for her and her aunt. How much longer could they tolerate living on the sad pittance that Marianne earned as a day teacher, two guineas for twelve lessons, panicking lest she lose a student or two, which meant they would have to skip a meal or two until she found other students to make up for the diminished revenue? And no matter how many hours she worked she could never hope to earn much better than a subsistence. There was no future in it. If she took a job as a governess somewhere, her aunt would be left alone, and they would still have the expense of keeping up the flat. How could they improve their lot?

"We will go into business for ourselves," the aunt declared.

Marianne saw how impractical that was. They had no money with which to start a business—they barely had enough to put bread on the table. And what else did she know but teaching?

Then Jane Pirie said that Marianne and she must open a school of their own, and Jane Pirie had the wherewithall to do it.

"But how will you be able to work with her?" the aunt asked. "She has the grace and couth of a herring seller. Who would send their daughters to be taught by her?"

"She is very intelligent, Aunt. And she has met with great success as a governess. Anyway, she would not join the school immediately. She will need to finish out her agreement with the Campbell family, and she will not be free for almost half a year. I will open the school and get the students. I will establish everything. You will help me. You will be the housekeeper—or the business manager, if you like. And who knows what will happen in half a year. In any case, the tone and atmosphere of the school will be set then."

Perhaps Marianne did not really mean to defraud her friend. But whatever heat she may have once felt for her had long since cooled (not to be revived until the summer of 1810). Marianne simply saw the way to a fuller life before her, and Jane Pirie was willing to provide the vehicle by which Marianne might travel that road. Marianne had neither the desire nor the inclination just then to look very far down the path to the point at which Jane stood there awaiting her. As for Mrs. Woods, six months was as good as a lifetime. Who could know where any one of them might be in six months? She and her niece would open the school, and perhaps Jane Pirie would marry or die before the time came for her to join them.

"Maybe," I say, "but I doubt it. Mrs. Woods may have had a hidden agenda, but I am sure that her niece did not. I think that Marianne believed at least that she loved Jane as much as Jane loved her. What Mrs. Woods saw as Jane's lack of polish, Marianne saw as her forcefulness and honesty. She admired her energetic confidence in dealing with the world. When Jane wanted something, she put everything into getting it. Nothing would stop her. It was a divine monomania that awed Marianne, all the more because she knew she did not possess it.

"I am sure they both entered into their bargain in the best faith. I doubt that even Mrs. Woods had larceny in her heart. She was silly and self-indulgent, but not thieving. Things went awry not because of anyone's malicious intent, but because the wrong mix of personalities came together."

"The beauty of this case, my darling," Ollie says, "is that you can believe of it whatever you wish to believe."

FEBRUARY 26, 1812, 10:00 A.M.

LORD CRAIGIE: This is a most painful discussion, and I have tried to relieve myself from the feelings it is apt to excite by confining my attention as much as possible to the questions of law and of evidence that are involved in it.

The pleas that have been urged are twofold: 1. The good faith of the defendant when she made the statements on which this suit is founded; and 2. The truth of those statements.

As to the first plea, it was clearly her duty to communicate the information to those persons to whom she had previously recommended the mistresses as being well qualified to take charge of children. She did this in good faith, having belief and confidence in the veracity of her granddaughter, who had never, in any essential degree, deviated from the truth.

As to the second plea, the truth of what the defendant had asserted against the plaintiffs: that, it seems to me has been well proven by the evidence. What has been sworn in this court would not only convince an individual like the defendant herself, but also the conscience of a Judge.

In the laws of most countries, and particularly in those of England, the testimony of Miss Munro, who seems to me to be a witness of unquestionable credit, would have been sufficient by itself to prove any crime of which the plaintiffs could be guilty. Her testimony, from what I could see in the transcripts, is indisputably clear, precise and positive with regard to the plaintiffs' gross indecencies. It is vain to assert that she was misled and deceived by Miss Cumming. She swears to circumstances which fell directly under her own observation, and which must render the plaintiffs unworthy of a place in the society of virtuous and modest women. And, although in Scotland it is held that the evidence of one witness, without anything else, is not sufficient to prove a criminal act, we do not require two witnesses swearing directly to the same act. One witness of full credit, if supported by collateral evidence, whether arising from the conduct of the accused parties or establishing circumstances previous or subsequent to the act that would show it was likely committed, will be enough. And here there is corroborative evidence of all the kinds I have mentioned.

In addition to this, if any addition were necessary, we have the evidence of Miss Cumming. A great deal has been said, and in my opinion far too much, with regard to this young lady. But I do not see that she is to be considered as a false or perjured witness. As to the material facts, all of which are confirmed by Miss Munro, I have not the least distrust of her testimony. Even if her evidence had not been taken, however, it seems to me that the rest of the testimony is such that I, both as a man and a Judge, must believe it.

On the whole, therefore, it appears to me that the decision of this court which was made last year ought to be affirmed, and that the defendant ought to be acquitted.

10:35 A.M.

LORD GILLIES: It appears to me that the major question in this case centers on whether or not Miss Marianne Woods and Miss Jane Pirie are guilty of indecent carnal knowledge of each other. I have perused the transcripts with great care, and I cannot believe they are. Matters not only perfectly innocent and natural, but perfectly common and, I may almost say universal in this country, are there presented as presumptions of guilt. The defendant's evidence tries to lead your Lordships to believe that whenever two young women form a friendship together, and that friendship ripens into intimacy, if ever they venture to share the same bed, that becomes a proof of guilt. What are we to think of this? Are we to say that every woman who has formed an intimate friendship and has slept in the same bed with another is guilty? Where is the innocent woman in Scotland?—If any such is known to your Lordships, she is not known to me, whose friendships do not ripen into intimacies which would permit her to sleep in the same bed with her friend when necessary.

I ask, in the case of women in their rank of life, is it not the natural and uniform practice to partake of the same bed? I am sure that I am not altogether ignorant of the manners of this country. I cannot think or admit that it furnishes any presumption against the plaintiffs because they formed a friendship of great warmth and they sometimes slept in the same bed together. These are the natural presumptions of innocence in my mind.

In like manner, the defendant's counsel has presented the whole conduct of the plaintiffs as suspicious, though I think their conduct was always accounted for by the circumstances. They visited each other at night because they had no opportunity of meeting together in the day time, when they were constantly occupied. These visits being paid, it was natural that they should invite each other into bed if no fire was going in the room, so this is no circumstance of suspicion. God forbid that that time should ever arrive when a lady in Scotland, standing at the side of another's bed in the night time, should be suspected of guilt because she was invited into it.

It is said that they tried to conceal their visits. I have no doubt of that. Whether they went to each other's bedsides with the infamous motives that have been imputed to them, or whether they went there on account of school business, it was natural that they should wish to conceal it. It is not a creditable thing that such business should have been necessary, which it was, on account of their quarrels. I may be told that even that was an indecency; but if they were not moved by the passion of lust in paying these visits, I say it was merely indecorum, which did not, in the slightest degree, justify the accusation against them.

I will not say much more as to the improbability of the charge, because that was fully dwelt upon formerly. But it does appear to me very improbable, if not incredible, in a moral point of view. I don't mean to deny that the existence of the crime has been alleged before now, and perhaps believed. But such reports and such belief do not in my mind prove its existence. I am happy to express my belief that to this moment, no such crime was ever known in Scotland or in Britain. I do believe that the crime here alleged has no existence.

But there is still another difficulty that the defendant has not sifted, and I put the question now: Is it more improbable that Miss Cumming should have invented the story or that the plaintiffs should have been guilty of the crime? Which is the most improbable of the two? For your Lordships are forced to make a choice. Whether it is more improbable that this girl from India should have invented such a charge, or that the mistresses should have committed this crime? I have no hesitation in saying that it is infinitely the most improbable of the two that the mistresses should have done it. And with all the inconsistencies in Miss Cumming's evidence, I have no hesitation in saying that I reject it altogether. I am sorry for it, respectably connected as she is.

Nothing then remains but the evidence of Miss Munro, for I will not dignify with the name of evidence the testimonies of Mary Brown and Miss Stirling. Miss Munro's mind was in a morbid state. She was worked on by the superior address of another, and she appears to me to be rather of a weak mind to begin with. Now, my Lords, what does she swear to? She saw one person come to the bed of another, both females,—the one asks the other to come into bed; and Miss Munro thinks that a proof of guilt. If her mind had not been perverted, how could she possibly have thought so? I ask, what would have been her impression if her mind had not been perverted? I say that if it had not, she would have forgot the whole circumstance within twenty-four hours.

I think what she says of the day time kissing and caressing is proof of what I say. That was not seen by her alone, but by every girl in the school—yet not one of them thought it more than ordinary female friendship, except Miss Munro. If this is not proof of her mind having been corrupted by Miss Cumming, I don't know what would be so.

I cannot get over it. I believe Miss Munro to be a true witness. I have not the least suspicion of her veracity. But I believe that her mind was distempered, that it was filled and abused with erroneous impressions,—that she was in the situation of Othello, so well described by Shakespeare. And Miss Cumming was to her Iago.

I believe there is nothing more to say, except that I am very sorry for the consequences to Lady Cumming Gordon. But that does not in the smallest degree weaken the opinion I have formed as to the merits of this case, and as to the judgement which this Court should pronounce.

August 6, 1982

So on February 26, 1812, the Court ordered Dame Helen Cumming Gordon to pay damages to the plaintiffs because her actions had deprived them of their livelihood and the reputations on which their livelihood depended. Marianne and Jane must have felt a bittersweet vindication. They must have celebrated, at least in their hearts. But after the horror and terror of the preceding fifteen months, could they have celebrated together? Now they no longer had the romantic friends' privilege of unselfconsciousness. Now they knew (whether or not they had known before), as well as women in our century know, that love between females may be more, or other than, an effusion of the spirit—and if it is, society's ire can be a swift sword. Heaped upon all their earlier trouble, could this terrible knowledge have permitted them to remain together without shame and anger?

Nor did their problems end there. According to the forty-eighth volume of *The Laws of King George III*, chapter 151, paragraph 15, as of July 4, 1808, "appeals to the House of Lords shall be allowed where there is a difference of opinion among the judges of the said Division." The judges had voted 4 to 3 against Lady Cumming Gordon, as narrow a margin as had before voted in her favor. Her appeal, represented by all the printed testimony, speeches, and other documents, was sent off to London to be heard in the House of Lords.

In *Bleak House,* which was written forty years later, Charles Dickens depicts people grown old and broken as they waited, sometimes sixty years, for their cases to be settled in the English courts. He exaggerated only somewhat. Miss Woods and Miss Pirie must have been aware of the notorious inefficiencies of the English court system. They may have been confident that the House of Lords would decide in their favor, just as the Court of Session finally did, and that they would be awarded enough money on which to live out their days. But there was no way of anticipating when the decision of the House would be forthcoming, and in the interim they had to find a way to eat.

The only work they knew was teaching. Word of the suit and the reasons behind it must have spread quickly among the upper classes. Probably there were few families who could afford to hire a governess who would not have known of Lady Cumming Gordon and her travail. How could the mistresses hope to find work if they stayed in Edinburgh?

What they should have done, of course—what Ollie and I agree we would have done once it became apparent that the suit would be dragged out for years—is taken each other's hand and run off, to England, Ireland, America, the Continent, anywhere. But I think we could do that because no matter who might tell us we are unnatural or wicked, we know that we love each other and (ironic thanks to the sexologists) that sex is natural to love. We know with an unshakable conviction that we are right. But no matter what had been the nature of Marianne and Jane's love for each other, after those months in court they could have had no unshakable convictions about its rightness anymore. Perhaps the girls' accusations were true. If that were so, even if the women hadn't understood before with what utter disgust their society would view sex between females, after being made to sit through the testimony and the judges' speeches, they could never again escape from the blast of that knowledge. How could they ever again make love without hearing those horrible courtroom words? It would have been no better if the accusations were lies. They would now be suspicious themselves of every gentle look, every soft touch or kiss that passed between them.

Ollie says that the difference between us and them is that we have spent all our adult years battling our society's silly notions about what we are, and the fight has made us strong. The mistresses never had to fight. Their moral muscles were puny, and they would have been felled by the first blow. But I believe that a more important difference is that we know we are not alone—all the people who really matter to us understand what we are to each other, and we have scores of friends like us. If the mistresses really were lovers, there would have been no one in the world they dared to tell. They would have felt entirely isolated. The first attack would have shattered them. And they would have known that in order to gather forces to help them fight off the attack, they would have had to lie about what they meant to each other.

So they did not run off together. Marianne Woods and her aunt went to London, where Marianne begged of the friends she had made at Camden House Academy and was finally hired to come in a couple of hours a day to teach literature. It probably had been in her mind since the suit began that she might have to call on friends outside of Edinburgh, and it was for that reason that she did not ask them to write a character for her, even though her lawyer must have told her it would help her case to produce good references.

Jane Pirie remained in Edinburgh and sought a position. Probably she brought to her quest a sort of bitter, ironic stubbornness, such as one might have who believed that the world was made up of malicious numbskulls, and it was her job to show them their uncharitableness and ignorance, no matter if it killed her. Of course she found nothing, and it is doubtful that her brooding presence raised Edinburgh to an awareness of its deficiencies.

She lived in a small flat, first with a maid and then by herself, until her savings ran out. In 1813 she moved back with her father to Lady Stairs Close, into the flat where she had grown up. How could she have kept the story of her tragedy from him? And if she told him, what words could she have used to describe it? Would he have believed in her innocence, or would he have believed that God does not allow the innocent to suffer, that if she was suffering she could not be entirely without guilt?

She was bereft of everything. She had lost her money, her

name, her profession, and worst of all, her beloved friend, whom she probably now saw as more treacherous than all her enemies together. She was not yet thirty. Can so young a life really stop with such finality even while one keeps living? Most people today have several lives. If the job does not work out, if the spouse or lover fails us or dies, we try another. People were not so flexible in 1812.

The Case Before the House of Lords

When the House of Lords agreed to hear an appeal in the early nineteenth century, neither the principals nor their witnesses were permitted to appear before that august body. The transcripts of all the previous proceedings of the case were forwarded to the House of Lords, and counsel for both parties again presented their position, either orally or in writing, generally on the basis of the contents of the transcripts. The counsel was usually a London attorney who was in consultation with the original lawyer on the case, since it would have been difficult in those days of uncertain court schedules and inefficient transportation for an attorney outside of London to be available when the House of Lords was ready for him.

The plaintiff and the defendant in a case had nothing more to do but hope.

The transcripts of *Woods and Pirie against Dame Cumming Gordon* were forwarded to the London attorneys after some slight difficulty. John Clerk and George Cranstoun requested the forwarding on April 14, 1812. The Court of Session postponed consideration of their request until May 21, 1812, but finally agreed that the transcripts must be forwarded, stipulating that the attorneys would submit receipts for the transcripts, employ them only as the House of Lords instructed, and give assurances that "the uses to which counsel applies the transcripts shall be proper and suitable to the precaution against publicity adopted by the Court in this case."

James Chalmers of Westminster, who was the attorney for

many of the titled in London, conducted the appeal for Lady Cumming Gordon. He submitted an Appeal Notice to the House of Lords on March 17, 1812. Marianne Woods and Jane Pirie were notified to respond to it in writing on or before April 28, 1812, and Chalmers was informed that he would be asked to present his case before the Lords upon receipt of Woods and Pirie's response. But since the transcripts had not yet arrived by the end of April, Chalmers asked for a delay in the date when he was to be scheduled to present the case. The delay was approved. It is not clear when the transcripts finally arrived in London, but both parties remained silent until December 1, 1812, when James Campbell, a London attorney whom the mistresses had obtained through the help of John Clerk, submitted an Answer to the Appeal Notice. The House then ordered that the case be heard "on the first vacant day for cases after those already appointed."

More than three years later, at the beginning of 1816, the House of Lords had still not made a move to hear the case. The mistresses' attorney submitted this petition to the House:

February 21, 1816, Petition to the Right Honourable the Lords Spiritual and Temporal in Parliament Assembled

Re: Dame Helen Cumming Gordon, Appellant
    Marianne Woods and Jane Pirie, Respondents

The humble petition of the Respondents showeth,
    That this case stood in the rolls to be taken up some time ago,
    That it is of the greatest importance to the Respondents.—Both parties are prepared, and since the counsel on both sides will be under the necessity of attending their circuits in fourteen days hence, the Respondents, who can ill afford taking other counsel, and who labour under great disadvantages until the case is heard, humbly
    Pray that this case, which stands in the rolls above those now in hearing, may be appointed to be heard on Monday, the 4th day of March, or on such other early day as your Lordships shall be pleased to appoint.
                (Signed) *James Campbell,*
                Counsel for the Respondents

Miraculously, the House of Lords declared on February 23, 1816 "that the prayer of the said petition should be complied with." It seemed that finally the case would be settled. Notice of it appeared in the London newspapers, in terms that probably whetted the appetite of those who enjoyed scandal while maintaining the absolute secrecy of the case—e.g., the *Anti-Gallican Monitor* for February 25, 1816:

PARLIAMENTARY NEWS

There is a most extraordinary appeal set down to be argued at the Bar of the House of Lords. The appellant is Lady Cumming Gordon against Miss Woods and Miss Pirie, respondents. The latter two ladies kept a female boarding school in Edinburgh, and, by propagation of a scandalous story, their establishment was, in one day, totally ruined. They brought action in the Court of Session against Lady Cumming Gordon for defamation. The story was of such a nature as to induce the Lords to swear all the agents and parties to secrecy, although, by the practice of the Court of Session, the papers of the case were printed. A judgement was pronounced in March 1812 against Lady Cumming Gordon for damages and costs, and the young ladies were allowed to prove the amount of their damages. Against the decree Lady Cumming Gordon appeals. The case in the House of Lords, as in the Court of Session, will be heard with *shut doors.*

But if the mistresses were relieved to think they were near the end of this tortuous ordeal, they were precipitous. On March 4, 1816, James Chalmers, Lady Cumming Gordon's London attorney, petitioned the House of Lords to delay their hearing of the case. "This is a case of a very singular and delicate nature," he wrote them, "and the Appellant conceives and is advised that it is not stated in the complete way it ought to have been on her part in the printed transcript delivered to the House, which was hastily prepared." He asked that the Lordships give his client leave to submit any additional arguments as may be thought proper, and, of course, that the mistresses "be given opportunity then to put in any additional arguments on their part if they think right." His petition was granted on March 12, 1816.

AUGUST 12, 1982

Jane Cumming would have been twenty-one in 1816—no longer a girl, but still suffering as a result of what had been either the childish maliciousness or the prodigious misfortune of her girlhood.

I surprise myself: I had always disliked the bullying little Mary Tilford character that I played as a twelve-year-old, and I despised Jane Cumming when I first encountered her. But now that I have seen her intimidating "ancestral home" and have considered her life in India and in Scotland, I think I understand why she would be bitter or revengeful or anything. Whether she was a liar or only an unwilling observer in this drama, I have almost as much sympathy for her as for my two ladies.

I have been able to find nothing more about her. She never appears in the Edinburgh Postal Directory; there is no record of her marriage or death in the Scottish Record Office; her grave is in none of the cemeteries around Gordonstoun or Altyre or Forres, where her grandmother is buried.

Ollie says, facetiously I hope, that we need to go to Patna or Bengal and search for her there. But I am sure she never returned to India. She would have been even more a stranger in India, despite her looks, than in Britain. What did she have left there? Her mother and grandfather had given her up, conceded that their claim on her was insignificant if an Anglo was willing to recognize her. And what would she have had to say to them after living all those years in an Anglo world, learning to think as Anglos thought, despising the East as they did? I do not think one just sloughs off that sort of childhood indoctrination. But even if she did, in what language would she have been able to communicate in India? I stopped speaking the language of my immigrant mother when I was six years old, and it is not my language anymore. I barely understand it. English must have become her language as much as it has become mine. India would have been only the dimmest memory to her, just as my birthplace is to me.

But I do not believe that she could have made a life for herself in Britain either. The others all might have kept on with their lives. It would not have been easy, certainly, but it would have been possible. Marianne Woods managed to function well enough, although she had to leave Edinburgh to find a job. Jane Pirie probably never functioned well after the school broke up, but if she had been more flexible, less bitter, truly strong, as I think she once appeared to be to Marianne, she would have been able to pick up the shards of her life and reassemble them, just as Marianne apparently did. Lady Cumming Gordon, if she finally came to see the women as innocent, must have believed herself an old fool or, if she continued to think they were guilty, must have been embittered toward the legal fools who betrayed her. But she was sheltered by her scores of children and grandchildren and her money. She would have been scarred but essentially all right in the end.

Jane Cumming could never have been all right again. Most of the Cumming Gordon family were not fond of her to begin with. After this, they must have loathed her. She had caused Lady Cumming Gordon grief and embarrassment, not to mention a good deal of money. Whether she was a liar or merely jinxed, one of those doomed always to suffer and be damned, she was trouble to everyone around her. I would guess that in the midst of all those court battles, at least some members of the family must have tried to persuade Lady Cumming Gordon to ship her back to India and be done with her.

I think, however, the good Lady would have been prevented from doing that by her religious superstitions if nothing else. Yet how could she have lived with the girl? And how could she love her? Even if she continued to want to believe in Jane Cumming's veracity, surely she must have had some twinges of doubt, and that must have strained her feelings of charity toward the creature who had meant little but anxiety and trouble for her from the very beginning.

Jane Cumming must have resided with Lady Cumming Gordon after the school was closed, since it seems to have been almost impossible for the former scholars to get accepted into another reputable school, and she, having been more central to the scandal than the other girls, would have had even more difficulty than they. How uncomfortable the daily encounters with her grandmother must have been. Even if the grandmother claimed to continue to believe, Jane would have realized that the woman had moments of doubt and that she resented her during those moments.

Did she marry? Would her husband have known the story and always wondered, if he believed it, whether she hadn't been corrupted by what she saw in her bed when she was a very young woman? But I do not think she married. I think that the tale spread everywhere among the small aristocracy of Scotland, and that this scandal, coupled with her dark skin and illegitimacy, meant the end of her as a social being.

I think when she came of age Lady Cumming Gordon gave her a small legacy and cast her out, and she lived loveless and friendless. How could she have been anything other than miserable? She had been spoiled by great expectations—even though they may always have been unrealistic. She was petulant and lazy; she had been made luxurious and snobbish—all very unpromising characteristics for a stranger with a small legacy and no skills and no friends.

But as despicable as I think she probably was, I see her as a victim from the start, and a victim of everything I hate most in our civilization: the stigma attached to "illegitimacy," the prejudices of the master race, the privileges of wealth that permit the wealthy to buy people and to use them as pawns. Of course I am rankled by the outrages the mistresses had to endure—and I am angry with Jane Cumming because she was the direct cause of their ruin. But I feel the injustice she suffered almost as much as I feel theirs.

For the next three and a half years there was no action whatsoever on the appeal of *Woods and Pirie against Dame Cumming Gordon* in the House of Lords. Whatever additional arguments James Chalmers felt obliged to submit have been lost to posterity, as have been James Campbell's response to those arguments. In the meantime, Jane Pirie must have been clothed, fed, and sheltered only by the grace of her relatives. She could find no work.

Finally, on July 9, 1819, the House of Lords ordered that "the case wherein Dame Helen Cumming Gordon is Appellant and Marianne Woods and Jane Pirie are Respondents be taken into consideration Monday next."

The following Monday, after a brief discussion of the appeal, the House of Lords issued this terse statement: "It is ordered and adjudged by the Lords Spiritual and Temporal in Parliament assembled that the Petition and Appeal be hereby dismissed from this House, and that the said judgement of the Court of Session therein complained of be hereby affirmed."

The *London News* for Sunday, July 18, 1819, reported the speech of the Lord Chancellor:

PARLIAMENTARY DECISIONS

In the curious case of appeal, Lady Cumming Gordon, appellant; Marianne Woods and Jane Pirie, respondents, which was heard in the House of Lords with shut doors, the Lord Chancellor gave judgement on the twelfth of July, at which time he spoke to the following effect:

My lords, this is a case in which I would take the liberty to move your Lordships to give judgement without saying much upon it. It is the case *Woods and Pirie v. Lady Cumming Gordon,* a case of a very singular nature, and perhaps of such a nature that the less it is discussed publicly the better. My Lords, in the first instance the Court of Session by their decision held that her Ladyship was liable for damages to the ladies who complained. My Lords, upon as attentive a consideration as I have been able to give the circumstances of that case, it does not appear to me that there is any error in the judgement of the Court of Session. However, the extent of the damages which ought to be paid is a matter for future consideration, which will require a very temperate and a very prudent deliberation, *regard being had to all the circumstances which occur in the case.* But I do not think, whatever difference of opinion there might be about the amount of damages, that it is possible to say that this is a case in which she is not liable for damages *to some extent;* and if she is liable for damages to any extent, it seems to me that the decision of the Court of Session ought to be affirmed. I beg, therefore, to move your Lordships that the judgement be affirmed.

We can enter into no other explanation of this singular case except to say that it was action for damages brought by the plaintiffs, Mesdames Woods and Pirie, of Edinburgh, who keep a Lady's boarding school, against Lady Cumming Gordon, for having spread sundry reports of a nature tending to the ruin of their establishment.

The report of the case in the Edinburgh papers was even less informative. The *Edinburgh Weekly Journal* for July 21, 1819, stated in its "Parliament: Scottish Appeals" section only:

LADY CUMMING GORDON v. WOODS

On the curious case of Lady Cumming Gordon v. Woods, their Lordships, on the suggestion of the Chancellor, who observed that the less said on the case the better, Affirmed the judgement of the Court of Session.

PART IV

The Settlement

AUGUST 16, 1982

Early in 1815, Sir Archibald Dunbar must have announced to his wife Helen that they would leave Edinburgh and return to Elgin, where he had an estate. All Lady Cumming Gordon's children were now married and scattered throughout Scotland and England. If her favorite, Helen, was leaving Edinburgh she no longer had reason to remain there. Gordonstoun had been taken over by her eldest surviving son, Sir William, and she had given Altyre House to her younger son, Charles. However, she had the life rent on a house in Forres, and since that was close to Elgin and her two family estates, she determined to go there.

Perhaps her decision to leave Edinburgh also had something to do with the chagrin she must have felt over the suit. It was scandalous, regardless of whether or not the courts would vindicate her. At worst, she had been made a dupe by a scheming child. And even at best, it was known everywhere in Edinburgh, at least in her circles, that not only had her poor grandchild been subjected to the grossest indecencies because of Lady Cumming Gordon's bad judgment in selecting mistresses, but that also she herself had been forced to mouth descriptions of those indecencies in order to put an end to the school. Either way, it must have been repulsive to her, and she would have been relieved to go where fewer people were likely to have heard of the affair.

When she received word in the summer of 1819 from her London lawyer that the House of Lords had decided against her, she would have felt it as a very heavy blow had she not sustained one even more dreadful a short time before: Lady Helen Dunbar had contracted scarlet fever and in a matter of days she was dead. She was just forty-two years old.

Lady Cumming Gordon had little time to react to her lost suit that summer, since she was deep in mourning for her daughter. When her lawyers told her that the House of Lords had set no sum that she must pay in damages, and that it would be prudent for her to make a low offer to the mistresses before they presented an exorbitant demand, she probably answered that she had no mind to think about the disgusting women and their suit now, and they must all have the decency to let her mourn in peace.

But, of course, the suit would not go away. When, at the beginning of 1820, the women demanded from her almost ten thousand pounds, she informed her lawyers that she intended to pay not one penny.

They must have remonstrated with her. "The law is the law," they probably said. "You must pay. We can offer a lesser amount—you need only tell us how much. But you must pay something."

"We will appeal it again," she must have insisted.

They would have informed her that there was no appeal from the House of Lords.

"Then let them throw me in prison," perhaps she said. "Not one penny will I give those monsters." Finally, however, she told her lawyers they might offer two thousand pounds.

They convinced her to offer three thousand.

Did she ever admit to anyone that she might have made a mistake? How difficult it must have been for a woman in her position, the daughter of Sir Ludovick Grant of Grant, the widow of Sir Alexander Penrose Cumming Gordon of Gordonstoun and Altyre, a gray-haired matriarch, the mother of two Members of Parliament, to make such an admission.

But surely she must have had moments alone when she understood that she had been foolish and culpable, that she had sinned in not treating fellow mortals with the Christian decency that would have recognized at least their right to explain themselves before she blasted them off the face of respectability. Or did women of her class and temperament ever come to that understanding?

Ollie and I agree that she is the villain of the piece, however protective of innocence she thought she was. Whether the mistresses were in fact guilty or not, she owed them a rational inquiry, an opportunity to explain themselves, and, if they could not, a chance to leave the country rather than to face exposure.

The Case in Scotland, Again

The mistresses had won against Lady Cumming Gordon's appeal to the House of Lords and that should have been the end of their struggle. In fiction the climax and conclusion of this drama would have occurred long before this. But in fact it continued to drag on. Because the courts did not set a monetary figure on the extent of Lady Cumming Gordon's guilt, Marianne Woods and Jane Pirie now had another battle before them. How could they get her to pay what they believed she owed them if the courts did not support them in the demand for a particular sum? The slow, tortuous legal process was not over; it had only entered another stage. Marianne and Jane were cheated of any clear feeling of victory. But how often are victories clear and the joy of them unmitigated in real life? Don't they almost always become like ashes in the exhaustion of an endless-seeming wait for them?

On November 30, 1819, nine years after the inception of the trouble, James Moncreiff, who had become John Clerk's law partner, submitted a petition to the Court of Session for "Miss Marianne Woods and Miss Jane Pirie, lately residing at Drumsheugh near Edinburgh." He reminded the Lords of Session that some years ago his clients were "under the painful necessity of instituting before your Lordships a suit for reparation of one of the deepest injuries that was ever inflicted on two individuals, against Lady Cumming Gordon, widow of the late Sir Alexander Cumming Gordon of Altyre and Gordonstoun, Baronet." Since the House of Lords, lately deliberating on the case, had found in favor of his clients, as had the Court of Session earlier, it was his understanding, Moncreiff wrote, that his clients must now ask permission to submit to the Lords of Session a statement of the damages claimed by them, so that the lords might decree the amount of reparation the defendant must pay. The lords, without committing themselves to any action, permitted the plaintiffs to submit such a statement, which was presented by Moncreiff:

January 28, 1820, Statement of the damages claimed by Miss Marianne Woods and Miss Jane Pirie, against Lady Cumming Gordon

As your Lordships know, the school of the plaintiffs enjoyed extraordinary success from its inception until November 1810. At that time the school was full, both with five day scholars and twelve regular night boarders, who paid forty pounds per annum. The plaintiffs also had at that time an immediate prospect of adding seven more day scholars. In fact, so great was the success which had attended their efforts that the plaintiffs had decided to rent a larger house beginning the following Whitsunday, so that they might take an increased number both of boarders and day scholars.

However, the calumny of the defendant suddenly and unexpectedly produced a disgrace so grievous to the plaintiffs that they were overwhelmed and compelled immediately to abandon their establishment. This happened shortly after the new term of Martinmas, 1810. Since they had no previous notice, they were under the necessity of paying house rent, as well as servants' and housekeeper's wages for which no return was or could be obtained. They were also forced to sell their furniture, having no other means of discharging their obligations. Because of their desperate circumstances, that furniture was sold for scarcely more than one-third of its actual value.

The effect of the slander against them was not only to ruin their successful school, but to render it nearly, if not altogether, impossible for either of them ever properly to employ the accomplishments which had been the study of their lives. Through the friendship and sympathy of one or two individuals, Miss Woods was, after a time, able to earn a very scanty subsistence for herself and a near relation, an aged lady, who depended upon her for support. Miss Pirie, on the other hand, although she too had well wishers who were anxious to help her, as she did not choose to leave her native country, was not so fortunate. She was, in point of fact, totally ruined, and has ever since been entirely disabled from employing whatever talents she may possess, and the acquirements of many years, either for her profit or her bare subsistence. Her health suffered severely from the deep grief and anxiety produced by the defendant's calumny and by the investigations which it rendered necessary. She has ever since been much less capable of exertion than she was before. This can easily be proven if your Lordships should require it.

It is clear from the experience of the plaintiffs that no decision of a tribunal, even the House of Lords, can ever do away the effects of such calumny upon the individual or upon the public mind. The plaintiffs are thankful that they have so far obtained protection from the laws of their country. But it is one of the peculiar qualities of a charge of this nature that no proof of innocence, however clear, can ever erase the first impression which the very telling of such a story produces. So that, regardless of the plaintiffs' efforts, and even had Miss Pirie's health not been impaired as a result of this libel, the plaintiffs will never again enjoy that exceptionally fine standing in society which they once claimed.

In light of the above, the plaintiffs submit these claims:

From the time the school was shut down to the present, they have already lost approximately £10000, but the plaintiffs are willing to accept £6000 for this loss.

In addition, they have incurred very serious legal expences, both in this Court and in the House of Lords. The sum of those expences is £783.

Lastly, the plaintiffs claim *solatium* for the injury to their feelings, their health, their private comfort, and their respectability in society. Miss Pirie in particular has suffered so severely in her health and constitution as certainly to embitter the remainder of her days, and in all probability greatly to shorten her life. Though Miss Woods, from better fortune, has not suffered so much personal injury, this cause has been and will be a source of perpetual unhappiness to her, probably for her whole life. But the plaintiffs, assuming they will be given full recompence for their actual losses, will claim only £2000 for solace—a sum which must appear moderate in the extreme to those who can enter at all into the state of their feelings or understand the situation into which they have been plunged for nine years by this extraordinary calumny.

The list of damages is as follows:

	Per annum
Twelve night boarders, for £40 per annum	£ 480 0 0
Charges for extra courses taught to these boarders by Misses Woods and Pirie	448 16 0
Twelve day scholars at £25 per annum	300 0 0
Charges for extra courses taught to these scholars by Misses Woods and Pirie	448 16 0
Total	£1677 12 0

The household expences, under all the circum-stances, would not have exceeded £500, but call them	£600	
House rent, taxes, wages	95	
	695	
Yearly profit		1677 12 00
		− 695 00 00
		982 12 00

According to these data, the claim of damages stands thus:

Loss on furniture, rent, wages, etc.	£	450	00	00
Loss on profits		6000	00	00
Expences for attorneys, court costs, etc.		783		
	£7233	00	00	

Solatium	2000	00	00
	£9233	00	00

In respect whereof, etc.

(Signed) *James Moncreiff*

On April 7, 1820, the Lords of Session required the defendant's counsel to respond to James Moncreiff's statement within thirty days. Exactly thirty days later, George Cranstoun submitted this response for Lady Cumming Gordon:

May 7, 1820, Replies for Lady Cumming Gordon to the Statement of Damages Claimed by Miss Marianne Woods and Miss Jane Pirie

The defendant wishes to point out first that the yearly profits which the plaintiffs claim they would have enjoyed is founded on the supposition of their future and increasing success. It is clear through the evidence that has been established in this case that such success would have been highly improbable. Your Lordships will recall the state of mutual dissension and quarrelling in which these parties, by their own account, were at that time living. That alone will satisfy you of the extreme improbability of their even continuing together, far less of advancing the school in public estimation. In addition, it must be pointed out that the chief cause of the plaintiffs' success during the time they operated the school was the exertions of the defendant on their behalf.

Secondly, Miss Pirie has claimed that she has been unable to earn her living since the school was broken up; but if Miss Woods has done so, it does not appear why

Miss Pirie might not have done the same if she had made proper exertions. And now, if the decision lately announced by the Supreme Tribunal of the country, the House of Lords, has cleared their character in the opinion of the world (and surely the plaintiffs will not maintain the contrary), what is to prevent them from making as much by their own exertions as if the present suit had never taken place?

Next, the plaintiffs also claim £2000 in the name of solatium for injury to their feelings. The defendant wishes to point out their own responsibility in this regard: though the plaintiffs have been acquitted of the actual charge made against them in its most aggravated form, they have been proved guilty of such improprieties and imprudences as to excite suspicion and to lead others to form unfavourable constructions of their conduct. They are, therefore, not entitled to the same compensation as if they had acted with perfect propriety and had given no grounds whatever for misconstruction. Their suspicious behaviour, as your Lordships know, was not only sufficient to colour the opinion of the defendant, but also on one occasion to fix the opinion of a majority of this Court, whose first judgement found the defendant not guilty. The conduct on the part of the plaintiffs which led to such conclusions in your Honours' minds must, to say the least of it, have been in no common degree suspicious, and must greatly diminish any claim of damages owing to them.

Finally, a circumstance which is always allowed to affect the amount of damages due is the fortune and means of the party who is found liable. Indeed, it is plain that if this were not attended to the penalty would fall most unequally on individuals: the same sum which inflicted but a trifling fine upon one party, would amount to total ruin on another. This principle clearly applies to what is strictly called *damage incurred* or *loss* as well as *solatium*. Suppose that reports to the plaintiffs' prejudice had been circulated by a servant or other person in that rank of life: could they have seriously made such a claim as they now do for damages to the amount of nearly £10000? It is plain they could not.

Now, the defendant avers that her only fortune and means of living is an annuity for her life of £800, with the liferent of a house and garden in Forres. Upon this your Lordships are left to judge how heavily will fall any sum of damages to be allowed to the plaintiffs, in addition to the legal fees which the defendant has already had to pay in the amount of £943. She has been able to save nothing, her whole income being barely adequate to support her.

On March 1, 1820 the plaintiffs, through their counsel, sent us an offer to accept the sum of £5000 in full of all demands. On this the defendant will only say that the plaintiffs had the best reason to know that such an offer would never be listened to by her, and therefore, that the ceremonious tender of it made upon their part is the merest affectation.

In respect whereof, etc.

(Signed) *George Cranstoun*

This was only the start of a paper war that was to continue into the following year. On June 1, 1820, James Moncreiff responded curtly to Cranstoun's statement for Lady Cumming Gordon:

The plaintiffs wish to point out that it was in their power to use arrestments of the defendant's annuity at the beginning of this suit. That would have secured a sufficient fund for their claim of damages at this period. They were assured that it was not necessary to do so because the defendant's sons had undertaken by a bond to become liable for whatever damages should ultimately be found due, and all discussion ended there. Lady Cumming Gordon's financial situation may indeed be as she presents it, although the absurdity of her claiming penury will be immediately apparent when her situation is compared to that of the plaintiffs. However, since there is a bond undertaken by her sons, regardless of her personal finances, she has access to the amount claimed by plaintiffs.

This, of course, only occasioned another response from George Cranstoun instead of an attempt to settle the matter. On July 5, 1820, Cranstoun wrote the Court:

> The defendant must confess herself unable to comprehend the force of the plaintiffs' reasoning. The interference on the part of her sons, arising from filial duty toward their parent, was solely intended to prevent her from being distressed by her only means of subsistence being withdrawn or locked up, while, as they believed, the plaintiffs would never be able to substantiate any claim against her. It is a material fact in the consideration of this matter that the caution given by the defendant's sons has not enriched her to the extent of one penny in the meantime. She has found her whole income but barely adequate to her support, and has expended it all along in the way. It humbly appears to the defendant, then, that the circumstance of her sons having undertaken to pay what damages *might ultimately be found due,* ought not in the slightest degree to affect your Lordships' judgement as to the amount of those damages, one way or another.

It appears that by this time the Second Division of the Court of Session considered itself sick of the case, at least for the time being. The lords summoned the two attorneys, chastised them for not having been able to bring about cooperation among their clients, told them they must try to reach a settlement out of court, and warned them that if they could not come to some agreement the only solution was to refer the case to a jury court and start the proceedings over again. I suspect that the lords used the threat of a jury court as a ploy to frighten the two parties into agreement. Considering the judges' strong determination to keep the subject matter of the case secret from the public, it is doubtful they would have been willing to submit it to a jury court with all the publicity that would have been attendant on such a move.

Perhaps the attorneys tried to reach a settlement in good faith, but their clients were obdurate. Not only did Miss Woods and Miss

Pirie need the money they hoped to get from Lady Cumming Gordon, but they also wanted to hurt her significantly, financially if in no other way. Lady Cumming Gordon, for her part, wanted to lose as little money as possible, and she also refused to accept emotionally her defeat and what it meant in terms of her legally acknowledged role as a dupe and a fool. A half year after the Court ordered the lawyers to reach a settlement, they still had made no progress. I wonder if, in a case like this, where it seemed impossible that the parties would ever reach agreement, the lords would not have usually ordered the defendant to pay the ten thousand pounds, or six thousand or four thousand—if the defendant were a lesser personage than Dame Helen Cumming Gordon.

On December 14, 1820, George Cranstoun wrote a lamenting note to the Lords of Session, begging that they intervene, but also that they cease to consider having the case reopened before a jury court. Cranstoun must have felt at this point that he could do nothing to budge his client from her intransigency, let alone Miss Woods and Miss Pirie. He probably prayed that their lordships would take the case out of his hands and let him be done with it.

> My Lords,
>
> When this case last came up in your Court, some of your Lordships expressed regret that it had been again brought before you. You seemed to think that it ought to have been settled out of Court by compromise, and you suggested that perhaps the only solution now was to refer it to a jury.
>
> Since then, the defendant has again tried to reach a compromise with the plaintiffs on the sum to be paid by her. But after full consideration, and with every desire to have the matter settled out of court, her counsel does not feel it warranted to advise her to pay the extravagant demand made upon her.
>
> Therefore, it has become necessary that the case should again come before the law for a decision, and the defendant felt it right to repeat her desire that your Lordships would take up the case yourselves rather than send it to a jury. It is hoped that you would decide upon it at a consultation out of court (if you think fit), and an-

nounce from the Chair, without discussion, your judgement as to the amount of damages. The defendant believes that in no other way can the case be so suitably decided, with so little publicity, delay, or expence, since your Lordships are perfectly acquainted with all the particulars of the case and the circumstances of the parties.

It appears to the defendant that the case is not suited to appear before a jury. From the nature of its details your Lordships formerly saw it fit to have the case carried on with shut doors, and you ordered all papers to be returned into the hands of the Court and sealed up. From similar views, no *viva voce* pleadings took place in the House of Lords, but the decision was made on the printed appeal documents. The motives for such secrecy, of course, still weigh heavily against giving a renewed and increased publicity to the case such as would necessarily arise from a trial by Jury Court.

Furthermore, before a jury could assess the damages, it would be necessary for them to try the whole case over again. Now, besides the further disclosure which your Lordships are desirous to avoid, it would be extremely difficult, indeed impossible, to bring forward all the evidence once again and at this late date.

The defendant, therefore, pleads against a trial by Jury Court. She does so from no fear that a jury, properly masters of the case, would order her to pay damages even in the amount that she has voluntarily offered to pay, but for the reasons stated above.

It will be recollected, too, that the case came into the Court, testimony was taken, and judgement given here almost four years before the Jury Court was established in Scotland. Consequently, it is not imperative on your Lordships to send it to a Jury Court to assess damages.

(Signed) *George Cranstoun*

On December 15, 1820, the Court of Session accepted involvement in the case again. The judges formally notified the plaintiffs' attorney that his clients would be allowed to respond to Cranstoun's note of December 14. On February 21, 1821, more than ten years after the case opened, James Moncreiff responded for Miss Woods and Miss Pirie:

My Lords,

The plaintiffs can assure your Lordships that it is with great regret that they find themselves still under the necessity of coming before you for judgement in this case. But they feel that they have already gone a great deal further in their concessions than they ought to have done. They cannot help thinking, through their attempts to effect a settlement, that the defendant has never yet brought herself to look upon that case with the realization that there has been a final judgement against her, and that the only remaining question is what shall be considered as sufficient damages for such an injury.

The plaintiffs have previously stated damages at upwards of nine thousand pounds. They adhere to this, but they also formerly agreed to settle for five thousand pounds for the sake of a speedy and final resolution. When your Lordships, without intimating any opinion one way or another, then stated they would prefer the case be settled out of court rather than have it come before them again, the plaintiffs said they would settle for four thousand pounds, making it clear at the same time that this was the lowest they would accept. The defendant, however, declined this proposal and offered to pay thirty-five hundred pounds, as a supposed halving of the difference between the two parties. But, in fact, the offer to accept the four thousand pounds was itself more than a halving of the difference for the plaintiffs.

For insuperable reasons, it is impossible for the plaintiffs to accept less. That they have lost on the furniture, etc. in breaking up the establishment, even the defendant cannot deny. That the calumny was calculated to prevent the plaintiffs from obtaining other employment must also be admitted. That, in the case of Miss Pirie, at least, it did produce this effect completely, despite great efforts by her friends to help her find employment, can be proven instantly. That even Miss Woods, though more fortunate, has been able to earn a bare subsistence with very hard labour, is equally certain. That the plaintiffs are entitled to a sum of money in solace must also be admitted.

Let the account then be stated in any way, and your Lordships will see the distance between the reparation the defendant offers and what is appropriate for such an injury.

The defendant offers	£3500	00	00
Deduct expence of attorneys, court costs, etc.	783	16	5
	2716	3	7
Divide this between Miss Woods and Miss Pirie, it leaves to each	£1358	1	9½
Let Miss Pirie's *actual* loss for the *past* years *alone* be considered, and let it be taken only on what Miss Pirie might have earned as governess—it cannot be less than what she did earn before the school was set up, *viz.* at least £130 or £140 a year including bed, board, washing, etc. Take that for ten years only, it will be	£1400	00	00

Thus there is not one farthing for loss of the furniture, etc.—not one farthing for loss of the school or the prospects of success,—NOT ONE FARTHING FOR SOLACE. And Miss Pirie is left at last with her health totally destroyed,—without the means of doing anything for her own support. It is impossible that this can be justice.

The proposal last made by the plaintiffs, out of respect for your Lordships' request that the matter be settled out of Court, entailed already great sacrifice. Miss Woods, it is true, has been able to live, though with great difficulty, without contracting debts. And after paying all the expences, her share of the balance might secure her against want and enable her to live with more comfort. Miss Pirie is differently situated. She has unavoidably contracted very considerable debts. Her share of the sum demanded would have enabled her to pay her debts and have left a very moderate amount indeed, perhaps near to a thousand pounds, to save her from positive beggary. But it is plain that if the defendant's offer were accepted, nothing whatever would remain to Miss Pirie.

The question of payment for solace must also be considered. Could it be stated at less, for such unheard of calumny, than one thousand pounds to each of the plaintiffs? And yet the defendant has refused to settle the matter for four thousand pounds to compensate for all the plaintiffs' losses and embarrassments. The plaintiffs feel confident that whether by a verdict of the jury or by the judgement of your Lordships, *upon evidence,* they will obtain a much larger sum for damages.

However, the plaintiffs wish to state that they cannot acquiesce to the case being taken up again on any other basis than that of proving the actual losses sustained, since both your Lordships and the House of Lords have already given the verdict on the defendant's calumny.

Moreover, while the plaintiffs are ready to submit to a jury trial for the question of reparations, they believe that the issues raised by the defendant regarding the expences, delays, and publicity of a jury trial are entitled to consideration. But they want to emphasize that however painful the discussion may be, they are not afraid of any disclosure in the face of any jury of their country, and they have not a shadow of doubt that the jury's verdict will satisfy the defendant as to the moderation of their proposal for a settlement.

(Signed) *James Moncreiff*

The court records stop with the document of February 21, 1821. Either Dame Cumming Gordon or the mistresses must have agreed out of court to accept less or to offer more. I can find little else about this unhappy trio.

Jane Pirie's father must have died in 1814. In that year his name was dropped from the Edinburgh Postal Directory and she was listed as being the sole inhabitant of the flat at Lady Stairs Close. In 1817 she moved to a smaller and cheaper flat at 36 Bristo Street. Shortly after the suit was settled she must have left Edinburgh. She was still living at the Bristo address in 1821, but the directory lists no Jane Pirie for 1822. I am certain she would not have married: she was almost forty then, and her temperament would not have permitted it at any age. How ironic and dismally appropriate it would have been had she died the year after she finally squeezed some money out of the woman who, as she saw it, had destroyed her.

Lady Cumming Gordon died on January 1, 1832, as though she knew that year would bring the finish to an era and she preferred not to see it. It was the same year Sir Walter Scott, the most beloved Tory of his day, died. Just before Scott's death, when he was already visibly ailing, he was howled down at a general election meeting for opposing reform. That election brought a great majority for the Whig government and the passage of the Scottish Reform Bill, which extended the vote to the middle classes, in July 1832. That year was the end of what is known as the Romantic period in literature, and it was the beginning of the end of the very rigid divisions between classes in Britain. I believe Lady Cumming Gordon would have loathed such democratizing.

It does not appear that Marianne Woods ever returned to Edinburgh unless she married and changed her name. But I think it probable that after her last experiment in sharing her life with one who loved her, she would have determined to remain solitary.

I found only one other trace of the Woods family. In 1865 a gentleman wrote to the editor of an Edinburgh journal, *The Era:*

SIR,—Wandering a few weeks ago through the Old Calton Burying Ground, I observed that a tombstone erected to the memory of Mr. Woods, a popular actor and teacher of elocution about the end of the last and beginning of the present century, had been removed. On inquiry, I found that the tombstone, which from the first had never been properly erected, had been gradually loosened by the necessary excavations of the sexton in its vicinity, and had finally been blown down in one of the late violent storms of high wind to whose action the Old Calton Burying Ground, from its elevated position, is peculiarly exposed. I was also informed by the intelligent and gentlemanly Recorder that he did not know any surviving relatives of Mr. Woods to whom he might write requesting the re-erection of the monument.

Mr. Woods was, for thirty years, a leading actor in the Edinburgh Theatre. I have been informed by one or two old citizens of Edinburgh that his private character was irreproachable, and I know an old clergyman of the Established Church who used to quote as an authority, from which there was no appeal, "Mr. Woods, the player." I have also been informed that Mr. Woods was an intimate friend of Scotland's glorious poet, Robert Burns. All of this surely is reason sufficient why Mr. Woods' tomb should not be allowed to perish. The sum required to re-erect the monument is a mere trifle, two pounds, two shillings—two guineas. Surely some of your readers will subscribe a trifle for this purpose.

OLD MORTALITY

The monument was reerected in 1866, and an inscription was added: WILLIAM WOODS, FRIEND OF POETS FERGUSSON AND BURNS, FAVOURITE ACTOR, EDINBURGH 1770 TO 1802. Ann Quelch, the mother of Mrs. Woods, is buried not far from him, but there is no sign of his wife's grave there, or of Marianne's.

So they have eluded me after all. And yet, I think I am able to guess well enough what became of them. Marianne Woods, despite her secret horror, grew into the quiet grace and superior calm that marked my associate preacher at St. Giles's. She had suffered—however, life must go on. Her aunt died a few years after the settlement, and it saddened Marianne, but she got over it after a plausible time. She made pleasant friends and grew fond of London. It no longer terrified her as it had when she was young. She thought of Jane Pirie with sadness sometimes, and with shame. But she never wrote—and Jane Pirie never wrote to her. Marianne was a survivor. Nothing other than physical sickness and death could destroy her, perhaps because outside of a commonplace sense of responsibility, nothing ever touched her very deeply.

The two Janes, namesakes and bedfellows, shared a common fate. They lived out their lives in small flats, making the pennies stretch, alone and angry and bitter. They became eccentrics. Their clothes were dirty and out of date, not merely because they could not afford better, but because they were empty of the desire and energy that it took to pass themselves off as being like the rest of humanity. They haggled violently with shopkeepers and landlords and neighbors, who were to them embodiments of the world's treachery. They spat in the streets. Children who passed them believed or pretended they were witches and ran from them, sometimes shrieking.

They were entirely careless of themselves, yet if threatened with death, they would have fought. Both had a spiteful stubbornness that mandated their physical survival. They would not give up the ghost and let the world go on smugly without them. But the world took no notice of their determination, nor of the time when that determination finally wore itself out.

I do not think they died of any dramatic cause such as starvation. Lady Cumming Gordon's conscience would not have permitted Jane Cumming to be in want, though she would have given her her deserts by withholding abundance. If Jane Pirie ended up with a thousand pounds from Lady Cumming Gordon after she paid her lawyers and the other debts she had accumulated over a dozen years, the sum invested at 5 percent per annum would have yielded her fifty pounds. Two pecks of potatoes were one shilling, three pence; a pound of beef was seven pence; a pint of milk, six pence; a pound of candles was a shilling. She could have survived on fifty pounds a year, though narrowly.

But my sorrow for her is not because I think she suffered hunger or cold. Her *loneliness* is unbearable to me. I wish I could reach across the centuries to her and lift her heaviness and hatred. I wish I could send her Ollie, who can be so light when lightness is needed, so comforting and giving that Jane Pirie would feel herself yanked from her moroseness and anger.

Our summer is over. I can't help feeling somewhat guilty that Ollie spent her vacation on my work, but she says that she needed this distance from her manuscript, and that now she sees how to proceed with the revisions. I tell her I will take dictation for her, type, photocopy, collate, do anything she wants me to, and that she is what Jane Pirie must have hoped to find in Marianne Woods. We return to New York this P.M.

Index